Intermediate Accounting

FOR

DUMMIES®

by Maire Loughran

WILEY

John Wiley & Sons, Inc.

Intermediate Accounting For Dummies®

Published by
John Wiley & Sons, Inc.
111 River St.
Hoboken, NJ 07030-5774
www.wiley.com

Copyright © 2012 by John Wiley & Sons, Inc., Indianapolis, Indiana

Published by John Wiley & Sons, Inc., Indianapolis, Indiana

Published simultaneously in Canada

LIMIT OF LIABILITY/DISCLAIMER OF WARRANTY: T
REPRESENTATIONS OR WARRANTIES WITH RESPEC
THE CONTENTS OF THIS WORK AND SPECIFICALLY D
OUT LIMITATION WARRANTIES OF FITNESS FOR A P.
CREATED OR EXTENDED BY SALES OR PROMOTION.
CONTAINED HEREIN MAY NOT BE SUITABLE FOR EVI
UNDERSTANDING THAT THE PUBLISHER IS NOT ENG
OTHER PROFESSIONAL SERVICES. IF PROFESSIONAL
A COMPETENT PROFESSIONAL PERSON SHOULD BE
AUTHOR SHALL BE LIABLE FOR DAMAGES ARISING
TION OR WEBSITE IS REFERRED TO IN THIS WORK
OF FURTHER INFORMATION DOES NOT MEAN THAT
THE INFORMATION THE ORGANIZATION OR WEBS
MAY MAKE. FURTHER, READERS SHOULD BE AWA
WORK MAY HAVE CHANGED OR DISAPPEARED BET
WHEN IT IS READ.

For general information on our other products and services, please contact our Customer Care Department within the U.S. at 877-762-2974, outside the U.S. at 317-572-3993, or fax 317-572-4002.

For technical support, please visit www.wiley.com/techsupport.

Wiley also publishes its books in a variety of electronic formats and by print-on-demand. Some content that appears in standard print versions of this book may not be available in other formats. For more information about Wiley products, visit us at www.wiley.com.

Library of Congress Control Number is available from the Publisher.

ISBN: 978-1-118-17682-5 (pbk); ISBN 978-1-118-22719-0 (ebk); ISBN 978-1-118-24022-9 (ebk); ISBN 978-1-118-26483-6 (ebk)

Manufactured in the United States of America

10 9 8 7 6 5 4 3 2 1

WILEY

Intermediate Accounting

FOR

DUMMIES®

About the Author

Maire Loughran is a certified public accountant and a member of the American Institute of Certified Public Accountants. Her professional experience includes four years of internal auditing for a publicly traded company in the aerospace industry, two years as an auditor in the not-for-profit sector, and even some experience as a U.S. federal agent. Her public accounting experience includes financial reporting and analysis, audits of private corporations, accounting for e-commerce, and forensic accounting.

Maire is a full adjunct professor who teaches graduate and undergraduate auditing and accounting classes. Interested in many different business-related fields, she is the author of *Auditing For Dummies*; *Financial Accounting For Dummies* (Wiley); *Close, Consolidate & Report For Dummies*, an IBM Limited Edition; a guide to starting a home-based business; as well as the *Arts and Crafts Business Guide* for About.com.

Dedication

To my much-loved son Joey, who serves his country aboard the USS *Harry S. Truman:* I am prouder of you than mere words can ever describe. And to my late husband Jeff, so long gone from our lives, but never absent from our hearts.

Author's Acknowledgments

To the Ursuline nuns and Jesuit priests who provided me with a stellar education, and to my parents, who selflessly footed the bill.

To my agent, Barb Doyen, for all her hard work and support.

And to Tracy Brown, Krista Hansing, Ron De Witt, and Robert Garrett for their months of editing, follow-through, and advice.

Publisher's Acknowledgments

We're proud of this book; please send us your comments at http://dummies.custhelp.com. For other comments, please contact our Customer Care Department within the U.S. at 877-762-2974, outside the U.S. at 317-572-3993, or fax 317-572-4002.

Some of the people who helped bring this book to market include the following:

Acquisitions, Editorial, and Media Development

Project Editor: Tracy Brown

Acquisitions Editor: Stacy Kennedy

Copy Editor: Krista Hansing

Assistant Editor: David Lutton

Editorial Program Coordinator: Joe Niesen

Technical Editors: Ron De Witt, Robert Garrett

Senior Editorial Manager: Jennifer Ehrlich

Editorial Manager: Carmen Krikorian

Editorial Assistant: Rachelle Amick

Art Coordinator: Alicia B. South

Cover Photos:
© iStockphoto.com / Hongqi Zhang

Cartoons: Rich Tennant
(www.the5thwave.com)

Composition Services

Project Coordinator: Patrick Redmond

Layout and Graphics: Carrie A. Cesavice, Corrie Niehaus, Mark Pinto

Proofreader: The Well-Chosen Word

Indexer: Claudia Bourbeau

Publishing and Editorial for Consumer Dummies

    Kathleen Nebenhaus, Vice President and Executive Publisher

    Kristin Ferguson-Wagstaffe, Product Development Director

    Ensley Eikenburg, Associate Publisher, Travel

    Kelly Regan, Editorial Director, Travel

Publishing for Technology Dummies

    Andy Cummings, Vice President and Publisher

Composition Services

    Debbie Stailey, Director of Composition Services

Contents at a Glance

Table of Contents

Introduction

*I*ntermediate accounting takes *financial accounting,* which is the language of business directed to the external user of the financial statements, to the next level. It fleshes out all the topics that your financial accounting class briefly touches upon and serves as a bridge between basic financial accounting and *advanced financial accounting,* which really gets into the nitty-gritty of handling financial transactions.

Along the way, you still encounter your old friends, the income statement, balance sheet, and statement of cash flows. And while preparation of the financial statements stays the same no matter what type of financial accounting class you take, intermediate accounting assumes you have a basic understanding of financial accounting and introduces you to more advanced accounting scenarios. For example, you get into inventory issues beyond cost flow assumption and find out about more advanced leasing topics such as residual value.

Although all business students have to take some form of financial accounting class, usually only students interested in pursuing a career in this field move on to intermediate accounting. Plus, intermediate accounting is a prerequisite for advanced financial accounting in many schools, which is a must-take class to prepare for the certified public accountant (CPA) exam.

After years spent in the classroom as both a professor and a student, I've realized that many accounting textbooks are, well, boring. My purpose in writing this book is to breathe some life into the subject of intermediate accounting and make it more understandable.

If some time has elapsed between your first financial accounting class and your intermediate accounting classes (intermediate accounting is normally taught in a series of three classes), you may need a refresher in the basics. If that's the case, and you have the time, I recommend reading another of my books, *Financial Accounting For Dummies* (published by Wiley), which is your beginner's reference guide to the financial accounting topics I discuss in this book.

About This Book

This book, like all *For Dummies* books, is written so that each chapter stands on its own. I always assume that whatever chapter you're reading is the first one you've tackled in the book. Therefore, you can understand the concepts I explain in each chapter, regardless of whether it's your first chapter or your last.

However, certain terms and concepts pertain to more than one subject in this book. To avoid writing the same explanations over and over, whenever I reference a financial accounting term, method, or other type of fact that I fully explain in another chapter, I give you a brief overview and direct you to the spot where you can get more information. For example, I may suggest that you "see Chapter 10" (which, by the way, discusses accounting for inventory).

Also, in this book, I talk about intermediate accounting in terms of its lowest common denominator. I avoid using jargon that only accounting majors with a few accounting classes under their belt will understand.

Please keep in mind that the list of intermediate accounting topics and methods I present in this book isn't all-inclusive. I simply can't cover every possible nuance and twist covered in your intermediate accounting textbook — after all, it's probably more than 1,000 pages! This book is meant to illuminate the rather dry presentation of topics given in all the intermediate accounting textbooks from which I've taught, providing a perfect companion to the intermediate accounting textbook your professor is using.

Conventions Used in This Book

Following are some conventions I use that you'll want to bear in mind while reading this book:

- ✔ I introduce new terms in *italic,* with an explanation immediately following. For example, *manufacturing companies* make the products that *merchandising companies* sell to consumers like you and me.

- ✔ Accounting terms tend to be like alphabet soup. I never assume that you remember the term behind the acronym. (Goodness, sometimes I have a brain-freeze moment, too!) The first time I introduce an acronym in a chapter, I spell it out and place the acronym in parentheses. For example, I may discuss the Financial Accounting Standards Board (FASB), which is the private-sector body establishing generally accepted accounting principles (GAAP) for all nongovernmental entities. (Ha ha, I slipped in two there!)

- ✔ I use **bold** text to highlight key words in bulleted lists.

✔ All web addresses are in `monofont` typeface so that they're set apart from the rest of the text. When this book was printed, some web addresses may have needed to break across two lines of text. If that happened, rest assured that I haven't put in any extra characters (such as hyphens) to indicate the break. So when using one of these web addresses, just type in exactly what you see in this book, as though the line break doesn't exist.

What You're Not to Read

I would love it if you read every word of this book, but I realize that people lead busy lives and sometimes just want to get the specific information they need. So if you're under a time crunch, you can safely skip the following without jeopardizing your understanding of the subject at large:

✔ **Material marked with a Technical Stuff icon:** These paragraphs contain extra intermediate accounting information that, while useful, isn't critical to your understanding of the topic at hand.

✔ **Sidebars:** These gray-shaded boxes contain asides that I think you'll find interesting but that, again, aren't vital to understanding the material your professor discusses in class.

Foolish Assumptions

I assume you have a rudimentary knowledge of accounting, since you have to take other accounting prerequisites before tackling intermediate accounting. I'm also guessing you're one of the following people:

✔ A college intermediate accounting student who just isn't "getting it" by reading (and rereading) the assigned textbook. (I've seen that deer-in-the-headlights look many times in my classroom.)

✔ A nonaccounting student currently enrolled in a business curriculum who liked financial accounting and has decided to take intermediate accounting, too. Maybe you're taking it as an elective or you're considering changing your major to accounting.

✔ A business owner (particularly someone operating a small business with gross receipts of less than $1 million) who wants to have a better understanding of the financial statements prepared by the in-house or external accountant.

✔ A brand-new accountant working in financial accounting who needs a plain-talk refresher of more advanced accounting concepts.

How This Book Is Organized

To help you find the financial accounting facts you need, this book is organized into parts that break down the subject of intermediate accounting into easily digestible portions that relate to one another.

Part I: Introducing Financial Accounting and Standards

This part introduces you to the world of financial accounting. I initiate you into the purpose, constraints, and responsibilities of financial accountants. I also provide an overview of the three financial statements. You learn how to enter accounting transactions into a company's books through the use of journal entries. You also find out about the general ledger, which records applicable transactions taking place in a business during a particular accounting cycle. Fair value accounting also gets its share of airtime in this part of the book.

Part II: Preparing and Using Financial Statements

A nice refresher, this part walks you through the proper preparation of the income statement, balance sheet, and statement of cash flow. As an extra goodie, you find out about the time value of money from the perspective of both the investor and the creditor. I walk you through simple and complex interest and show you how to account for deferred annuities and long-term bonds.

Part III: Homing in on Current and Noncurrent Assets

Parts III and IV of the book concentrate on different sections of the balance sheet. This part contains two on current assets. The first discusses cash and accounts and notes receivable. *Accounts receivable* generally originate with customer transactions. You find out about accounting for the different types of debt hanging out on the balance sheet as notes receivable. The second chapter discusses inventory. You find out about the different types of inventory and the costs associated with them. *Inventory cost flow assumptions,* which is how the cost of inventory moves from the balance sheet to the income statement, is also a topic of discussion.

The remaining chapters look at *noncurrent assets*, which are the assets a company feels it will still have at least 12 months past the balance sheet date. You learn about two types of noncurrent assets: *tangible,* which have a physical presence, and *intangible,* which you can't touch and feel. You also learn how to use depreciation to move the cost of tangible assets from the balance sheet to the income statement and how to use amortization and impairment to move the cost of intangible assets from the balance sheet to the income statement. Wrapping up Part III is a discussion about *research and development costs,* which are costs a company incurs to investigate new business processes or products.

Part IV: Analyzing Debt and Equity

The flip side of the balance sheet asset equation, Part IV talks about debt (yuck) and *equity,* which shows the combined total of each owner's investment in the business. Part IV discusses both current and noncurrent debt. Chapter 14 is all about the short-term claims payable by the company, and Chapter 15 discusses accounting for long-term obligations under various debt scenarios.

Part V: Accounting for Advanced Intermediate Issues

Here I delve into other, more advanced financial accounting topics, like accounting for income taxes and leases. You find out how to fix inadvertent mistakes in the financial statements. I also cover how to account for a change from one accounting method to another and what to do when you find out an accounting estimate is incorrect.

Part VI: The Part of Tens

I wrap up the book by explaining ten ratios helpful for evaluating the relative merits of investing in or lending money to a company. I also provide a quick look at ten common disclosure notes to the financial statements.

Icons Used in This Book

Throughout the book, you see the following icons in the left margin:

Text accompanied by this icon contains useful hints that you can apply during your class to make your studies a bit easier and more successful.

When you see this icon, warm up your brain cells, because it sits next to information you want to commit to memory.

Looking for what not to do while preparing for any graded objectives in your financial accounting class? Check out paragraphs next to this icon; they alert you to what can trip you up while taking this class.

This icon includes information that enhances the topic under discussion but isn't necessary to understand the topic.

Where to Go from Here

Each chapter stands on its own, so no matter where you start, you won't feel like you're coming in on a movie halfway through. Your motivation for purchasing this book likely dictates which chapters you want to read first and which you'll read only if you have some spare time in the future.

If you're an intermediate accounting student, flip to the chapter explaining a topic you're a little fuzzy on after reading your textbook. Business owners can get a good overview of the financial accounting process by starting with Chapters 1 and 4; these two chapters explain the nuts and bolts of financial accounting and its concepts. Otherwise, check out the table of contents or the index for a topic that interests you, or jump in anywhere in the book that covers the intermediate accounting information you're wondering about.

Part I
Introducing Financial Accounting and Standards

The 5th Wave · By Rich Tennant

©RICHTENNANT

"This ledger certainly paints a picture of the company. Edvard Munch's 'The Scream' comes to mind."

In this part . . .

You get a refresher course on financial accounting basics. This tutorial includes briefly going over the three financial statements: the income statement, balance sheet, and statement of cash flows. You review the nuts and bolts of accounting for financial transactions that show up on these financial statements.

In addition to explaining the financial statements, Chapter 1 provides info on how the financial statements are used. You explore the three standard-setting agencies that offer guidance to financial accountants and dictate how to handle all the transactions in your intermediate accounting course. Before you finish the chapter, you read over the accountant's code of professional conduct.

Chapter 2 explains the Financial Accounting Standards Board's (FASB) conceptual framework of accounting, which defines the boundaries of accounting. Along the way, you find out who the external users of the financial statements are and identify the objectives of financial reporting. Plus, you find out what basic assumptions users make when reviewing financial statements.

How to value financial transactions on the balance sheet is the subject of Chapter 3. I explain fair value, which is the price an asset will fetch in an open marketplace. You also dig into the future of fair value, especially in the international market.

The last chapter in this part, Chapter 4, explains basic accounting terms. You also find out how to book accounting transactions, investigate the difference between journals and ledgers, and work thought how to prepare a trial balance.

Chapter 1

Seeing the Big Picture of Financial Accounting

*M*ost people don't buy a title like *Intermediate Accounting For Dummies* on a whim in the bookstore, so I assume you have good reason for picking up this book. Most likely, you're preparing for or in the midst of starting your series of classes on intermediate accounting. Or perhaps you're gearing up to take the certified public accountant (CPA) exam and are looking for a plain-talk explanation of some tested topics. Maybe you're a business owner wanting to get a better handle on financial statement preparation. Then again, maybe you're just curious about the inner workings of the wonderful world of accounting. Whatever brought you here, welcome.

In this chapter, I talk about the background of financial accounting including key challenges to preparing financial statements. I also introduce you to the alphabet soup that is the three financial accounting standard-setting bodies: the SEC, FASB, and AICPA.

This chapter also introduces generally accepted accounting principles (GAAP), which defines for financial accountants the acceptable practices in the preparation of financial statements in the United States and addresses the recent Codification, which restructures GAAP into a more user-friendly format.

This chapter provides an overview of the financial accounting code of professional conduct and rules and regulations that set the standards for professionalism for financial accountants and certified public accountants. These standards give you a roadmap to follow when you're trying to figure out how to handle various accounting transactions taking place during day-to-day business operations. In particular, I explain integrity, objectivity, independence, and due care.

Ready to jump into the pool of financial accounting? Time to go back to the beginning, to the early days of financial accounting.

Financial Accounting: Seeing Where It All Began

Financial accounting involves the process of preparing financial statements for a business. This extravaganza involves three major components: accounting information, type of business entity, and user of the financial statements.

The three financial statements are the income statement, balance sheet, and statement of cash flows.

Following is a brief description of each:

- ✔ **Information:** Any accounting transactions the business completes during the accounting period. These transactions include generating revenue from the sales of company goods or services, paying business-related expenses, buying company assets, and incurring debt to run the company.

- ✔ **Business entity:** The company incurring the accounting transactions. Important in this consideration is the type of business entity; some accounting transactions require different treatment, depending on the type of entity.

  The three types of business entities are sole proprietorships (one owner), corporations, and flow-through entities, like a partnership.

- ✔ **User:** The persons or businesses that need to see the accounting transactions organized into financial statements to make educated decisions of their own. More about these users comes in the "Providing results for the users of the financial statements" section of this chapter.

  The next few sections give you more information about the three different financial statements and various users of the financial statements.

This book and your intermediate accounting textbook home in on the corporate business entity. Corporations are separate legal entities, with oversight by a board of directors and owned by its shareholders.

Preparing financial statements

The number one objective of financial accounting is to prepare financial statements that accurately reflect business operations and are understandable by those using the financial statements. You've taken your prerequisites to intermediate accounting, so you're well aware of the fact that accountants can't just throw accounting transaction data on the statements.

Rules govern how the accounting must be done, and they're called *generally accepted accounting principles (GAAP)*. I discuss them later in this chapter, in both the "Developing financial standards" and "Explaining Codification" sections. These rules pertain to both how the financial accountant shows the accounting transactions and on which financial statement the transactions appear.

But first, you get a mini-refresher on each of the financial statements:

- ✔ **Income statement:** This financial statement shows the results of business operations consisting of revenue, expenses, gains, and losses. The end product is net income or loss. I talk about the income statement again in Chapter 5. Here are just the basic facts on the four different income statement components:

  - **Revenue:** Gross receipts the company earned by selling its goods or services. More information about recognizing revenue comes in Chapter 20.

  - **Expenses:** The costs to the company to earn the gross receipts. Part V of this book contains more information on various expenses.

  - **Gains:** Income from non-business-related transactions, such as the sale of a company asset. Chapter 11 gives more information on the sale of assets, which can lead to gains and losses.

  - **Losses:** The flip side of gains — for example, losing money when selling the company car.

  The income statement is finite in what it reflects. For example, it may report net income for the 12-month period ending December 31, 2012. Any accounting transactions that take place before or after this 12-month window do not show up on the report.

- ✔ **Balance sheet:** The balance sheet has three sections: assets, liabilities, and equity. Standing on their own, they contain valuable information about a company. However, a user has to see all three interacting together on the balance sheet to form an opinion approaching reliability about the company. Chapter 6 gives you more information on preparing the balance sheet.

The balance sheet shows results from the first day the company opens to the date on the balance sheet.

Consider the basics about each balance sheet component:

- **Assets:** Resources a company owns, such as cash, equipment, and buildings. Part III of this book discusses current and long-term assets.

- **Liabilities:** Debt the business incurs for operating and expansion purposes. Chapters 14 and 15 discuss current and long-term l iabilities.

- **Equity:** The amount of ownership left in the business after deducting total liabilities from total assets. See Chapter 16 for more information on equity.

Since your intermediate accounting textbook is all about the corporation, your main areas of equity focus are stock, retained earnings, and additional paid-in capital.

✔ **Statement of cash flows:** The statement of cash flows contains certain components of both the income statement and the balance sheet. The purpose of the statement of cash flows is to show cash sources and uses during a specific period of time — in other words, how a company brings in cash and for what costs the cash goes back out the door.

The statement of cash flows combines both the income statement and the balance sheet, but it's finite in nature, showing cash ins and outs for only the reporting period.

Developing financial standards

I'm certainly not implying that preparing financial statements is a frivolous pursuit (quite the opposite!), but for now, I want you to liken preparing financial statements to a game. As in any game you play, whether it be athletics, board games like Monopoly, or computer games, without clear-cut, unambiguous rules, players in the game have no idea of their standing. Are they winning or losing?

Well, the same is true of accounting for financial transactions. And the rulebook defining acceptable practices in the preparation of financial statements in the United States is GAAP.

GAAP is the result of a witch's brew of more than 2,000 accounting documents forged during the last 60 years. In the past, generally accepted accounting principles were a collaborative effort among several standard-setting bodies — for example, the Financial Accounting Standards Board (FASB), the Emerging Issues Task Forces (EITF), and the American Institute of Certified Public Accountants (AICPA). At the AICPA, this is the specific task of the Accounting Standards Executive Committee (AcSEC), which is a senior technical committee composed of 15 CPA members of the AICPA.

Just to add a little excitement to the mix, how financial accountants view GAAP changed in 2009 with the adoption of FASB Accounting Standards Codification. You find more information on these standard setters and Codification in the "Getting to Know Key Financial Accounting Players" section of this chapter.

Providing results for the users of the financial statements

The information in the financial statements enables users to evaluate whether they want to become financially involved with the company. Involving the use of ratios and measurements, a topic I cover in Chapter 22, users of the financial statements evaluate the relative merit of one company over another by analyzing the company's historic performance.

Okay, so just who are these much-ballyhooed users of the financial statements? Users fall into three categories: existing or potential investors in the company, individuals or businesses thinking about extending credit terms to the company, and governmental agencies such as the Securities and Exchange Commission (SEC) that want to make sure the company is fairly presenting its financial position.

Although each user is different, they have a common need: assurance that the information they're looking at is both materially correct and useful. *Materially correct* means the financial statements don't contain any serious or substantial misstatement. To be useful, the information must be understandable to anyone not privy to the day-to-day activities of the company.

Investors and creditors sit at different ends of the table, but they share one characteristic: They're looking for a return in exchange for allowing the business to use their cash. Government agencies don't have a profit motive. Depending on the agency, it just wants to make sure the company is abiding by all tax codes, regulations, and GAAP.

Investors buy stock in the company. Examples of creditors are banks, automobile financing companies, and the vendors from which a company purchases its inventory or office supplies.

Identifying reporting challenges

The biggie reporting challenge is producing financial statements that are both materially correct and timely. *Materially correct* means the financial statements don't contain any serious or substantial understatement or omission. *Timeliness* relates to the users having the financial information while it's still relevant. After all, what good is financial information to investors if it's reported so far after the date of the statements that it's no longer true?

Timeliness is so important that the Securities and Exchange Commission (SEC) requires publicly traded companies to issue certain financial reports as soon as 60 days after the end of the financial period.

See Chapter 19 for more information on correcting financial statement errors.

Another reporting challenge is accounting for and determining *fair value,* which means companies record or disclose. See Chapter 11 for what assets are worth in an open marketplace instead of at historic cost.

This topic has been the subject of heated debate, as some argue that using historic cost doesn't show the true economic impact of the assets on the financial statements. Others counter by saying that fair value reporting can adversely affect the economy. Find out more about this contentious topic in Chapter 3.

Getting to Know Key Financial Accounting Players

This section discusses the three primary players in the financial accounting game. I also discuss GAAP, which defines the acceptable practices in the preparation of financial statements in the United States. In addition, I give you some information on the recent Codification, which restructured GAAP into a more user-friendly format.

First up, you get to find out about the standard setters.

Identifying standard-setting organizations

The three organizations primarily in charge of setting U.S. GAAP are the Securities and Exchange Commission (SEC), the American Institute of Certified Public Accountants (AICPA), and the Financial Accounting Standards Board (FASB).

SEC

In response to the stock market crash of 1929 and the ensuing Great Depression, the Securities Exchange Act of 1934 created the SEC. The SEC's mission is to make sure publicly traded companies tell the truth about their businesses and treat investors fairly by putting the needs of the investors before the needs of the company.

Publicly traded companies are those whose stock is available for sale in an open marketplace, such as the New York Stock Exchange.

The SEC is run by five commissioners, who are appointed to five-year terms by the President of the United States. Their terms are staggered, and no more than three commissioners can be from the same political party at the same time. These commissioners ride herd over the SEC's power to license and regulate stock exchanges, the companies whose securities trade on them, and the brokers and dealers who conduct the trading.

The enforcement authority given by Congress allows the SEC to bring civil enforcement against individuals or companies alleged to have committed accounting fraud, provided false information, or engaged in insider trading or other violations of the securities law. The SEC also works with criminal law enforcement agencies to prosecute individuals and companies alike for offenses, which include a criminal violation.

AICPA

After reading about the SEC's enforcement over publicly traded companies, you may be wondering who's making sure privately traded companies toe the line. Well, look no further! This responsibility goes to the AICPA.

Through the AICPA's senior technical committee, the Auditing Standards Board (ASB), the organization is responsible for establishing auditing and attestation standards for nonpublic companies in the United States. The purpose of a financial statement *audit* is to gather enough evidence about a company's documents to be able to issue an opinion on whether the financial statements are free of material misstatements.

The ASB has 19 members, most of whom either work for public accounting firms such as KPMG LLP or are university professors, governmental accountants, or other workers in the field of accounting. Members serve one- to three-year terms and are jointly nominated by the director of the AICPA Audit and Attest Standards Staff and the ASB chair. The responsibilities of approving the nominations fall to the AICPA Board of Directors.

A financial accountant provides an *attestation service* when issuing a report on a subject that is the responsibility of another person or business. For example, a company can hire you to calculate *net accounts receivable,* which is what customers owe the company, minus an allowance for uncollectible accounts (see Chapter 9), making sure your figures match the company's amount showing on the balance sheet.

The AICPA also has a Code of Professional Conduct by which its members must abide. I discuss the tie-in between being a member of the AICPA and following the ethical responsibilities of financial accountants in the "Considering Ethical Responsibilities" section of this chapter.

FASB

Before you get into the meat and potatoes of FASB, you need a little history lesson! Resulting from some congressional criticism of the standard-setting work being done by the AICPA, the Financial Accounting Foundation (FAF) was established in the state of Delaware as a nonprofit corporation.

The FAF, in turn, established the *Financial Accounting Standards Board* (FASB), which, ta-da!, is currently the private-sector body establishing GAAP for all nongovernmental entities.

Governmental entities follow procedures set up by the Governmental Accounting Standards Board (GASB).

The FASB has five full-time members, who are selected by the FAF. All are required to have knowledge of accounting, finance, and business. For more info on the FASB, accounting standards, and FAF, check out the FASB website at www.fasb.org/home.

The FASB further formed the Emerging Issues Task Force (EITF) in 1984 to help identify emerging accounting issues in need of standardization. The EITF consists of accounting professionals who meet six times a year with nonvoting members of the SEC and FASB to mull over current economic, business, and industrial developments.

Recognizing generally accepted accounting principles

GAAP defines for financial accountants the acceptable practices in the preparation of financial statements in the United States. The preponderance of the information I provide in Parts II, III, IV, and V of this book directly ties back to GAAP. Specifically, GAAP tells financial accountants exactly how financial data has to show up on the income statement, balance sheet, and statement of cash flows.

As I mentioned already, GAAP was, in the past, a collaborative effort among several different standard-setting bodies. I discuss all three of them earlier in this chapter: the Financial Accounting Standards Board (FASB), the Securities and Exchange Commission (SEC) and the American Institute of Certified Public Accountants (AICPA).

But hold on to your hats! How financial accountants view GAAP changed in 2009 with the adoption of FASB Accounting Standards Codification, which I discuss in the next section.

Explaining Codification

As of July 1, 2009, the FASB Accounting Standards Codification (ASC) became the single source of authoritative GAAP in the United States. Before you get in a dither, keep in mind that the Codification doesn't change GAAP; it organizes GAAP in a more user-friendly fashion and consistent format across the board for all GAAP topics.

FASB allows free, albeit limited, access to the Codification. To check this out, go to `http://asc.fasb.org/`. On the right side of the page, click *Order Professional or Basic View.* Then at the bottom of the page, under *Basic View — Free Access,* click the Select button and follow the order registration instructions.

Access is free, but for some reason, your free access comes with an expiration date. You get an e-mail asking you to renew the free access before your expiration date. If you forget, no biggie. You can renew next time you go to the Codification, regardless of whether your expiration date already passed.

After you complete the log-in procedure, on the Basic View home page, browse the topics on the taskbar at the left to see how to apply GAAP for accounting topics such as revenue (which I discuss in Chapter 20 of this book); assets, liabilities, and equity (I discuss all three in Parts III and IV of this book); and financial statement presentation (for more info, see Part II of this book). Each topic allows you to drill down to more detailed information. For example, if you select *Equity,* you can further select *Stock Dividends and Stock Splits* (see Chapter 16 in this book for more information on stock) to find out how to account for stock transactions under GAAP.

The ASC professional version annual subscription costs $850. However, ask your financial accounting instructor if your school has academic accounting access. If so, you have free access to better search functions, allowing for a fully functional view of the Codification.

Introducing international accounting standards

Your intermediate accounting textbook goes into this topic a whole lot more than your basic financial accounting textbook. In the last few decades, business has increasingly spanned borders. The U.S. was content to rely only on U.S. GAAP for many years, but since the 1970s, there's been an increasing demand for international accounting standards, to deal with the increasing international aspects of U.S. companies.

The first organization to work on harmonizing international accounting standards worldwide was the International Accounting Standards Committee (IASC), formed in 1973. The International Accounting Standards Board (IASB) preceded the IASC. Currently, the IASB has promulgated approximately 50 International Financial Reporting Standards (IFRS) in use by more than 130 countries.

Noting that the IASC dates back to 1973, it's clear to see that converging FASB and IASB standards is an ongoing process. Indeed, it's been ten years since the FASB and IASB agreed to converge in "The Norwalk Agreement." Added to the mix is the SEC, which is pushing to have the FASB act as an endorsement (vs. convergence) body for the IASB standards in the U.S.

This is a hot accounting topic that will take center stage in the accounting arena for the foreseeable future. For more information, visit the FASB website at www.fasb.org/intl/convergence_iasb.shtml.

Considering Ethical Responsibilities

Just as you probably follow your own personal code of conduct, every profession should operate following ethical guidelines. In other words, you must always attempt to do the right thing, regardless of whether doing the right thing is at that particular moment best for you personally. Linked to staying true to ethical responsibilities are such items as adhering to high standards of business behavior and fostering an atmosphere of trust and mutual respect between employees and customers.

Following the accountant's code of conduct

Most professions that require state licensing have to abide by that state's code of conduct. In the case of financial accountants, this licensing is in the form of being designated as a certified public accountant (CPA).

In addition to state codes, your code of conduct as a financial accountant comes from the *AICPA,* which is the national professional organization for all CPAs. You don't have to be a member of the AICPA to be a CPA. If you're serious about your profession, membership has many rewards such as automatically informing you about new accounting and auditing standards.

Since the AICPA Code of Professional Conduct is for nonpublic companies, you're probably wondering about codes of conduct to follow when auditing publicly traded companies. All publicly traded companies' standard of professional conduct comes from The Public Company Accounting Oversight Board (PCAOB) of the SEC. (The acronym PCAOB is pronounced "Pee-Ca-Boo.") The Sarbanes–Oxley Act of 2002 established PCAOB.

But what if you're a financial accountant who isn't a CPA or a member of the AICPA? Do you still have to worry about abiding by a code of conduct? Well, of course you do. Any profession that lacks ethical behavior will descend into chaos. Financial accountants must have high professional standards, a strict code of professional ethics, and a commitment to serving the public interest. They achieve these goals through their integrity, objectivity, and independence.

Having integrity

In the world of financial accounting, integrity means you act according to a code or standard of values. You demonstrate integrity when you do the right thing, regardless of whether doing so is best for you personally.

Accountants must follow specific rules, standards, or guidance. You read about these different standards and rules throughout the rest of this book. For example, Part II shows you the right way to prepare financial statements, Part III homes in on accounting for assets, and Part VI delves into accounting for debt and equity.

Understanding the AICPA's effect on the Code of Conduct

You may be wondering what the big deal is about the AICPA Code of Professional Conduct, since membership in the AICPA isn't mandatory. Well, to practice as a CPA, you must be licensed by your state, which does recognize the authority of the AICPA. State and federal courts consistently hold that all practicing CPAs, regardless of membership in the AICPA, must follow the professional ethical standards contained in their Code of Professional Conduct. Find out more about the Code of Professional Conduct at www.aicpa.org/About/code/sec50.htm.

Keep in mind that you have to follow both the form and the substance of technical and ethical standards. Substance over form is a pretty common expression, but you may not understand exactly what it means. Form represents the tangible; you also may think of it as following the letter of the law. Substance represents an implied fact.

For intermediate accounting, integrity means that you prepare financial statements to the best of your ability, keeping in mind that doing so may not be the same as completely agreeing with the way the user of the financial statements prefers them to look.

In the same vein is the fact that you don't record a transaction in such a way that you hide the true effect of the transaction, regardless of whether you are following form. In other words, you must show the true nature (substance) instead of hiding a negative financial event behind form.

Integrity also requires you to be objective, remain independent, and show due care. Objectivity and independence are somewhat interrelated. Showing due care means you're competent and diligent. I discuss each in more detail in the next few sections of this chapter.

Maintaining objectivity

Accountants must be *objective,* meaning impartial and intellectually honest. Being *impartial* means you're neutral and unbiased in all decision-making processes. You base your opinion and reporting only on the facts, not on any preconceived notions or prejudices. Remaining *intellectually honest* means that you interpret rules and policies in a truthful and sincere manner, staying true to both their substance and their form.

Therefore, despite what one person may tell you, until all the facts are revealed, you keep an open mind. And always keep in mind that whether the users of the financial statements *perceive* the accountant to be objective is just as important as the fact that the accountant is actually 100 percent objective.

Achieving independence

Many types of public accounting services, such as auditing services, require the financial accountant be independent in both fact and appearance. Being *independent* while providing services means that you have no special relationship with or financial interest in the client that may cause you to disregard evidence and facts when evaluating your client.

What does it mean to be independent in both fact and appearance? The biggie is that you avoid any perceived conflicts of interest: You don't perform services for any client with whom you have either a personal or a non-audit-related business relationship. For example, if you have a significant financial interest with a major competitor of your client, your client may question whose best interests you have in mind while performing the accounting services.

The concept of independence and objectivity differs somewhat, depending on whether the financial accounting work is in public accounting or private accounting. In public accounting, the financial accountant (most likely a CPA) works for an accounting firm, providing services such as auditing or financial statement preparation for clients. In private accounting, you do accounting work for your own employer rather than for a client. Obviously, you can't strive for independence when you're doing accounting work for your own employer, so in private accounting, objectivity is key.

Taking due care

When providing services, you must be competent and practice diligence. In addition, due care means you plan and supervise adequately any professional activity for which you are responsible. For example, your boss has the responsibility to make sure you understand how you are to handle your piece of the financial accounting pie and to supervise you to make sure you stay on course. Due care on your part as an accountant means you follow the instructions of your manager and ask questions if some accounting transaction comes up that you don't understand.

Competence means you have the education and experience to be able to do the job. Maintaining competence requires a commitment to professional development by taking continuing education classes throughout your career.

Each state requires a certain number of continuing education classes to recertify your CPA license. Most states require 80 hours of continuing education every two years, with 20 of those hours in accounting and auditing.

Diligence means you work to the best of your ability, showing concern for the best interest of the user of the financial statement while remaining consistent with your responsibilities and serving the public trust. It also means you provide information in a timely fashion.

Chapter 2

Walking Through the Conceptual Framework of Financial Accounting

*T*he calculator may seem mightier than the sword, but accountants are beholden to certain rules of practice. They have to follow the rules on their preparation, which are called *generally accepted accounting principles (GAAP)*. GAAP is the law, but every law needs a body to interpret it, and the world of accounting is no exception. The Financial Accounting Standards Board (FASB) is a nonprofit, non-government-affiliated organization that interprets GAAP and sets guidelines and practices for accounting.

This chapter introduces you to the FASB's conceptual framework of accounting. This framework defines the boundaries of accounting by providing accountants with methods for booking accounting transactions, defines key terms for the users of the financial statements, and shows the correct way to prepare financial statements.

Along the way, you find out who the external users of the financial statements are and read about the objectives of their financial reporting. I also explain the primary and secondary qualities of accounting information and walk you through the basic elements of all three financial statements.

Plus, you find out what basic assumptions users make when reviewing financial statements. For example, a biggie is that the business is a *going-concern,* which means it will remain in existence for at least 12 months past the balance sheet date. You also find out about the basic cost, revenue, and matching principles used in financial statement preparation.

Who Needs a Conceptual Framework?

Accounting dates back to the Stone Age as a way of figuring out the supply and demand of commerce. Before we had stores and cash registers, man needed some way to make sure there was an equitable trade of good for good or good for service. Coming forward into the present, with trading going beyond near geographic areas, accountants needed rules to follow to make sure their work product was understandable, comparable, and reliable.

However, not a lot of standard setting hit the accounting biz until the Great Depression of 1929. The Financial Accounting Standards Board (FASB) didn't begin the process of spelling out a framework of financial accounting concepts until the mid-1970s.

Your intermediate accounting textbook probably has an overview of the framework for financial accounting, the Conceptual Framework in a sort of pie chart. In the spirit of keeping with standard practices, I use a similar chart here, in Figure 2-1.

Figure 2-1:
Mmmm,
Conceptual
Framework
pie!

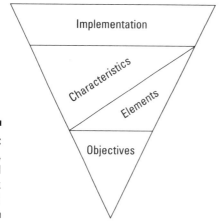

Implementation

Characteristics

Elements

Objectives

FASB CONs

Nope, they aren't jailbirds! The FASB organizes its conceptual framework into Statements of Financial Accounting Concepts (CON). Following is a brief description of each by Statement of Financial Accounting Concept (SFAC) number:

SFAC No. 5: "Recognition and Measurement in Financial Statements of Business Enterprises": Discusses how transactions record on the financial statements (for example, using historic cost rather than fair value).

SFAC No. 6: "Elements of Financial Statements": Defines terms that show up on the financial statements, such as what an asset is.

SFAC No. 7: "Using Cash Flow Information and Present Value in Accounting Measurements":

Talks about using estimated future cash flows as a basis for measuring an asset or a liability.

SFAC No. 8: Conceptual Framework for Financial Reporting: Chapters 1 and 3 discuss the goals and purposes of accounting, along with the qualities that make accounting info useful.

You can find the full text of each CON available at www.fasb.org/jsp/FASB/Page/SectionPage&cid=1176156317989

FASB CONs also address nonbusiness organizations, such as private nonprofit hospitals, and some SFACs have been superseded or replaced.

At the narrow tip of the pie, the first level is the objective of financial reporting. In the middle are the characteristics of accounting information and the elements of financial reporting.

Finally, the third level (the wide piece of the pie, by the crust) is the "how" of implementing the concepts. This level includes recognition, measurement, and disclosure.

The information in the next sections of this chapter provide some general background on why financial accounting standards work the way they do and what they attempt to accomplish. Ready to get chewing on this accounting piece of pie? I start with the objective.

Knowing the Objective

The first piece of the pie points out that financial accounting is the process of classifying and recording all events that take place during the normal course of business. These events include earning revenue, paying bills, bringing in gains, and incurring losses.

The results of all these events are then arranged on the correct financial statement: the balance sheet, income statement, or statement of cash flows. I give you more information on all three in the section "Identifying the Elements of Financial Statements," coming up in this chapter. The company then reports these results to the external users of the financial statements.

External users include investors, creditors, banks, and regulatory agencies such as the IRS and the SEC (see Chapter 1). However, you have to remember that sticking all these accounting events on the right financial statement isn't an end in itself. The facts and figures shown on the financial statements give the people and businesses using them a bird's-eye view of how well the business is performing.

The internal users of the financial statements are employees, department heads, and other management — all folks who work at the business.

This point is important. The external users evaluate the information so they can make reliable, informed investment and credit decisions. An individual's decision to invest (and keep investing) in one business over another can make the difference between being able to retire early to live on investment proceeds or bagging groceries after retirement at the local supermarket to make ends meet.

Respecting Statement Characteristics

The middle piece of the pie discusses what financial accountants have to do to serve the needs of the external users, beyond merely organizing accounting events into financial statements. Just as adding salt instead of sugar to a cookie recipe puts your end result out of whack, not adding the right ingredients to your financial statements gives users the equivalent of an inedible cookie.

So what sort of characteristics do you need to make sure are present for financial statement preparation to totally serve the needs of your users? Two biggies are relevance and faithful representation, which I explain in the "Primary" section of this chapter.

Other fundamental qualities that make financial accounting useful for external user decision making are comparability and consistency (see the "Secondary" section for more info). Following is an explanation of each, starting with the primary qualities.

Primary

Accounting information must be *relevant,* which means it's capable of affecting the user's decision-making process. The financial statements have to give the users enough info that they can form opinions about the final outcome of past events and how any present or future events may shake out. This info is also known as *predictive value.*

The financial statements also need to give users enough info that they can tell whether any opinions they made about events that have come to fruition were indeed correct. This info is known as *confirmatory value.*

Materiality also ties in with relevance. *Materiality* is the importance accountants place on accounting transactions, based on their overall significance. Accountants and auditors bandy about the term *materially correct,* which means that nothing is missing or has been added to the financial statements that would cause an informed user to come to an erroneous conclusion about the financial standing of the company.

What makes this constraint interesting is that what's material for one business may not be material for another. You have to consider the size of the business, the amount of the financial statement transaction, and how significant the transaction is when comparing to the financial statements as a whole.

Timeliness is also a big deal with relevance. The users need to have the relevant material before it loses its capacity to influence the decision-making process. Look at it this way: If you find out a day after the sale ends that something you wanted to buy was marked 50 percent off, that information is now of absolutely no value to you.

Another biggie is *faithful representation,* meaning that what's on the financial statements actually happened; the company didn't make anything up to show better results. The financial statements are *complete* — that is, the company didn't "forget" to match all expenses with revenue, and the statements are free from error. They also have to be *neutral,* which means the company doesn't suppress unflattering information.

No financial statement can be totally free from error. Besides the fact that it's impossible to eliminate all *de minimis* errors and still produce a financial statement in a timely fashion, many financial statements contain estimates, which may change as future events play out.

Financial statements aren't worth the paper they're written on unless their users can rely on the fact that the representations made within the financial statements are verifiable, neutral, and materially correct. For example, if the income statement shows $10 million of sales, these sales must actually have taken place — they can't be merely the best guess of company management (or what company management wants the users to think occurred).

Secondary

Two secondary qualities are comparability and consistency. *Comparability* means that the financial information is prepared in such a way that it can be weighed against companies in similar industries or past financial statements for the same company.

Consistency means that the same accounting events are handled in a similar fashion, period after period. For example, the company doesn't just willy-nilly switch methods to recognize revenue. Changing it up midstream causes old financial statements results to be skewed when comparing with the current one.

In some instances, a company can change accounting methods. See Chapter 19 for more information and how to report it to satisfy the consistency standard.

The information on the financial statement has to be understandable to anyone who's not privy to the internal workings of the business. Of course, having the data be understandable is relative.

Basically, however, the financial information must be laid out in a fashion that users with a reasonable understanding of the business world (and a willingness to do research on specific topics, as needed) can ferret out all important accounting facts about the business.

Identifying the Elements of Financial Statements

The second concept that shows up in the middle piece of pie is an explanation of the proper preparation of financial statements. From prior accounting classes taken as prerequisites to intermediate accounting, you know there are three financial statements: the balance sheet, the income statement, and the statement of cash flows.

GAAP rules pertain to both how the financial accountant shows the accounting transactions and on which financial statement the transactions appear.

You get into all the details of different accounts and how they show up on the financial statements in other chapters in this book. For now, I just want to give you a refresher on the three financial statements, their purpose, and what types of accounts show up on each.

I stress the term *financial accountant* in some instances throughout this book because other types of accountants (such as tax accountants) don't follow GAAP. In fact, tax accountants have to prepare their records for use in preparing tax returns in accordance with the Internal Revenue Code, which varies from GAAP. See Chapter 17 for more information on accounting for income taxes.

Balance sheet balancing act

The *balance sheet* shows the health of a business from the day the business started operations to the specific date of the balance sheet report. The balance sheet has three sections: assets, liabilities, and equity. Following is a thumbnail sketch of the three:

- ✔ **Assets:** Resources a company owns, such as cash, equipment, and buildings
- ✔ **Liabilities:** Debt the business incurs for operating and expansion purposes
- ✔ **Equity:** Amount of ownership left in the business after deducting total liabilities from total assets

Standing on their own, they contain valuable information about a company. However, a user has to see all three interacting together on the balance sheet to form an opinion approaching reliability about the company.

A *classified balance sheet* groups like accounts together. For example, all current assets, such as cash and accounts receivable, show up in one grouping. Likewise, all current liabilities, such as accounts payable and other short-term debt, show up in another grouping. This structure assists users of the balance sheet so they don't have to go on a scavenger hunt to round up all similar accounts.

Figure 2-2 shows a simple balance sheet. If you want to see a totally blown-out one, check out Figure 6-4.

Hill Landscaping, Incorporated
Balance Sheet
December 31, 2013

Assets:

Current assets

Cash	$ 32,500		
Accounts receivable	10,000		
Total current assets		$ 42,500	

Long-term assets

Notes receivable - long-term	15,000	

Property, plant, and equipment:

Machinery and equipment - net of depreciation	123,500	
Total assets		$ **181,000**

Liabilities & Equity

Current Liabilities

Accounts Payable	$ 35,700	

Long-Term Liabilities

Note payable	15,000	
Total Liabilities		$ **50,700**

Stockholders' Equity

Capital Stock:	100	
Retained earnings	130,200	
Total Stockholders' Equity		**130,300**
Total Liabilities & Equity		$ **181,000**

Figure 2-2:
Classified
balance
sheet.

Note two important points about the balance sheet:

- ✔ The date on a balance sheet is always the last day of the accounting period reflected on the statement.
- ✔ Assets must always equal the total of liabilities plus equity. If they don't, the balance sheet doesn't balance — and then something is definitely wrong!

This balancing act is known as the fundamental accounting equation. Get it? Balance sheet — balancing act? Another way to state it is net assets equals equity. Using the term *net assets* is the same as saying "assets minus liabilities."

Eager to talk more about the balance sheet? Check out Parts III and IV of this book. Part III covers current assets and noncurrent assets, and Part IV delves into debt and equity.

For a more detailed look into stockholders' equity many companies also prepare a statement of changes in stockholders' equity showing stockholders' equity at both the beginning and end of the year.

Income statement elements

The income statement shows the business's income, expenses, gains, and losses. The end product of these transactions is net income or loss.

Some also call the income statement a statement of profit and loss, or P&L. GAAP also refers to this report as statement of income because the income statement shows not only income and expenses from continuing operations (which basically is revenue minus expenses), but also income from myriad sources, such as the gain or loss that results when a company sells an asset (see Chapter 11). Read more on the income statement in Chapter 5.

Here's information on each of the four different income statement components:

- ✔ **Revenue:** Gross receipts earned by the company selling its goods or services
- ✔ **Expenses:** The costs to the company to earn the gross receipts
- ✔ **Gains:** Income from non-business-related transactions, such as selling a company asset
- ✔ **Losses:** The flip side of gains, such as losing money when selling the company car

It's important to note that the date for the income statement is for a defined period rather than for the entire life of the company, as with the balance sheet. Figure 2-3 shows a simple income statement.

Hill Landscaping, Incorporated
Income Statement
For the Year Ending December 31, 2013

Sales:			
Sales			$ 187,400
Less: Sales discounts	$ 15,200		
Sales returns and allowances	5,250		20,450
Net sales			$ 166,950
Cost of goods sold:			76,375
Gross profit			$ 90,575
Operating expenses:			
Selling expenses	$ 15,370		
General and administrative expenses	35,600		
Total operating expense			50,970
Operating income			$39,605
Other revenues:			
Gain on disposal of fixed asset	$ 15,135		
Dividend income	3,200		18,335
Other expenses:			
Interest expense			2,595
Income before taxes			55,345
Provision for income taxes			16,604
Net income			$38,741

Figure 2-3: Income statement.

Statement of cash flows elements

The purpose of the statement of cash flows is to show cash sources and uses during a specific period of time — in other words, how a company brings in cash and for what costs the cash goes back out the door. Therefore, the statement of cash flows contains certain components of both the income statement and the balance sheet.

The statement of cash flows has three different sections classifying all cash receipts and payments:

- ✔ **Operating:** The sources and uses of cash in the operating section come from revenue, expenses, gains, losses, and other costs.

- ✔ **Investing:** This section shows sources and uses of cash from debt and equity purchases and sales; purchases of property, plant, and equipment; and collection of principal on debt.

- ✔ **Financing:** You report activities such as long-term liability (paying or securing loans beyond a period of 12 months from the balance sheet date) and equity items (sale of company stock and payment of dividends) in the financing section.

Figure 2-4 shows a simple statement of cash flows. Can't wait to really dive into the statement of cash flows? Check out Chapter 7 to read more about each section and how to prepare one.

Financial statements, made to measure

Communicating with parties interested in the business via the financial statements requires the measurement of all accounting transactions. *Measurement* refers to the fact that every accounting event must have a cost or a value to be recognized on the financial statements. You may be confused by the difference between cost and value. Well, don't feel as if you're alone. This issue can be a thorny one even among seasoned financial accountants.

For example, the method a merchandising or manufacturing company opts to use to value its ending inventory (see Chapter 10) definitely affects financial statement measurement. A few different methods are allowable under generally accepted accounting principles (GAAP). Depending on the method the business uses, the value of inventory on the balance sheet and the associated cost of goods sold on the income statement can vary wildly.

Hill Landscaping, Incorporated
Statement of Cash Flows
For the Year Ending December 31, 2013

Cash Flows from Operating Activities:	
Cash received from customers	$ 75,800
Cash paid to suppliers	(45,960)
Net cash provided by operating activities	29,840
Cash Flows from Investing Activities:	
Proceeds from sale of equipment	$ 15,000
Purchase of land	(45,000)
Net cash used for investing activities	(30,000)
Cash Flows from Financing Activities:	
New long-term borrowing	$ 22,500
Payment of long-term debt	(7,500)
Payment of dividends	(5,000)
Net cash provided by financing activities	10,000
Increase (decrease) in cash	9,840
Cash balance, January 1, 2012	22,660
Cash balance, December 31, 2012	32,500

Figure 2-4:
Statement
of cash
flows.

Explanatory notes accompany the financial statements and contain information that isn't readily available through review of the figures on the statements. They show how or why a company handles various transactions. For
example, notes to the financial statements tell the reader what type of method
the company uses to depreciate its assets (see Chapter 12). Chapter 21 gives
you ten common explanatory notes to the financial statements.

Finally, it's time to move on to the big piece of the pie. The next few sections in this chapter discuss recognition, measurement, and disclosure concepts. You start with financial statement assumptions, continue with accounting principles, and finish with financial statement constraints.

Making Assumptions

Users of the financial statements make certain assumptions about them. Your intermediate accounting textbook discusses four: going-concern, economic entity, monetary unit, and periodicity.

From your prerequisite accounting classes, you probably have at least a passing understanding of going-concern. The other three aren't as hot topics and may have you scratching your head somewhat wondering what the heck they are.

Don't worry — by the time you finish reading this section, you'll have a complete understanding of all four. I kick it off with everyone's favorite: the going-concern principle.

Going-concern principle

The going-concern principle means the business will still be operating more than 12 months past the balance sheet date. Many events, both within and outside the control of a business, can affect its ability to continue as a going concern.

Reporting parent and subsidiary

An exception to the Chinese wall of economic entity is merging the activities of a parent and a sub for reporting purposes. A *parent business* owns more than 50 percent of another business. This investee is the subsidiary. Financial statements for parents and subs have to be consolidated — the two entities are treated as one business. Revenues and expenses are reported together, with the investment in the sub reported on the parent's balance sheet as "Investment in Sub."

Consolidated financial statements are prepared for parent companies and include all the assets, liabilities, revenue, expenses, and other gains and losses of all its subsidiaries. For example, say that Corporation Alpha is the parent and Corporation Beta and Chi are subs. Corporation Alpha's financial statements must include all accounting information for Beta and Chi.

Following are just a few:

- ✔ **Rapid technological change:** If a business can't keep up with the advances in its field and has inventory that becomes obsolete, going-concern can be a serious consideration. For example, no one wants a cellular phone so big and clunky that it can double as a paperweight.

- ✔ **Expiring patents:** Pharmaceutical companies that don't have a long-range plan to deal with the lack of revenue from expiring patents may soon be out of business.

- ✔ **Availability of financing:** If a company is having problems paying short-term debt, having access to loans with low interest rates can mean the difference between being a going concern and having to close its doors.

To qualify as a going concern, a company has to be able to generate and/or raise enough capital to pay its operating expenses and make appropriate payments on debt.

Economic entity

This info means that the company is separate and distinct from any shareholders, corporate officers, or any other closely related individual or business entities. In other words, the company has to report the results from operations and balance sheet accounts without comingling the financial affairs of owners and managers.

This stipulation is important for users of the financial statements so they can make an informed decision on whether to invest in or loan the company money. It's so important that if there are material *related party transactions*, such as a company making a salary advance to an employee/shareholder, it must be disclosed in the notes to the financial statements (see Chapter 21).

Being an accountant in private practice, it can be horrifying to see how many corporate officer/employees tend to use corporate assets as their own private piggybank. Per most state statutes regulating business entities, this act removes the barrier between business and individual eliminating the limited liability advantage of incorporation.

Rules were (sometimes) made to be broken

Based on the unique facts and circumstances of the revenue transaction, it can be okay to deviate somewhat from the earned and realizable criteria for revenue recognition. Two good examples are the percentage-of-completion method for long-term contracts and the installment-sale method.

Here's a thumbnail sketch of both:

Percentage-of-completion method: Use this method when you record revenue from long-term contracts in stages. You recognize revenue, cost, and gross profit throughout the life of each contract, based on a periodic measurement of progress. It's considered to be advancing revenue recognition (see Chapter 20 for more information). This method is also

discussed as a note to the financial statements (see Chapter 21).

Installment sale method: This method of revenue recognition takes place whenever purchases are made but not fully paid for at point of sale or delivery and, thus, do not fully record as revenue at the point of sale.

The theory behind delaying recognition for financial statement purposes is that the risk of not collecting on the installment sale receivable is greater than an accounts receivable. Therefore, to cover the realizable aspect of revenue recognition, the revenue is booked as it is received. See Chapter 20 for more information. This method is also discussed as a note to the financial statements (see Chapter 21).

Monetary unit

In accounting, we measure items in dollars (for the U.S.). And these dollar measurements don't adjust on the balance sheet or income statement to take into account fluctuations in valuation. For example, except in extremely rare circumstances, financial accountants don't report the effects of inflation or deflation.

This subject gets more complex when a corporation is multinational and, thus, dealing with monetary units other than the dollar. Your intermediate accounting class doesn't cover this, but you can read more about multinational corporations and currency conversions at www.fasb.org/summary/stsum52.shtml.

Periodicity

To give the users of the financial statements timely information they can use, financial statements have to issue with regularity. The periodic cycle of financial statement preparation is usually monthly, quarterly, or yearly.

Keep in mind that the shorter the time frame, the less likely the financial statements will be faithful representations of the financial facts and circumstances of the business. For example, an income statement for the year ending December 31, 2013, would be more accurate and reliable than a report showing the results of a one-month period.

Sticking to Your Principles

Accountants follow basic principles when booking accounting transactions. These principles reign supreme over the recognition of costs and revenue, matching, and disclosure. This section gives you a thumbnail sketch of each, referencing other chapters in the book when necessary.

Historic cost

Assets and liabilities report on the balance sheet at *historic cost,* which is acquisition price plus (in the case of fixed assets like equipment) the cost of any major modifications. Recording transactions at historic cost is good for the users of the financial statements because the costs are verifiable.

Verifiable means that two people looking at the same transaction will come to a similar conclusion. For example, two people adding up invoices relating to a certain expense will come up with the same grand total.

Fair value, a market-based rather than historic cost measurement, is the topic of Chapter 3.

If anything other than historic cost is used to value a transaction, the accounting for the same type of transaction may vary wildly, based on who was doing the valuation and what method that person was using. In other words, a dollar today is the same as a dollar next month.

Revenue recognition

Financial accounting GAAP (see Chapter 1) guidelines state that you record revenue when it's earned and realizable and record expenses when they're incurred. Wondering what the criteria are for earned and realizable? The *earned criteria* are satisfied when the vendor satisfactorily performs on its contract with the customer. *Realizable* means that the vendor has an actual expectation of collecting the money for the job from the customer.

Cost-benefit down the drain

Years ago, the bookkeeper at one of my clients spent 5 hours tracking down the reason why the company bank reconciliation was off by $2.00 to make sure the bank hadn't made a mistake. Yikes! Now, was this an effective and efficient use of that bookkeeper's time and salary expense? Well, no, of course not. Let's say she was paid $10/hour. It cost the company $50 for her to confirm the operating account bank balance was indeed off by $2 and it wasn't just an inadvertent mistake on the part of the bank.

The accrual method takes cash out of the equation because money changing hands doesn't determine whether you recognize a transaction. Thus, a company has accounts receivable, which shows as money customers owe to the business and accounts payable, which shows all money a company owes to its vendors.

Matching

Under GAAP, a business must associate all relevant expenses to recognized revenue during an accounting period. Your textbook probably puts this as "Let the expense follow the revenue."

The mainstay of accrual accounting, you record revenue when it's earned and realizable and record expenses when they're incurred, regardless of whether money changes hands at the time of the transaction.

A good example of matching is a fixed asset purchase. Under GAAP, the cost of buying a fixed asset (see Chapter 11) goes to the balance sheet and then is systematically written off over the asset's useful life through depreciation (see Chapter 12).

Full disclosure

Accountants have to provide any additional information users need to explain the numbers on the financial statements. They do this with notes to the financial statements (see Chapter 21) or with supplementary information.

A good example of supplementary information is management discussion and analysis. Management for a manufacturer of food-related products may discuss how obesity trends are expected to affect the business.

Important notes to the financial statements discuss the depreciation method in use and the methods the company uses to figure allowances and inventory valuation.

Accepting Financial Accounting Constraints

Perfection in financial reporting is the Great White Whale of accounting. You're just never going to reel it in into your financial statement boat. The major reason for this problem is that every day that slides by while you're wringing your hands trying for perfection is just one more step toward making the financial statements obsolete and unusable.

In addition to the whole timeliness aspect of financial accounting are cost/benefit, materiality, and treatment constraints. Plus, some industries have "special GAAP," in which they have to account for certain industry-unique transactions in a particular way.

Playing it safe

Financial accountants aren't daredevils! Being conservative means that, when in doubt, the financial accountant chooses the accounting treatment that has the least effect on revenue or expenses.

Keep in mind that the business shouldn't go overboard trying to minimize the risk of uncertainty. Sprinkled in with conservatism is neutrality, which means a company can't discriminate between financial facts merely to appeal to its users, and comparability, which is the ability to spot similarities and differences between two sets of financial statements.

Understanding cost-benefits

Associated with materiality (see the "Primary" section of this chapter for more info on materiality), this topic means you don't spin your wheels trying to tie down every accounting event. There's a limit to the amount of cost a company should incur for any reporting benefit.

Outside the GAAP

Before you exit this chapter, I want to give you some info on the different types of specialized GAAP that applies to particular industries. Any GAAP guide can give you the 411 on all of them. Following are just a few:

Gas and oil: This industry is all about mineral interests and the production of crude oil — including natural gas. The workflow of this industry focuses on finding properties that may contain the natural resources, conducting some exploration, developing the properties (for example, putting in oil wells), and, finally, acquiring or producing the natural resource. See Chapter 13 for more information.

Health care: Examples of health care entities are hospitals, nursing homes, surgery centers, and doctors' offices. A major issue with

this type of entity is the significant amounts of money that can be invested in drugs, linens, and other ancillary services. Most health care entities use the last-in, first-out method to value their inventories. See Chapter 10.

Motion picture: Issues include how to account for the production, sale, licensing, and distribution of the films, associated DVDs, and product-related merchandise. Accounting for the motion picture industry can be quite harum-scarum, since it's difficult to estimate earned revenue and related costs over the life of a film. To handle this problem, the motion picture industry figures an appropriate estimation method that, as accurately as possible, matches revenue and expenses to show the film's financial performance.

For example, imagine that an employee of a company spends five hours trying to track down some missing office furniture with a *de minimis* value to see whether the missing furniture needs to come off the balance sheet. This information involves a cost (the employee payroll). Generally, the cost of information should not exceed the benefits to users of financial accounting information in their decision making.

Preparing a *bank reconciliation* means you take the balance in the bank account per the bank as of a certain date, add in any deposits that got to the bank too late to hit the statement and subtract any checks the company has written that have not yet cleared.

Following industry practices

I wax on throughout this book about GAAP (see Chapter 1) because it's such an integral part of your intermediate accounting course. Although GAAP pertains to most nongovernmental entities, certain types of businesses have

GAAP tailored to the specialized industry. The inherent nature of each of these types of industries may require modified accounting principles, financial reporting presentation, and required or recommended disclosures.

Materiality also ties in with constraints. Basically, accountants have to decide which errors are material, fix them, and move along. Thus, another constraint is that no financial statement will ever be totally error-free.

Chapter 3

Invaluable Valuation

*T*his chapter gives a brief overview on valuation. It provides a refresher on historic cost while homing in on fair value measurements. I also report on current developments regarding the Financial Accounting Standards Board's (FASB) long-term goal of having financial assets and liabilities reporting on the balance sheet at *fair value* (what an unpressured person would pay in an open market place) instead of historic cost.

Assets are resources that a company owns, such as cash, equipment, and buildings. *Liabilities* are debts the business incurs for operating and expansion purposes.

You also read about various ways to figure and adjust fair value. This topic is a somewhat complicated accounting subject that I reduce to its most basic explanation, to help you get your feet wet in the subject. Still, this chapter gives you all the info you need to tackle this topic for your intermediate accounting class.

Introducing Valuation

After taking the financial accounting class that's the prerequisite for intermediate accounting, you probably have at least a passing remembrance of the concept of *historic cost:* Assets and liabilities go on the balance sheet at the acquisitions amount. For example, if a company buys a new desk and pays $2,000, the desk reflects in the fixed assets section of the balance sheet at the $2,000. Even if the company got a good deal and the desk is really worth $2,500, the balance sheet amount remains $2,000.

Defining financial assets and liabilities

Financial assets include cash, ownership in another business entity, or a contract that can lead to cash or other financial instruments, such as an option from another company.

Financial liabilities arise when a company has to give up cash or other financial instruments to another company. In contrast, nonfinancial assets include property, plant, and equipment.

Costs beyond the purchase price of assets like property, plant, and equipment can also reflect on the balance sheet. For more information on this topic, see Chapter 11.

Critics of the historical cost method find fault with the fact that it considers only the acquisition cost of an asset while ignoring the asset's current market value. The historical cost method focuses primarily on allocating the cost of an asset over its useful life. For more information, see Chapter 12, which is all about depreciation, a cost-allocation method.

Adding excitement to the mix, since the late 1980s, the FASB has been pushing to require all financial instruments and some other assets and liabilities to be listed at fair value rather than historic cost. Breaking this down to its most simple explanation, the value of the financial instrument adjusts up and down, depending on the fair value of the asset or liability as of the date of the balance sheet.

Of course, nothing in generally accepted accounting principles (GAAP) is as easy as it looks. I explain the concept of fair value in the next few sections of this book. Get a cup of coffee — it's time to get started!

Explaining Fair Value

In *fair value,* a company presents certain assets and liabilities on the balance sheet at a price received or given in an orderly transaction between market participants. Goodness, what a mouthful! Need an example to make this a bit clearer? Basically, a company reports securities it owns on the balance sheet at the current market rate, or the amount of money the company would be able to sell them for if it wanted to.

This value is also known as the security's *exit price.* The exit price assumes that no duress is involved in the sale and that it applies regardless of whether the company wanted to or was able to sell the security at the date of fair value measurement. For example, the company isn't forced to sell the security to have the funds to make payroll. In fact, some sort of contract may prohibit the company from selling the security for a certain period of time after purchase. Such a situation doesn't preclude fair value measurement.

Fair value assessment assumes a hypothetical transaction to sell the asset or get rid of a liability at the measurement date, which is the date of the balance sheet.

Here's a bit of history, for the interested: After the failure of 747 savings and loans in the 1980s, FASB issued Statement No. 107, "Disclosures about Fair Value of Financial Instruments," in 1991. Since Codification (see Chapter 1), it is now a part of Accounting Standards Codification (ASC) 825 "Financial Instruments," which requires entities to supplement their historical cost financial statements with disclosures about the fair values of financial instruments that those statements report. See Chapter 21 for more info on disclosure notes.

Some items for which fair value is never used are investments in subsidiaries, lease financial assets, and liabilities. See Chapter 18 for more info on leases and deposit liabilities, which is money the holder is required to eventually pay back.

Making fair value fair again, post-Enron

The Enron debacle in 2001 ushered in the Sarbanes–Oxley Act of 2002 (SOX) and further prompted the FASB to establish SFAS 157. Under Codification, it is now referred to as ASC 820: "Fair Value Measurements and Disclosures." This ASC defines fair value, gives a framework for measuring fair value, and provides disclosure guidance for fair value measurements.

I find my students are still fascinated by the events leading to the meltdown at Enron. Basically Enron was going a bit crazy with their accounting treatment for fair value. The unrealistic accounting was signed off on by their accounting firm – the now defunct Arthur Andersen and approved by the Securities and Exchange Commission (SEC). Unfortunately for the lower ranking employees at Enron, large bonuses were paid to upper Enron management based on grandiose fair value assessments that never came to fruition.

At the end, all employees at Arthur Anderson and Enron lost their jobs and health insurance benefits. Many Enron employees and retirees lost their entire retirement savings, having been invested Enron shares that value bottomed out at .40 per share.

Techniques for measuring fair value

Fair value measurement involves some basic assumptions. For one, you can't have an accurate measurement of fair value unless you figure it based on what the asset is worth or what the liability would transfer for in an appropriate marketplace — in other words, its *principal market.* For example, you find out fair value of gold in a precious metal marketplace, such as Monex, not in a marketplace that specializes in pork belly futures, such as the Chicago Mercantile Exchange.

Failing to find a principal market place, the valuation comes from the most advantageous market for the asset or liability.

You also have to quantify the *market participants,* which are the buyers in the principal or advantageous marketplace. For example, the market participants can't be *related parties,* which means they're somehow associated with the business and have either a real or a perceived vested interest in the outcome of the valuation. The company also must have a working knowledge of the asset or liability so that it can come up with an accurate valuation. In addition, the company has to be willing to sell or transfer the asset/liability, regardless of the fact that this situation is likely hypothetical.

Fair value also takes into account the specific attributes of the asset or liability at measurement date. These attributes include the condition of the asset and credit risk. For example, fair value measurement of a building takes into consideration the neighborhood in which the building sits and the overall condition of the building.

Except for U.S. Treasury bonds, which are considered risk-free, since they're backed by the U.S. government, credit risk is generally present in most financial assets. Fair value therefore adjusts based on the risk associated with the asset or liability.

Figuring out highest and best use

Highest and best use applies to nonfinancial assets and takes place when considering the asset in such a way that maximizes its value.

Two concepts are important in gaining at least a working knowledge of "highest and best" use: whether the valuation is "in use" or "in exchange." Here's a quick definition of each:

   ✔ **In use:** This valuation method applies when the company gets the most bang for its buck when it uses the asset with other assets as a group. For example, consider the land on which a manufacturing plant sits. As raw land, it's not as valuable as it is when considered in combination with the value of the plant.

✔ **In exchange:** Use this valuation method when the maximum value for the asset comes when considering the asset on a stand-alone basis. For example, imagine that a manufacturing company has various types of equipment. If a particular piece of equipment is more valuable when considered solo rather than as a part of the whole group, you would use the concept of in exchange to figure the fair value at measurement date if the asset is sold in an open marketplace.

"Highest" and "best use" normally apply only to assets, not to liabilities.

Participating in the marketplace

ASC 820 outlines four potential markets for assets and liabilities subject to fair value accounting: active exchange, dealer, brokered, and principal-to-principal. Here's a quick explanation of each:

✔ **Active exchange:** These markets are stock exchanges in which fair value closing prices for the financial asset or liability are readily available. As of the publication of this book, the major five stocks exchanges, in order, are as follows:

- **NYSE Euronext:** Located in New York City, it covers the U.S. and Europe economies.

- **NASDAQ OMX:** Located in New York City, it also covers the U.S. and European economies.

- **Tokyo Stock Exchange:** Located in Tokyo, it cover the Japanese economy.

- **London Stock Exchange:** Located in London, it covers the U.K. economy.

- **Paris Stock Exchange:** Located in Paris, it covers the French economy.

✔ **Dealer market:** In these markets, participants buy and sell for their own account, using their own money via the telephone or computer. In the U.S., they are known as over-the-counter (OTC) markets. Examples include *forward contracts,* which are agreements between two parties to buy or sell an asset in the future at the price agreed upon today.

✔ **Brokered market:** These markets match buyers with sellers. The *broker,* the individual doing the matchmaking, isn't trading his own securities, nor is he operating from any inventory of securities. For example, imagine that you want to buy 100 shares of stock in AT&T. You call your stockbroker, who facilitates the transaction for you but doesn't ever own the shares of AT&T during any part of the transaction.

✔ **Principal-to-principal:** The actual parties to the transaction negotiate directly with each other, without using a middleman. For example, Company A has a widget machine, and Company B is willing to pay a certain amount to purchase it.

Modeling Valuation

Three valuation techniques are used under ASC 820: market approach, income approach, and cost approach. Selecting the correct approach requires applying professional judgment, expert knowledge about the particular asset or liability, and expertise in valuation techniques.

The FASB emphasizes in ASC 820 that the valuation technique must be consistent among similar assets and across reporting periods — for example, for the years ending December 31, 2012, 2013, and 2014. However, if contemporaneous info shows that a prior valuation approach is no longer giving the best fair value measurement, the company is required to change valuation approaches.

Account for a change in valuation approach as you would for a change in accounting estimate (see Chapter 19).

Valuation is a complex subject. The next few sections of this chapter give you enough information to understand related topics in your intermediate accounting class. Further details are reserved for advanced finance and advanced financial accounting classes.

Marketing multiples

Using the market approach, you look to current prices for either the same or comparable assets. An example is the use of *market multiples*. You consider the range of prices for the asset in an open marketplace, taking into account many different factors to determine where in the range of prices the fair value for the asset at hand lies.

For example, say that a measurement is done to figure the price a machine would fetch in its current condition and geographic location, factoring in the cost to transport and install the machine at various potential buyer locations. Applying professional judgment and expert knowledge about the particular asset or liability, the market participant with expertise in valuation techniques reckons the fair value range to be from $30,000 to $35,000.

Matrix pricing, which considers the stated interest rate, maturity date, and credit rating, is used for debt.

Discounting cash flows

The *income approach* converts future cash flows or earnings for the asset to a discounted present value amount (see Chapter 8 for more information on future and present value calculations) for fair value.

The income approach also uses option-pricing models, which financial analysts use to calculate the value of a stock option. *Stock options* are benefits that allow employees to purchase a special number of shares of the company stock at a determined date. Ta-da! There's also a multiperiod excess earning method that measures fair value of intangible assets. Examples of *intangible assets* are copyrights and patents (see Chapter 13).

Going back to the machine example in the "Marketing multiples" section, imagine that, using the cost approach, the fair value for the same machine, facts, and circumstances ranges from $30,000 to $41,000. How could you figure out which approach best represents fair value?

Basically, the entity must decide which of the two approaches uses the least subjective adjustments. Plus, in this case, the market approach ($30,000 to $35,000) overlaps the cost approach ($30,000 to $41,000) and is narrower in scope. All things being equal, the market approach probably gives the best fair value.

Most option-pricing models in use today are based on the model Fischer Black and Myron Scholes developed in 1973.

The multiperiod excess earning method relates well to intangible assets because they normally bring in revenue over an extended period of time.

Adjusting replacement cost

This method of fair valuation bases itself on the current replacement cost of the asset in question. You're probably thinking, "Finally, something that makes sense and is easy to remember!" With this measurement, you considering the cost to the market participant to buy or make an asset of comparative use, adjusting for obsolescence.

In this accounting transaction, obsolescence goes beyond mere depreciation (see Chapter 12). It also takes into account technological improvements, wear and tear, and economic factors.

Joining Forces: The FASB and the IASB

The *Financial Accounting Standards Board* (FASB) is currently the private-sector body establishing GAAP for all nongovernmental entities. The International Accounting Standards Board (IASB) has promulgated approximately 50 International Financial Reporting Standards (IFRS) in use by more than 130 countries. See Chapter 1 for more information on each of these agencies.

In 2002, the FASB and the IASB got together and hammered out an agreement to bring together U.S. GAAP and IFRS. Fast-forwarding to May 2011, prior to this date, no IFRS defined fair value. The IASB had pretty much endorsed the U.S. GAAP definition of fair value.

However, in May 2001, the IASB released its own standard, IFRS 13, "Fair Value Measurement," for use in the countries that followed IFRS. Although ASC 820 and IFRS 13 are fairly consistent, a few differences stand out, notably in disclosure requirements. A biggie is that, under GAAP, *nonpublic entities,* which are companies whose stock isn't traded in an open marketplace, are exempt from some fair value disclosures. No such exclusion exists under IFRS.

Chapter 4

Reviewing the Accounting System

There's no getting around it: you must have a system in place to collect financial information in order to effectively and efficiently produce accurate financial statements. This process of collecting, sorting, and entering accounting data into business accounting software is called the *accounting cycle.* It's perhaps not the most stimulating of activities, but following a systematic accounting cycle helps reduce errors and provides a consistent approach to business accounting.

In this chapter, the first step is to get up to speed on the language of accounting. Feeling a little hazy on whether you debit or credit an asset to increase it? Can't quite remember what accounts go on which financial statement?

No worries — this chapter has you covered. In this chapter, you'll also walk through the accounting equation, acquaint yourself with the five types of accounts, and look at how you adjust them via journal entries and posts to the ledgers. Finally, you see an example of a six-column worksheet for a trial balance, adjustments, and adjusted trial balance.

The Language of Accounting

Whether you took your intermediate accounting prerequisite courses last semester or a few years ago, you probably can use a refresher course in accounting terminology. The following sections define the key terminology that you'll want to understand in your intermediate accounting course and beyond.

The accounting equation

The *accounting equation* (also called the *fundamental accounting equation* or the *balance sheet equation*) proves that all accounting transactions in the financial statements are equal and opposite. The equation is as follows:

Assets = Liabilities + Owners' equity

A truncated version of this equation states the following:

Net assets = Owners' equity

The shorter version of the equation just moves liabilities to the other side of the equals sign; *net assets* are all assets minus all liabilities. If you feel a little fuzzy on difference in assets, liabilities, and equity accounts, the following section clears things up, plus gives you the dish on revenue and expenses.

Assets, liabilities, and equity are balance sheet accounts. The other two types of accounts are revenues (income) and expenses, shown on the income statement, which I discuss later in this chapter.

Familiarizing yourself with accounts

A company's *chart of accounts* is an index of the financial accounts that a business uses in its accounting system and that it posts to its *general ledger* — the record of all financial transactions within the company during a particular accounting cycle. (You take a closer look at the general ledger later in this chapter.)

Companies use charts of accounts to organize their finances and separate expenditures, revenue, assets, and liabilities to get a clear picture of the financial standing of the company. The chart of accounts contains account names and account numbers. Most accounting software programs use a similar numbering sequence, shown in Table 4-1.

Table 4-1	Numbering Sequence: Accounting Programs
Number Sequence	**Account Type**
1,000 to 1,999	Assets
2,000 to 2,999	Liabilities
3,000 to 3,999	Equity
4,000 to 4,999	Income

Number Sequence	Account Type
5,000 to 5,999	Cost of goods sold
6,000 to 7,999	Operating, general, administrative expense
8,000 to 9,999	Non-business-related items of income and expense

A computerized system may have classifications and subclassifications of accounts based on the type of account or category. For example, a system may classify all cash accounts in the 1,100–1,199 series, accounts receivable in the 1,200–1,299 series, and so on.

The chart of accounts isn't a financial report. It's merely a list of all accounts you've previously set up to handle the company transactions. Here's a description of the chart of accounts cast of characters:

- ✔ **Assets** are resources a company owns. Chapters 6, 9, 11, and 13 discuss all the typical types of business assets. Some examples are cash, equipment, and vehicles.

- ✔ **Liabilities** are debts the company owes to others. See Chapters 14 and 15 for the complete scoop on liabilities. The biggie liabilities you encounter in your intermediate accounting class are accounts payable, notes payable, and bonds payable.

- ✔ **Owners' equity** is what's left over in the business at the end of the day — a company's assets minus its debts. Equity components differ depending on the type of business entity. There are three basic entities: sole proprietorships, corporations, and flow-through entities such as partnerships. Check out the "What's mine is mine: Ownership" section of this chapter for the ABCs of equity.

- ✔ **Income** is revenue the business takes in for the products or services it sells. It doesn't include income from any other sources not related to the main purpose of the business. Those go in as nonbusiness income. See the bullet point on non-business-related items of income and expense, at the end of this list, for more information.

- ✔ **Cost of goods sold (COGS) expenses** directly tie back to products a business either makes or wholesales. Examples are direct labor and raw materials. You can find more information about COGS in Chapters 5 and 10.

Whether a business is a manufacturer or merchandiser affects how COGS shows up on the income statement. Accounting for a merchandising company COGS is easier than a manufacturer. That's because the merchandiser only has one class of inventory to keep track of: goods the business purchases from manufacturers for resale while the manufacturer has to account for all the bits and pieces plus the labor involved in making goods available for sale.

Service companies that don't make or sell a tangible product, like a dentist or doctor, won't have a COGS.

✔ **Operating, general, and administrative (G & A) expenses accounts** reflect all expenses a business incurs while performing its business purpose that do *not* directly relate to making or wholesaling a product — in other words, any expense that's not a COGS. Some examples are rent, office salaries, and postage expenses. Find more about these types of expenses in Chapter 5.

✔ **Non-business-related items of income and expense** is the classification used for money brought in or spent that generally accepted accounting principles (GAAP) state are not directly related to business. For example, if a company sells an asset at a loss, that's an example of a nonbusiness expense. More about this topic comes in Chapter 5 as well.

Defining debits and credits

At the core of accounting for transactions within a business is the *double-entry accounting system,* which means there must be two sides to every entry: Debits must equal credits and must affect more than one account.

When writing journal entries (see the "Analyzing Accounting Cycle Steps" section later in this chapter), debits show up on the left side of an entry and credits on the right. Each category of account has a "normal" balance that allows the financial statements to balance. Table 4-2 shows the "normal" balances for each type of account and the action you take to add or subtract from an account.

Table 4-2	"Normal" Balances for All Account Types		
Account Type	*Normal Balance*	*Increase It*	*Decrease It*
Asset	Debit	Debit	Credit
Liability	Credit	Credit	Debit
Equity	Credit	Credit	Debit
Income	Credit	Credit	Debit
Expense	Debit	Debit	Credit

Looking at financial statement types

Three types of financial statements exist: the balance sheet, the income statement, and the statement of cash flows.

While not one of the big three financial statements, the Statement of Changes in Retained Earnings shows the detail for the total owners' equity on the balance sheet.

I talk about each of the three in detail in Chapters 5, 6, and 7, respectively. For now, here's a thumbnail sketch of all three:

- **Balance sheet:** Reports assets, liabilities, and equity accounts, reflecting a company's financial position. Flip over to Chapters 6, 9, 11, 13, 14, 15, and 16 for more information. Whoa — that's a lot of chapters!

- **Income statement:** Shows all income (revenues) and all expenses the company incurs in producing the income. Income minus expenses shows business results for a specified period. See Chapters 5 and 20 for more information.

- **Statement of cash flows:** Shows all cash sources and uses for a specified period. Accountants pull the info for this financial statement from both the balance sheet and income statements. See Chapter 7 for more information.

What's mine is mine: Ownership

Who owns the business is a hot topic — and the focus of Chapter 6. However, it's important to briefly cover it in this chapter, too, because ownership changes, as the equity accounts show.

Earlier in the section "Familiarizing yourself with accounts," I named the three types of entities as sole proprietorships, corporations, and flow-through — for example, partnerships. Here are the equity ownership accounts appropriate for each:

- **Sole proprietorship:** The two unique equity accounts are owner's capital (owner contributions) and owner's draw (money the owner takes back out of the business).

- **Corporation:** Ownership in a corporation is reflected in the stockholders' equity section — specifically, paid-in capital, which is money the shareholders in a corporation invest in the business. This account is much more complicated than this short sentence warrants, so I cover the topic in more detail in Chapter 16.

- **Partnership:** The two unique equity accounts are partner's capital (contributions made by the partners) and partner's draw (money the partners takes back out of the business).

Intermediate accounting textbooks mostly use the corporate type of business entity in examples, which makes gaining an understanding of the information in Chapter 16 crucial to your success in your course.

Analyzing Accounting Cycle Steps

So far in this chapter, I've discussed how companies must have a system in place to collect financial information. The accounting cycle encompasses the steps to post a financial transaction to the financial statements and close a financial period.

Following the accounting cycle process helps reduce errors and provides a systematic approach to accounting — but how does all this work in the real world? The first step in the accounting cycle is understanding the who, what, where, and how much of each business transaction.

The transaction methodology

This section walks you through the rationale behind each accounting transaction within a business. The *transaction methodology* is a process for deciding how to handle whatever accounting event occurs within the company.

Accountants review the facts and circumstances of accounting transactions and determine which journal to use to record it. More on that later in this chapter. Accountants also determine which types of accounts are affected by these transactions, as well as which specific accounts to use. Finally, the dollar amount and date of each transaction needs to be determined.

Walking through a transaction

Your first task as an accountant is to know what's going on, what the transaction is, and what it's for. In this sample transaction, let's say the company has bought a new piece of business equipment. You have to figure out which accounts the transaction affects. For example, is the account an asset, a liability, owners' equity, revenue, or expense?

Fixed assets (check out Chapter 11 for more) definitely are affected by the purchase of business equipment; assuming that the business paid cash for the purchase, current assets also are affected (hop over to Chapter 9).

Then you have to figure out how to affect the accounts — is this a debit or a credit? Looking back to the rules of debits and credits in the "Defining debits and credits" section of this chapter, buying assets adds to that account, so it's a debit. Paying out cash reduces cash, a current asset, which is a credit. Finally, you have to make sure that all debits and credits for an entry *balance*, which means that all debits for a journal entry equal all credits for the same entry.

Dear diary: Using accounting journals

Accounting journals are a lot like that diary you may have kept as a child — or maybe still do keep! They're a day-to-day recording of business transactions that take place within a company's accounting department. Accountants call journals the "books of original entry" because no transactions get into the accounting records without being entered into a journal first. Two basic types of journals exist: general and special.

General journal

A general journal is a catchall type of journal for transactions that don't logically belong in one of the special journals. Transactions are recorded in the general journal via *journal entries* — I know, that's a shocker!

Depending on the size of the business, either all entries are recorded in the general journal or, in the case of a company with many special journals, only adjusting, reversing, or nonroutine entries are booked in the general journal. I discuss adjusting and reversing entries at the end of this chapter.

A general journal entry always includes the following:

- Date the transaction took place
- Chart of account titles and numbers
- Amount of the debits and credits
- Brief explanation of why the transaction is being booked

Want to see some journal entries in action? Check out the "Preparing the Trial Balance" and "Working with Worksheets" sections, later in this chapter.

Special journals

If a company has many similar transactions, it uses special accounting journals. Consider some examples of special accounting journals and some transactions they may contain:

- **Sales journals** record all sales a business makes to customers *on account,* which means no money changes hands between the company and the customer at the time of the sale.
- **Cash receipts journals** record cash sales, customer payments on account, or interest and dividend payments.
- **Cash disbursement journals** show any payment the business makes using a form of cash. These entries include purchases transactions or payments on debt.

- ✔ **Purchases journals** show purchases a company makes on account.
- ✔ **Payroll journals** record all payroll transactions, including gross wages, taxes withheld, and other deductions, such as health insurance paid by the employee, leading to net pay, which is the amount shown on the employee's check.

While an accrual-based business will have cash journals, a cash-based business won't have a sales or purchases journal as a cash-based business only recognizes transactions when cash changes hands.

Posting to ledgers

At this point, you may be thinking, "Okay, the journals are the books of original entry, but what happens then? How do these journal entries turn into financial statements?" Well, that's the next topic of conversation in this chapter.

The accounts and amounts from the journals, either debited or credited, show up in the *ledgers*, which are listings of each account belonging in the particular ledger. You're probably familiar with ledgers from your financial accounting prerequisite class, so I next review the use of the general and subsidiary ledgers.

Posting means that after the transaction is recorded in one of the journals, the information transfers (posts) to the general ledger. In today's computerized environment, this can be an automatic step.

Some accounting software requires that users select the posting command in the software's menu array, however. In that case, posting can occur at various times during a period and may depend on a company's accounting policies. Often an accounting supervisor must approve journal entries before they post.

General ledger

The *general ledger,* also known as the book of final entry, contains all the accounts for a company, from assets to expenses. The general ledger is a permanent financial summary of all amounts, which you previously entered in the general or special journals, and shows the activity (debits and credits) and the current balances of each account.

For a visual of the general ledger, picture a big book. Now imagine that each page in the book has a title that corresponds to an account from the chart of accounts.

For example, page 1 could be 1,001 Cash in Bank, with the total of all funds deposited in the bank account and all withdrawals against the fund for the financial period.

Subsidiary ledgers

Subsidiary ledgers store details on certain general ledger accounts, such as accounts payable in the purchases journal or payroll transactions in the payroll journal. The balance on the subsidiary ledger should agree with the balance for the controlling general ledger account.

For example, the single line item for accounts payable in the general ledger must equal the sum of all the transactions in the purchases journal.

Generally, accounts that include customer or vendor information, such as accounts receivable and accounts payable, have subsidiary ledgers to track detailed information. When a journal entry is posted relating to one of these accounts, it posts individually to the subsidiary ledger and also to the general ledger.

Preparing the Trial Balance

Whew! Here you are at the end of this chapter, ready to discuss closing out the financial period. At the end of the financial period, an unadjusted trial balance is prepared. A *trial balance* shows all the general ledger accounts and their debit or credit balances.

The unadjusted part of this equation means additional required journal entries have yet to be entered (hang tight — the adjusting journal entries discussion is coming up next).

You produce a trial balance for two main reasons:

- ✔ To supply evidence that the total debits equal total credits
- ✔ To provide information to help formulate any necessary adjusting entries

Although modern accounting software shouldn't allow this to happen, if the trial balance is "out of balance," the accountant must find the errors before financial statements can be prepared. Of course, other errors can show up in the trial balance, such as transactions being recorded in a wrong account.

Adjusting entries

To satisfy the ever-important matching principle (more in Chapter 2), accountants use two main categories of adjusting entries: accrual and deferral. At the heart of adjusting entries is the fact that the business has to account for events happening in one period that affect another, or vice versa. I explain accrual and deferral entries in turn:

- **Accruals:** These entries adjust revenue and expense accounts. For example, some interest income for the financial period might have been earned but not yet received. Or the company might incur expenses, such as employee payroll, that it hasn't yet paid.

- **Deferrals:** These entries adjust for contemporaneous accounting events (a fancy term for transactions that occurred within the current period) that the company needs to recognize in future financial periods. For example, payment of a 12-month magazine subscription in advance must be deferred and recognized over the subscription year, not entirely in the period the company makes or receives the payment.

A trial balance run after the adjusting entries are posted is called an adjusted or post-closing trial balance.

People who aren't savvy about financial accounting tend to think that adjusting entries fix mistakes. The side effect is that some do, but it's not the main purpose of this class of journal entry. See Chapter 19 for more information on correcting errors.

Closing out the books

After a company prepares the annual financial statements (income statement, balance sheet, and statement of cash flows), *temporary accounts,* which include all revenues and expenses, must be reset to zero. You do this to set the income statement (see Chapter 5) figures to zero so you know exactly how much revenues and expenses take place during each time period.

The good news is that modern accounting software does all the heavy lifting for the closing entries. After you select the appropriate command in the software, revenue and expense accounts reset to zero and then income or loss for the financial period transfers to the equity account. For a corporation, the equity account is retained earnings (more in Chapter 16).

If the owners of the corporation pay themselves dividends (or take distributions) during the period, the dividend or distribution account also must be reduced to zero. The other side of this entry goes to retained earnings. An accountant records and posts this entry.

Wondering what to do with balance sheet accounts? Well, how about nothing? Balance sheet accounts are permanent accounts. Until you cease using the account (for example, you close a bank account), no balance sheet accounts are zeroed out at closing.

Reversing Entries

After the shiny new financial period begins, you may need to reverse certain accrual or deferral entries. One good example is a payroll accrual.

Because the last day of a pay period rarely falls on the last day of a financial period, companies usually have wages earned but not yet paid to their employees as of the last day of the month. When this happens, payroll expense is recorded in the period the employees earn it; in the subsequent period, the original payroll entry reverses.

Figure 4-1 shows how this looks as a journal entry (to keep it simple, I omit the chart of account numbers for this and all other journal entries in this chapter) if unpaid wages total $15,000 on August 31, 2012. The August 31 journal entry reverses on September 1.

This setup keeps the accumulated year-to-date total of payroll expense correct because the first payroll run in September includes both the August accrual and the current September payroll expense.

August 31, 2012

Adjusting journal entry to book salaries earned but not yet paid:

Salary Expense	15,000
Salaries Payable	15,000

Figure 4-1: Adjusting and reversing wages payable entries.

September 1, 2012

Reversing entry used:

Salaries Payable	15,000
Salary Expense	15,000

As you will recall from your Introduction to Accounting class, debits are to the left and credits are to the right!

Not all accrual or deferral entries are reversed — just those that will have the actual expense or revenue booked in the next period.

Working with Worksheets

Imagining what a trial and adjusted trial balance looks like is hard unless you see one on paper. So to round out this chapter, I provide a very uncomplicated trial balance.

You have a few end-of-period adjustments to make, resulting in the adjusted trial balance. Figure 4-2 shows the trial balance, adjustments, and adjusted trial balance for the following facts and circumstances:

The accountants at Penway, Inc., prepare the following trial balance and adjusted trial balance. Adjustments consist of the payroll entry (which shows up as the (a) memo in the Adjustments column) from the earlier section "Reversing Entries," plus the following:

Physical inventory at year-end (see Chapter 10), shows that inventory totaling $100,210 remains on hand. The unadjusted trial balance shows inventory at $176,230. The adjustment (b) is $76,020 ($176,230 – $100,210). Here is the journal entry to adjust inventory to actual physical inventory on December 31, 2012.

Cost of Goods Sold	76,020	
Inventory		76,020

Interest expense accrued on the note payable is $480 (c). The journal entry to accrue this expense is to debit interest expense and credit interest payable for $480.

Penway, Inc.
Six–Column Worksheet for the Year Ending December 31, 2012

	Trial Balance		Adjustments		Adjusted Trial Balance	
	Debit	Credit	Debit	Credit	Debit	Credit
Cash	$32,340				$32,340	
Accounts Receivable	85,450				85,450	
Inventory	176,230			(b) 76,020	100,210	
Prepaid rent	12,500				12,500	
Equipment	96,000				96,000	
Accumulated depreciaton		$52,000				$52,000
Accounts payable		24,356				24,356
Note payable		12,500				12,500
Interest payable		1,410		(c) 480		1,890
Salaries payable				(a) 15,000		15,000
Unearned client fees		14,000				14,000
Income texes payable		5,000				5,000
Capital stock		50,000				50,000
Retained earnings		206,077				206,077
Revenue		160,000				160,000
Cost of Goods Sold	75,423		(b) 76,020		151,443	
Salary expense	18,750		(a) 15,000		33,750	
Interest expense			(c) 480			
Rent expense	11,250				11,250	
Utilities expense	4,600				4,600	
Depreciation expense	7,800				7,800	
Income taxes expense	5,000				5,000	
	$525,343	$525,343	$91,500	$91,500	$540,343	$540,823

Figure 4-2:
Trial balance, adjustments, and resulting adjusted trial balance.

Part II
Preparing and Using Financial Statements

The 5th Wave   By Rich Tennant

"I think I'm finally getting the hang of this accounting system. It's even got a currency conversion function. Want to see how much we lost in rupees?"

In this part . . .

I introduce the three financial statements: the income statement, the balance sheet, and the statement of cash flows. Companies use these financial statements to make important operating decisions. Potential investors and creditors also use them to decide whether to do business with the company. You can also use them to see how investments grow over time.

Kicking off this part is the income statement, which shows a company's revenue and expenses. This chapter gives you an overview on how to prepare an income statement and highlights the difference in setting up the income statement in a single- or multiple-step format. You also find out how to condense the income statement, and you see what happens if you have other comprehensive income, an item that normally shows up on the balance sheet instead of the income statement.

You explore each operating section of the income statement. Plus, you find out about irregular items that sometimes show up on the income statement, as well as special items such as allocating income tax expense and figuring earnings per share.

Chapter 6 provides a brief overview of the balance sheet, the financial statement that shows a company's assets, liabilities, and equity. Looking at the balance sheet, you can see how much debt the business owes and what resources it has to pay it.

Bringing up the rear of the financial statement lineup, the statement of cash flows records accounting transactions from both the balance sheet and the income statement. Its purpose is to convert accrual-based accounting to cash basis accounting. You find out about the three different sections of the statement of cash flows — operating, investing, and financing — and the type of accounting information you record in each.

Chapter 7 explains how to make money through the magic of simple and complex interest on investments. Find out how to figure the time value of money from the perspective of both the investor and the creditor. The chapter wraps up with a more advanced discussion of annuities (which are a series of payments), deferred annuities, and long-term bonds.

Chapter 5

Posting Income Statement Profit and Loss

*T*he bottom line for most companies when it comes to accounting comes down to two factors: How much did we earn and how much did we spend? When you prepare an income statement, you're putting in black and white what the company's revenue and expenses were during an accounting period. The final accounting of these revenue and expense items lets you know whether a company made a profit or lost money.

In this chapter, I walk you through the difference between setting up the income statement in a single-step format and using a multiple-step format, as well as how to condense the income statement. The chapter also looks at what happens if you have *other comprehensive income*, which normally shows up on the balance sheet instead of the income statement. Items of other comprehensive income include items such as foreign currency transactions and pension liabilities.

This chapter provides a tour of the income statement and fills you in on each operating section of the document. Plus, you find out about irregular items that sometimes show up on the income statement and special items such as allocating income tax expense and figuring earnings per share.

Finally, the income statement in all its glory is laid out on the table, from the entrée of gross revenues to the dessert, or net income after taxes. Time to dive in.

Making a Statement

The income statement shows the business's income, expenses, gains, and losses (more about each of these in the "Battling the elements" section of this chapter). It's also known as a statement of profit or loss, or P&L. Generally accepted accounting principles (GAAP) also refers to this report as statements of income.

This is because the income statement shows not only income and expenses from continuing operations, but also income from myriad sources, such as the gain or loss that results when a company sells an asset (see Chapter 11) it no longer needs.

Individuals and businesses use the income statement for specific reasons and must understand the limitations of the information shown on the income statement.

This chapter provides a brief introduction to the income statement. You can find more specific, account-driven information in Chapters 12, 17, 18, and 20.

What the information tells you . . .

The income statement represents a company's financial activity within a specified period of time — for example, one year ending December 31, 2013. An income statement is a company's financial statement that indicates how items of revenue interact with items of expense to cough up the business's net income. Therefore, the income statement is the statement to go to (not the balance sheet, which is a topic of Chapter 6) to effectively evaluate a company's potential growth.

Income statements prepared in accordance with GAAP (see Chapter 2) should give investors and creditors the accurate information they need to determine past financial performance of companies, predict their future performance, and assess their capability to generate future cash flow by producing net income.

And what it doesn't tell you

You can do the best job possible preparing an income statement, but it has certain inherent limitations. A biggie is that expense amounts depend on the accounting method the company uses to report them, such as the inventory cost flow assumption (see Chapter 10).

Some figures are the result of estimates, which means the company uses its best guess when deciding what to book how. Depreciating tangible assets, which asks for an estimate of both salvage value (how much the company feels it will receive when disposing of an asset) and useful life is a great example of this (see Chapter 12).

The information reflected on the financial statements allows its users to evaluate whether they want to become financially involved with the company. This decision is one they can't correctly make unless they have the opportunity to compare several years of net income. Involving the use of ratios and measurements, a topic I cover in Chapter 22, users of the financial statements evaluate the relative merit of one company over another by analyzing the company's historic performance.

Income statements have different sections. The main reason items of revenue and expense are separated and reported in these distinct sections is so the business owner can better use the income statement for decision making and to isolate problems with the way the business is being run. This explanation will make more sense to you after you review all the income statement parts later in this chapter.

Everything in Its Right Place: Formatting the Income Statement

GAAP dictates that certain accounts go on the balance sheet (see Chapter 6) and others go on the income statement. At no time can income statement accounts migrate to the balance sheet, and vice versa.

In addition, GAAP has strict criteria for where income statement accounts show up on the income statement. For example, revenue can't show up in expenses as a negative figure. The net effect is the same, but the users of the financial statements won't be able to effectively do comparative and ratio analysis (see Chapter 22) if the accounts aren't sitting all nice and pretty where they belong.

In the next few sections of this chapter, I take you through the four major elements of the income statement. You also see how to break out these elements depending on the type of format you use to prepare your income statements.

The statement of cash flows (see Chapter 7) doesn't have any accounts that you can call unique. This financial statement is a melding of all relevant income statement and balance sheet accounts.

Battling the elements

The four elements of an income statement are revenue, expenses, gains, and losses. It's a rookie mistake to equate revenue with gains and expenses with losses. You've probably got better things to do between semesters than obsess over accounting minutiae, so I give you a brief heads-up on the four here:

- ✔ **Revenue:** Gross receipts earned by the company selling its goods or services

- ✔ **Expenses:** The costs to the company to earn the gross receipts

- ✔ **Gains:** Income from non-business-related transactions, such as selling a company asset

- ✔ **Losses:** The flipside of gains, such as losing money when selling the company car

Combining the four elements, you prepare the income statement in two basic ways: the single-step and multiple-step formats. In the next section, you read about both and see an example of the single-step format. You find a full-blown, multiple-step format income statement at the end of this chapter.

Recognizing the single-step format

The single-step format groups revenue and gains; it also groups expenses and losses, providing a very truncated version of what happens to bring the company to net income or (loss).

Figure 5-1 shows an example of the single-step format. You can see, in addition to revenue and expenses, the calculation for basic *earnings per share (EPS) of common stock,* which shows net income allocated to investors based on how many shares of common stock they own. This figure is very important to your users of the financial statements (see Chapter 1) because it tells them how well their investment in the stock of the company is faring.

You walk through the EPS calculation later in this chapter in the "Figuring retained earnings" section.

Green and Blue Incorporated
Income Statement
For the Year Ending December 31, 2012

Revenues		
Net sales		$ 1,752,103
Dividend income		65,000
Gain on disposal of fixed Assets		25,135
Total revenue		
		1,842,238
Expenses		
Cost of goods sold		
Selling expenses		987,250
General & administrative expenses		100,000
Interest expense		589,120
Income tax expense		56,340
		38,335
Total expenses		
		1,771,045
Net Income		
		$ 71,193
Earnings per common share		
		$ 17.80

Figure 5-1:
Single-step
format.

Stepping up to the multiple-step format

The multiple-step format provides more information than the single-step method and is the preferred format for the vast majority of publicly traded companies. A *publicly traded company* is one whose stock is for sale to the general public, like you or me, on one of the stock exchanges such as the NASDAQ Stock Market also known merely as the NASDAQ.

The big differences between the single- and multiple-step formats are the following:

✔ The multiple-step format has a line item for gross profit and income from operations. This information is very helpful when doing Chapter 22 ratio analysis.

✔ The multiple-step format uses parentheses to indicate certain items that are subtracted rather than added. The single-step format assumes that the readers can figure out this information on their own.

Regardless of which method you use, the bottom-line net income doesn't change — just the presentation does. Expanding on the info in the "Recognizing the single-step format" section of this chapter, here are the subdivisions of operating revenue and expense elements that separately show up with the multiple-step format:

- ✔ **Net sales:** Net sales is the difference between gross sales and any relevant contra-accounts. The precipitating event with gross sales is an implicit or written contract between a company and its customer. The contract states that an agreed-upon good or service is to be provided for a set amount of money.

  Two contra revenue accounts you cover in your financial accounting class are sales discounts and sales returns and allowances. *Sales discounts* reflect any discount a business gives to a good vendor that pays early. *Sales returns and allowances* reflect all products that customers return to the company after the sale is complete.

  A company's gross sales revenue includes only transactions that relate to the purpose of the business. For example, a department store's revenue includes the gross amount of merchandise sold to customers.

- ✔ **Cost of goods sold:** The cost of goods sold (COGS) reflects all costs directly tied to any product a company makes or sells.

  Net sales minus cost of goods sold gives you gross profit.

  A service company, such as a doctor's or lawyer's office, does not have a COGS because it does not sell a tangible product.

- ✔ **Selling expenses:** These expenses are any expenses a company incurs to sell its goods or services to customers. Some examples are salaries and commissions paid to sales staff; advertising expense; store supplies; and depreciation (see Chapter 12) of furniture, equipment, and store fixtures the company uses for the purpose of selling or marketing its products. Typical retail shop depreciable items include cash registers, display cases, and clothing racks.

- ✔ **General and administrative expenses:** This category includes all expenses a company incurs to keep up normal business operations. Some examples are office supplies, officer and office payroll, nonfactory rent and utilities, and accounting and legal services.

  Gross profit minus all operating expenses, such as selling and general and administrative expenses, gives you income (or loss) from operations.

- ✔ **Other revenues/gains:** This section includes company income not related to its business purpose. An example of other revenue is the sale of a company vehicle for a gain or dividend income on investments the company holds.

✔ **Other expenses/losses:** This section includes costs the company incurs outside the bounds of business operations. Two types of expenses you typically see in this section of the income statement are interest expense and loss on disposal of an asset.

Income from operations plus other revenues/gain and minus other expenses/losses gives you income before taxes.

✔ **Income tax:** Before you figure the final total for net income or loss, you have to reduce income before taxes by subtracting a provision for the income tax the company will pay when it files tax returns. I discuss accounting for income taxes in Chapter 17. For now, just remember that, depending on many different factors, the business may owe federal or federal *and* state income tax — and maybe other types of income taxes as well.

You need to work through other income statement items, too, before you can really get a grip on preparing a multiple-step income statement. If you want a sneak peek, go to the section "Arriving at the Final Product," at the end of this chapter. Otherwise, it's time to get cranking with the other income statement goodies!

Managing the Misfits: Examining Irregular Items

The previous section reviews operational items of income and expense that directly relate to continuing operations. *Continuing operations* are the company's normal day-to-day activities doing whatever it's in the business of doing.

This section highlights *irregular items,* which are transactions GAAP classifies as outside the bounds of continuing operations. Irregular items include discontinued operations, extraordinary items, unusual gains or losses, changes in accounting principle, changes in estimates, and corrections of errors.

Wow, that's quite the list! You may not be familiar with some of these terms. Don't fret — following is an explanation of each.

Noting discontinued operations

Discontinued operations take place either when a segment of a business is regarded as *held-for-sale,* meaning the business is under a specific mandate to sell the segment, or when the segment has been disposed of during the accounting period. Both the following criteria must be met:

1. The operational results and *cash flow,* which are the sources and uses of cash (see Chapter 7), figures of the company's discontinued segment are or will shortly be removed from the continuing operations of the business.

2. The business will not have any significant involvement with the operations of the discontinued segment after it disposes of that segment.

To breathe a little life into this concept, imagine that a company that manufactures furniture has three different segments: tables, chairs, and entertainment centers. The company decides to concentrate on the most profitable two segments, tables and chairs, and sells its entertainment center segment to another manufacturer.

Under GAAP, you report any anticipated operational results from getting rid of the entertainment center segment (net of tax) and any loss or gain on the sale of that segment (also net of tax) on the income statement after income from continuing operations.

Figure 5-2 shows the income statement presentation of discontinued operations if the company incurs a loss of $250,000 from operating the segment prior to disposal and a gain on disposal of $50,000.

Extraordinary items

To meet the GAAP criteria for *extraordinary item* treatment, the item in question must be both something that occurs infrequently and, by its nature, something unusual. Meeting both criteria is hard.

One example that may meet these strict criteria is the results from litigation. If the company is a defendant in a lawsuit and a final judgment of a specific amount of monetary damages is awarded to the plaintiff, and this type of event is highly unusual, abnormal, infrequent, and unrelated to its ordinary business activities, GAAP allows it to be classified as an extraordinary item.

Figure 5-2 shows income statement presentation for an extraordinary litigation item. The company is awarded damages of $100,000, and tax on the damages is $25,000. Thus, the extraordinary items amount is $75,000 ($100,000 – $25,000).

Income from continuing operations		$ 1,650,000
Discontinued operations		
Loss from operation of discontinued entertainment center		
segment (net of taxes)	$ (250,000)	
Gain from disposal of entertainment center		
segment (net of taxes)	50,000	(200,000)
Income (loss) before extraordinary item		$ 1,450,000
Extraordinary gain from litigation, net of tax		75,000
Net income		$ 1,525,000

Figure 5-2: Income statement presentation for discontinued operating and extraordinary item.

Understanding unusual gains and losses

Sometimes a company has unusual or infrequent gains or losses that are material in amount and thus need to be stated separately, just like discontinued operations or extraordinary items.

What's material for one company may not be material for another. You have to consider the size of the company, the size of the unusual gain or loss, and any other factors that help you decide whether the issue is truly significant.

Usually these transactions report on the income statement in a single line item just before operating income. Figure 5-3 shows a simple example of how unusual gains and losses show up on the income statement.

Net sales	$ 20,000
COGS	8,500
Selling, general, administrative expenses	5,000
Unusual items	(2,000)
Income from operations	$ 4,500

Figure 5-3: Income statement presentation of unusual items.

In the notes to the financial statements (see Chapter 21), the company must explain each unusual gain or loss making up the total on the income statement. In Figure 5-3, the $2,000 could be one item or many. Whether it's 1 item or 100, it's important for the users to understand to their ability every line item showing up on the financial statements, which is why GAAP dictates disclosure note treatment.

Factoring in changes in principle

Although financial statement transactions have to report in accordance with GAAP, in some instances GAAP doesn't dictate only one way to handle the transactions.

Depending on what's going on, there may be many acceptable ways to handle the same event. Therefore, a change in accounting principle moves from one GAAP principle to an alternate that the business considers to be preferable.

When this happens, the company shows the change in accounting principle by making a retrospective adjustment to the financial statements. I really dig into this topic in Chapter 19.

Here are the steps for making a retrospective adjustment for a change in accounting principle:

1. Calculate the effect of the accounting change and adjust the carrying balances of any affected accounts to show the effect.

2. Take your offsetting entry to retained earnings.

3. Adjust any comparative prior-year financial statements so that the prior-year financial statements are on the same basis as the contemporaneous statement.

Discontinued operations, extraordinary items, and changes in accounting principle show up on the financial statements net of tax and after operating income or (loss) because the users of the financial statements want information on the earning power of the business. Earning power is the normal level of income the company earns in the current year and expects to earn in future years. Because the results of discontinued operations, extraordinary items, and changes in accounting principles, by definition, are irregular and infrequent, such items are separately identified on the income statement.

Calculating changes in accounting estimates

Estimates take place because sometimes, until the whole accounting transaction concludes, the company is probably not 100 percent sure how much revenue or expense to book. A good example of this is depreciation of *tangible assets,* which include property, plant, and equipment.

When depreciating assets, a company has to make two important estimates: how long it will be able to use an asset and the salvage value of the asset. *Salvage value* is how much a company assumes it will be able to get for a long-lived asset when it comes time to dispose of it.

Unlike changes in accounting principle, companies don't make a retrospective adjustment to the financial statements. Changes in accounting estimates have to be recognized in the current year and also prospectively, if appropriate. *Prospective treatment* comes into play when the change in accounting estimate affects both the current and future years *and* the effect of the change in accounting estimate shows up in the current financial statement and all applicable future financial statements. See Chapter 19 for more information about changes in accounting estimates.

Watching Out for Special Income Statement Items

You've been careful to correctly report all items of income and loss. Now it's time to put together the last few pieces of the income statement puzzle. I discuss these little gems in more detail in other chapters of this book. However, to keep you from having to flip back and forth while you check out the income statement at the end of this chapter, I give you a brief tutorial here, referencing where you can find more information about each.

We focus on tax allocations, earnings per share, and comprehensive income. You also find out how the balance sheet account retained earnings ties into the income statement.

Calculating the allocation for income taxes

After going through the prior sections of this chapter, you can see that income tax expense calculates on the taxable income that comes from adding operating income to other gains/revenues and subtracting other expenses/ losses. You also know that irregular items show up on the income statement net of tax. Look at Figure 5-2 for an example.

Calculating income tax expense in this manner has a special name, *intraperiod tax allocation.* You allocate income tax expense or benefit to continuing operations (normal day-to-day operations), discontinued operations (company segments no longer functional), extraordinary items (weird accounting stuff that's unusual), and prior-period adjustments (corrections of errors taken directly to retained earnings).

Figure 5-2 shows the netting effect, but I think it's helpful to see the underpinnings of the netting effect. Using the same info from Figure 5-2, Figure 5-4 breaks out the allocation for you for the extraordinary gain.

Want to have more tax-related fun (there are also interperiod tax allocations)? Check out Chapter 17.

Figure 5-4: Illustrating intraperiod tax allocation — extraordinary gain.	Income (loss) before extraordinary item	$ 1,450,000
	Extraordinary gain from litigation	$ 100,000
	Less: applicable income tax	25,000	75,000
	Net income	$ 1,525,000

If Figure 5-4 were an extraordinary loss, the $25,000 would show as a positive tax benefit.

Reporting earnings per share

Okay now, if you're an investor in a corporation, you're probably very interested in earnings per share (EPS) because it gives you a really good idea of how well your investment is doing. *Basic EPS* is net income minus preferred dividends divided by the weighted average of common stock outstanding.

Ay caramba! What does this mouthful mean? Well, I don't want to go into excessive detail in this chapter because Chapter 16 tells you everything you need to know about the subject for your intermediate accounting class.

For this chapter just keep in mind that two types of stock exist, common and preferred, and each has advantages and disadvantages. For your intermediate accounting class, your textbook gives the weighted average number of shares to you.

If the book doesn't flat out state it, you compute EPS yourself by adding beginning outstanding shares of common stock to ending outstanding shares of common stock and then dividing by 2. So if beginning is 5,000 and ending is 6,500 your weighted average is 5,750 [11,500 (5,000 + 6,500) ÷ 2].

Continuing with this information and using the net income amount from Figure 5-1 of $71,193, imagine that preferred dividends are $2,500 and the weighted average of common shares outstanding is 3,860. EPS is $17.80 ([$71,193 – $2,500] ÷ 3,860).

Companies must disclose EPS on the face of the income statement.

Figuring retained earnings

Retained earnings shows the company's total net income or loss from its first day in business to the date on the balance sheet.

Keep in mind, though, that dividends, a topic I discuss in Chapter 16, reduce retained earnings. *Dividends* are earnings paid to shareholders based on the number of shares they own.

For example, imagine that the company opens its doors on January 2, 2012. On January 2, retained earnings is zero because the company didn't previously exist. From January 2 to December 31, 2012, the company has a net income of $50,000 and pays out $5,000 in dividends.

On January 1, 2013, retained earnings is $45,000 ($50,000 – $5,000). To figure retained earnings as of January 1, 2014, you add or subtract the amount of income the company made or lost during 2013 (and subtract any dividends paid) to the $45,000 prior balance in retained earnings.

Figure 5-5 shows a retained earnings statement as of December 31, 2013. It includes 2013 income of $150,000 and cash dividends of $10,000.

Sometimes events happen that cause a company to have to restrict retained earnings. A portion is set aside and can't be used as a basis for declaring dividends. This situation happens often as a result of a clause in a contract: A lender may want to make sure the company doesn't pay out an excessive amount of its retained earnings, to ensure there's money for debt payments.

ABC Incorporated
Retained Earnings Statement
For the Year Ending December 31, 2013

Retained earnings January 1	$ 45,000
Add: Net income	150,000
Less: cash dividends	10,000
Retained earnings, December 31	$ 185,000

Figure 5-5:
Statement
of retained
earnings.

Studying comprehensive income

Comprehensive income encompasses gain and loss transactions that bypass the income statement and go directly to the balance sheet. It may seem weird to have an item of income showing up on the balance sheet. After all, isn't that what the income statement is for? Too true. However, revenue, expenses, gains, and losses that under GAAP are part of comprehensive income but aren't included on the income statement show up in the equity section of the balance sheet (see Chapter 6).

Sometimes the company produces a second income statement that shows the comprehensive income or shows a combined income statement reporting the whole ball of yarn. I discuss comprehensive income in more detail in Chapter 16. But I do want to give you some income statement info now. Figure 5-6 shows comprehensive income, net of tax, of $10,000, using net income from Figure 5-1.

If fair market value is more than cost, the value of the investment on the balance sheet and accumulated other comprehensive income increases. When fair market value is less than cost, the value of the investment and accumulated other comprehensive income decreases.

Green and Blue Incorporated
Comprehensive Income Statement
For the Year Ending December 31, 2012

Net Income	$ 71,193
Other comprehensive income,	
net of tax	10,000
Comprehensive income	$ 81,193

Figure 5-6:
Comprehensive income.

Condensing the multiple-step statement

A condensed income statement uses the multiple-step format but crunches all similar line items into one. For example, Figure 5-7 shows four different general and administrative expenses totaling $589,120. If condensing, the entire $589,120 shows up as a single line item, but with a supporting schedule detailing the various general and administrative expenses.

The following figure shows a portion of a condensed income statement, starting at gross profit and ending with operating income. It presents a cleaner and more compact income statement while still showing the same results from operations.

Note that A and B reference back to a supporting schedule that shows the detail in the following statement.

Gross profit		$ 764,853
Operating expenses:		
Selling expenses (see Note A)	$ 100,000	
General and administrative expenses (See Note B)	589,120	
Total operating expense		(689,120)
Operating income		$75,733

Arriving at the Final Product

Excitement has reached a fever pitch because now you see the multiple-step income statement in all its glory! In Figure 5-7, I take the information from Figure 5-1 and break it out into multiple-step format.

Green and Blue Incorporated
Income Statement
For the Year Ending December 31, 2012

Sales

Sales			$ 1,632,000
Less: Sales discount		$ 110,000	
Sales returns and allowances		10,103	120,103
Net sales			**$ 1,511,897**
Cost of goods sold			
Beginning inventory			$ 15,000
Add: Purchases		1,049,150	
Freight-in		25,600	
Cost of purchases		1,074,750	
Less: Purchase discounts	$ 53,000		
Purchase returns and allowances	9,500	62,500	
Net purchases		1,012,250	
Cost of goods available for sale		1,027,250	
Less: Ending inventory		(40,000)	
Cost of goods sold			987,250
Gross profit			$ 524,647
Operating expenses			
Selling expenses			
Sales salaries	$ 45,000		
Commissions	50,000		
Advertising expense	5,000	$ 100,000	
General and administrative expenses			
Office salaries	$ 209,794		
Office supplies expense	75,250		
Insurance expense	45,000		
Utilities expense	18,870	$ 348,914	
Total operating expense			448,914
Operating income			$ 75,733
Other revenues			
Gain on disposal of fixed asset		$ 25,135	
Dividend income		65,000	90,135
Other expenses			
Interest expense			(56,340)
Income before taxes			109,528
Provision for income taxes			(38,335)
Net income			$ 71,193
Basic earnings per share of common stock			17.80

Figure 5-7:
Multiple-
step income
statement.

Chapter 6

Reporting Assets and Claims: Keeping Your Balance (Sheet)

*T*his chapter provides a brief overview of the balance sheet, the financial statement showing a company's assets, liabilities, and equity. The data on the financial statements gives people and businesses using them a bird's-eye view of how well the business is performing. In this chapter, you see how to look at the balance sheet to identify how much debt the business owes and what resources it has to pay it.

I briefly explain the common assets a business may have and further break down the assets as either current or noncurrent (Part III of this book expands on the basics in this chapter). You also get info on long-term debt obligations businesses use to acquire their assets. As with assets, liabilities are classified as short and long term. I give you a brief heads-up on types of current liabilities and I also discuss basic long-term debt, such as mortgages and notes payable (Chapters 14 and 15 discuss liabilities in greater detail).

Finally, you get a thumbnail sketch (more info about equity in Chapter 16) of equity's relationship to assets and liabilities and the different types of equity accounts. Although the asset and liability sections of a balance sheet contain similar accounts that are slightly tailored depending on the purpose of the business, the equity section of the balance sheet is unique to the business's type of legal entity.

Classifying the Balance Sheet

The *balance sheet* shows the health of a business from the day the business started operations to the specific date of the balance sheet report. A *classified balance sheet* groups similar accounts. For example, all current assets (see Part III), such as cash and accounts receivable, show up in one grouping. Likewise, all current liabilities, such as accounts payable and other short-term debt (see Chapter 14), show up in another. This organization helps users of the balance sheet avoid having to go on a scavenger hunt to round up similar accounts.

The balance sheet is also referred to as the statement of financial position.

In addition, people who aren't accounting geeks may not know which accounts are short term versus long term or equity as opposed to assets. By classifying accounts on the balance sheets, the business gives information that's easy to use.

The balance sheet has three sections: assets, liabilities, and equity. Standing on their own, they contain valuable information about a company. However, a user has to see all three interacting together on the balance sheet to form an opinion approaching reliability about the company.

When keeping it simple makes more work

The other method of presenting a balance sheet, the *simple method,* willy-nilly throws all assets into one category and all liabilities into another category, with the equity section coming up last. The net effect of classified versus simple is the same, but the classified balance sheet gives more information about the financial position of the company than the simplified balance sheet.

Without this more detailed "classified" presentation, users of the balance sheet would have a tough time doing any sort of comparative or ratio analysis (see Chapter 22). For example, the liquidity position of the company can be known only if the current assets and current liabilities are easily identified. Likewise, shareholders want to know in detail the amount they've invested, the amount of retained earnings, profit made during the year, and the amount of dividend declared. All that info is more than a simple balance sheet shows.

Companies may prefer the simplified balance sheet because they want to maintain the confidentiality of their financial position instead of disclosing it to the public. However, this isn't an option for *publicly traded companies,* which are companies with a free exchange of their stock in the open marketplace. See information about the Securities and Exchange Commission (SEC) in Chapter 1 for more information about publicly traded companies.

Counting Your Assets

Assets are resources a company owns. They consist of both current and noncurrent resources. I explain the difference between the two in the next sections.

Current

Current assets are ones the company expects to convert to cash or use in the business within one year of the balance sheet date. Examples of current assets are cash, accounts receivable, and inventory.

This chapter closes out with a full-blown example of a balance sheet, so I give you the definition of a few different current assets here. Just keep in mind that you're getting the bare bones of each in this chapter, since I fully discuss current assets in Part III.

- **Cash:** Cash includes accounts such as the company's operating checking account, which the business uses to receive customer payments and pay business expenses, or an *imprest account,* which keeps a fixed amount of cash in it (such as petty cash). See Chapter 9 for more info on cash accounts.

- **Accounts receivable:** This account shows all money customers owe to a business for a completed sales transaction. For example, Business A sells merchandise to Business B with the agreement that B pay for the merchandise within 30 business days. See Chapter 9 for more information on accounts receivable.

- **Inventory:** Goods available for sale reflect on a merchandiser's balance sheet in this account. A merchandiser is a retail business, like your neighborhood grocery store, that sells to the general public. For a manufacturing company, a business that makes the items merchandisers sell, this category also includes the raw materials used to make items. See Chapter 10 for more information on inventory.

- **Prepaid expenses:** Prepaids are any expense the business pays for in advance, such as rent, insurance, office supplies, postage, travel expense, or advances to employees. They also list as current assets, as long as the company envisions receiving the benefit of the prepaid items within 12 months of the balance sheet date.

Lil' Orphan Assets

Any other resources the company owns go in the catchall category of "other assets." Security deposits are a good example of other assets. Say the company rents an office building and, as part of the lease, pays a $1,000 security deposit. That $1,000 deposit is reflected in the other assets account until the property owner reimburses the business at the end of the lease.

Noncurrent

Long-term assets are ones the company reckons it will hold for at least one year. Typical examples of long-term assets are investments and property, plant, and equipment currently in use by the company in day-to-day operations.

- ✔ **Fixed assets:** This category is the company's property, plant, and equipment. The account includes long-lived assets, such as a car, land, buildings, office equipment, and computers. See Chapter 11 for more information on fixed assets and Chapter 12 for information on moving the cost of fixed assets from the balance sheet to the income statement.

- ✔ **Long-term investments:** These investments are assets held by the company, such as bonds, stocks, or notes. More about stocks and bonds comes in Chapters 15 and 16.

- ✔ **Intangible assets:** These assets lack a physical presence (you can't touch or feel them). Patents, trademarks, and goodwill classify as noncurrent assets. You get more on intangibles in Chapter 13.

Reporting Debt and Other Liabilities

Not nearly as much fun as assets, the second category of accounts on a balance sheet is claims against the company. As with assets, these claims record as current or noncurrent.

Liabilities are claimed against the company's assets. Usually, they consist of money the company owes to others. For example, the debt can be to an unrelated third party, such as a bank, or to employees for wages earned but not yet paid. Some examples are accounts payable, payroll liabilities, and notes payable.

Presenting both assets and liabilities as current and noncurrent is essential for the user of the financial statements to perform ratio analysis. See Chapter 22, with a special eye to the liquidity ratios.

GAAP almost entirely prohibits the practice of netting assets and liabilities that relate to one another. GAAP narrowly allows it when a right of setoff exists, which involves special debt circumstances.

Current

Current liabilities are ones the company expects to settle within 12 months of the date on the balance sheet. Settlement comes either from the use of current assets such as cash on hand or from the current sale of inventory. Settlement can also come from swapping out one current liability for another.

At present, most liabilities show up on the balance sheet at historic cost rather than fair value (see Chapter 3). And there's no GAAP requirement for the order in which they show up on the balance sheet, as long as they are properly classified as current.

The big-dog current liabilities, which you're more than likely familiar with from previous accounting classes, are accounts payable, notes payable, and unearned income. Keep in mind that any money a company owes its employees (wages payable) or the government for payroll taxes (taxes payable) is a current liability, too.

I fully discuss current liabilities in Chapter 14. For now, here's a brief description of each:

- ✔ **Short-term notes payable:** Notes due in full less than 12 months after the balance sheet date are short term. For example, a business may need a brief influx of cash to pay mandatory expenses such as payroll. A good example of this situation is a *working capital loan,* which a bank makes with the expectation that the loan will be paid back from collection of accounts receivable or the sale of inventory.

- ✔ **Accounts payable:** This account shows the amount of money the company owes to its vendors.

- ✔ **Dividends payable:** Payments due to shareholders of record after the date declaring the dividend. More info about dividends comes in Chapter 16.

- ✔ **Payroll liabilities:** Most companies *accrue* payroll and related payroll taxes, which means the company owes them but has not yet paid them.

✔ **Current portion of long-term notes payable:** If a short-term note has to be paid back within 12 month of the balance sheet date, you've probably guessed that a long-term note is paid back after that 12-month period. However, you have to show the current portion (that which will be paid back in the current operating period) as a current liability.

✔ **Unearned revenue:** This category includes money the company collects from customers that it hasn't yet earned by doing the complete job for the customers but that it anticipates earning within 12 months of the date of the balance sheet.

Noncurrent

Noncurrent or long-term liabilities are ones the company reckons aren't going anywhere soon! In other words, the company doesn't expect to be liquidating them within 12 months of the balance sheet date.

From your accounting classes, you're probably familiar with notes and mortgages payable. I discuss the whole ball and chain of long-term debt in Chapter 15, but I want to briefly go over a couple points right now.

Also see the section "Keeping track of contingencies," later in this chapter, for another long-term liability.

✔ **Bonds payable:** Long-term lending agreements between borrowers and lenders. For a business, it's another way to raise money besides selling stock. See Chapter 15 for more information on bonds.

✔ **Long-term leases:** Capital leases (you record the rental arrangement on the balance sheet as an asset rather than the income statement as an expense; see Chapter 18) that extend past 12 months of the date of the balance sheet. Because the rental arrangement is recorded as an asset, the related lease obligation must be recorded as a liability.

✔ **Product warranties:** Report as noncurrent when the company expects to make good on repairing or replacing goods sold to customers and the obligation extends beyond 12 months from the balance sheet date.

I show how to prepare both the current and noncurrent liabilities section of the balance sheet at the end of this chapter in "Seeing Sections of the Balance Sheet."

Reporting Equity

Equity shows the owners' total investment in the business, which is their claim to the business *net assets* (the difference between assets and liabilities).

Whereas the assets and liabilities sections of a balance sheet contain similar accounts that are slightly tailored depending on the purpose of the business, the equity section of the balance sheet is unique to the business's type of legal entity.

Three basic types of business entities exist: sole proprietorship, flow-through, and corporation. In general, a *flow-through entity* involves income and loss the flow directly to the owners for taxation. Different types of flow-through entities exist, but this chapter discusses only the partnership.

The information in your intermediate accounting textbook centers on the corporate type of business entity, but it's also important to know the difference between that type and the other two basic types of entities.

Single owner

A sole proprietorship has only one owner. As the individual in charge of the whole shooting match, the single owner has complete control and decision-making power over the business. Owners aren't classified as employees.

Sole proprietorships aren't all moonlight and magnolias, however. The sole proprietor is personally liable for the debts and obligations of the business. Additionally, this risk extends to any liabilities incurred as a result of acts committed by employees of the company. Funding is usually by the owner rather than outside investors.

No real legal distinction is made between the owner and the business, so it's an inexpensive type of entity to start up and maintain. Few formal business requirements and minimal legal costs are involved in forming a sole proprietorship.

In most jurisdictions of the United States, the only legal requirement is that the sole proprietorship have adequate business licensing with the state, city, and county in which it operates.

The equity section of a sole proprietorship (see Figure 6-1) contains two accounts:

- ✔ Owner capital is the amount of money the sole proprietor invests in the business.
- ✔ Owner withdrawals represent distributions the owner makes to him- or herself.

Some sole proprietorships use a retained earnings account to hold income transactions. More about retained earnings comes in the upcoming "Corporation" section of this chapter.

Green Topiary

Statement of Owner's Equity

December 31, 2013

Thomas Green, capital January 1, 2013	$ 25,000
Year-to-date net income	8,000
Thomas Green, draw	(16,000)
Thomas Green, capital December 31, 2013	$ 17,000

Figure 6-1:
A statement of owner's equity for a sole proprietorship.

Partnership

A partnership must have at least two owners, with any percentage of ownership interest (as long as the combined total isn't more than 100!). As with the sole proprietorship, partners aren't classified as employees.

A partnership doesn't need to have two partners with a 50 percent share each. It can have many partners with all sorts of different interest percentages in the partnership.

Partners usually share the financial commitment of the business. They can bring different strengths to the table by pooling resources, expertise, and strengths. Most states have limited startup costs, and beyond the partnership agreement, there are few formalities.

As with typical family dynamics, partners can have shifting loyalties and, thus, may have a partnership fraught with disagreement. Partners may have different and conflicting goals for the business. They may show unequal commitment in terms of time and finances, leading to personal disputes. Partners are personally liable for business debts and liabilities. Depending on the partnership setup, partners may also be liable for debts incurred, decisions made, and actions taken by the other partner or partners.

Figure 6-2 shows a typical presentation for the equity section of a partnership. Partnerships mimic sole proprietorships, in that the equity section has capital and withdrawal accounts. Assume that Thomas Green and John Blue each have a 50 percent ownership in the partnership.

Green and Blue Partnership

Statement of Partner's Equity

December 31, 2013

	Tom Green Capital	John Blue Capital	Total Capital
Partner capital January 1, 2013	$ 12,000	$ 15,000	$ 27,000
Year-to-date net income	17,500	17,500	35,000
Partner draws	(10,000)	(2,000)	(12,000)
Partner capital December 31, 2013	$ 19,500	$ 30,500	$ 50,000

Figure 6-2: A statement of partners' equity.

Corporation

Saving the best for last, your intermediate accounting textbook mostly covers and gives examples of the corporate type of business entity. You get just a thumbnail sketch of it in this chapter; I go into the nitty-gritty of corporate equity in Chapter 16.

Partnering up!

State statutes in whatever state the partnership wants to operate spell out how to form and operate the partnership. In many states, the partnership has to prepare a written partnership agreement and file paperwork with the Secretary of State. Most states have provisions for both general partnerships and limited partnerships.

General partnerships: All partners are personally liable for any legal action taken against the partnership and for any debts the partnership owes.

Limited liability partnerships: Many states allow for limited liability partnerships, which basically means that if you're a limited partner, your liability for partnership debt is limited to your investment in the partnership. However, as a limited partner, you may not have any say in how the partnership is run.

The major advantage to incorporation is *limited liability,* which means that, unless debt is personally guaranteed, no individual retains responsibility for paying off debt. Other advantages are *continuity,* which means that, until the corporation is formally dissolved, it exists in perpetuity, and *easy transferability of shares,* which means you can sell your shares of stock in a corporation to anyone you want.

One major exception arises concerning the limited liability aspect of incorporation: the trust fund portion of the payroll taxes. Trust funds include the FICA and federal withholding amount withheld from employee paychecks. This amount doesn't include the employer FICA match.

You may not have the same type of personal intrigue in a corporation as you have in a sole proprietorship, but this structure does have disadvantages. For example, it costs money to incorporate. You also must follow the proper corporate formalities of organizing and running a corporation to receive the benefits of being a corporation, including completing legal and taxation paperwork and filing in a timely fashion.

Corporations have distinct equity accounts consisting of retained earnings, paid-in capital, and stock. I discuss each briefly:

- ✔ **Retained earnings:** This account shows income and dividend transactions. For example, imagine that the business opens on April 1, 2013. On December 31, 2013, it has cleared $100,000 but has also paid $20,000 in dividends to shareholders. Retained earnings is $80,000 ($100,000 – $20,000).

   Retained earnings accumulate year after year, ergo the "retained" in the account name. So if the business makes $40,000 in 2014 and pays no dividends, retained earnings on December 31, 2014, is $120,000 ($80,000 + $40,000).

   You may have seen the accounting equation truncated down to net assets equaling equity. However, keep in mind that although retained earnings is a source of assets, it's not an asset itself. It shows up in the equity section of the balance sheet because it's an investment by the owners, which increases their interest in the actual assets of the business.

- ✔ **Paid-in capital:** This element of equity reflects stock and additional paid-in capital. Corporations raise money by selling *stock,* a piece of the corporation, to interested investors.

   Additional paid-in capital shows the amount of money the investors pay over the stock's par value. *Par value* is the price printed on the face of the stock certificate. For example, if the par value of Green and Blue, Inc., is $20 per share and you buy 100 shares at $25 per share, additional paid-in capital is $500 [$5 ($25 – $20) × 100 shares].

Another stock account is treasury stock. Treasury stock is its own stock that the company buys back from its investors. Treasury stock is a part of equity but isn't a part of paid-in capital. More about accounting for treasury stock comes in Chapter 16.

Want to see all these accounts in action on the balance sheet? I show a fully developed corporate equity section at the end of this chapter in "Seeing Sections of the Balance Sheet."

Studying Advanced Balance Sheet Issues

The balance sheet is more than just the sum of its parts. So that the users can totally understand what they're looking at and properly interpret the potentially hidden meaning of the accounts and their balances, supplemental balance sheet information is a must.

To completely round out the balance sheet, the issuing company has to present information about contingencies, accounting policies, contractual requirements and obligations, and disclosure of fair values. Whew, that's a lot of work! Not quite sure how to get started? I explain each next.

Keeping track of contingencies

A *contingent liability* is a noncurrent liability that exists when a company has an existing circumstance as of the date of the financial statements that may cause a loss in the future, depending on events that haven't yet happened and, indeed, may never happen.

You typically record contingent liabilities in the footnotes to the financial statement (see the upcoming section "Balance Sheet Disclosure Issues") instead of as an actual part of the financial statements. However, if a loss due to a contingent liability meets two criteria, it must be accrued as part of the company's financial statement. You find more info on this type of extravaganza in Chapter 14.

Consider these two examples of common contingent liabilities:

- **Pending litigation:** The company is actively involved in a lawsuit that it hasn't yet settled.
- **Guarantee of obligations:** A business agrees to step in and satisfy the debt of another company, if needed.

Walking through accounting policies

The accounting principles a company follows and the methods a company uses to apply those principles are referred to as the company's accounting policies. At this point in your accounting studies, no one has to tell you that financial accountants use GAAP to record a company's accounting events affecting assets and liabilities.

Keep in mind that, in some instances, GAAP doesn't dictate only one way to handle accounting transactions. Depending on what's going on, there may be many acceptable ways to handle the same event.

For example, there are different ways to value ending inventory (see Chapter 10). Therefore, for comparability purposes, companies have to let the users know which method is in use.

Without this info, the users can't possibly do an effective evaluation of the relative merits of investing in one company versus another, since different valuation methods can cause wild fluctuation in income.

Keeping it legal

All significant contractual obligations affecting the balance sheet liabilities have to be disclosed in the notes to the financial statements. Just a few examples of contractual obligations are pension obligations, commitments to purchase new assets, and the obligation to maintain certain financial ratios.

Here's a brief description of each:

- ✔ **Pension obligations:** These obligations are funds a company holds that it eventually will have to pay out to retired employees.

- ✔ **Purchase commitments:** If a company has an obligation to make good on a material purchase that hasn't yet come to fruition, it must reveal the related pending liability.

- ✔ **Maintaining ratios:** To secure financing, sometimes a company has to agree to maintain a certain current ratio or amount of working capital. I discuss ratios in Chapter 22. However, so you don't have to flip back to that chapter, the *current ratio* is current assets divided by current liabilities and *working capital* is current assets minus current liabilities.

Banks and other lenders require a company to maintain certain ratios, to ensure that the company will have the current assets to pay back both the principal and interest portions of the debt in full and on time.

Applying legalities

As another example of keeping it legal, say that Sharkey Money Lenders agrees to accept a note receivable from Bad Mistake, Inc., for the amount of money Bad Mistake owes to Sharkey, with the contractual obligation that 60 percent of all annual profits go directly to Sharkey to liquidate the debt. The note payable on Bad Mistake's books originally records as a long-term liability, with a note in the financial statement explaining the arrangement (see the upcoming section "Balance Sheet Disclosure Issues" for more information on disclosure notes). Then each year as the profit shakes out, an amount equal to 60 percent of the profit moves from long-term liabilities to current liabilities.

Valuing accounts fairly

Many accounts on the balance sheet report at *historic costs,* which are static costs that are known — basically, cost plus any capitalized improvements. Fair value reporting (see Chapter 3) states that most assets are a market of some kind and that, to truly reflect the value of a company, these assets need to report at fair value. *Fair value* is what an unpressured person would pay for the asset in an open marketplace.

The Financial Accounting Standards Board (FASB; see Chapter 2) has been requiring some fair value measurements because they provide more transparency than reporting using historical costs. For financial instruments such as short- and long-term investments and debt, the company must follow a fair value hierarchy that gives insight into how it calculates fair value:

- ✔ **The company uses market prices for identical assets or liabilities.** For example, if the company owns stock in AT&T, it's pretty easy to find the market value of the stock at any point in time.

- ✔ **Less reliably, the company uses market prices for similar assets or liabilities.** The company may choose this method because it lacks access to info for identical assets or liabilities.

- ✔ **With the least reliable method of the three, the company may have no choice but to rely on its own fair value assumptions.** Some assumptions may be expected cash flow from the asset or liability or its present value; see Chapter 8 for more on figuring present value.

Crossing your assets and dotting your liabilities

If a company has an asset listing that has an associated liability, cross-referencing is done directly on the balance sheet. The following is an example of how this looks if a company pledges $200,000 of accounts receivable as collateral for a $100,000 working capital loan.

Showing in current assets:

Accounts receivable pledged as collateral on bank loan payable $200,000

Cross-referencing to this in current liabilities:

Bank working capital loan payable, collateralized by accounts receivable $100,000

Balance Sheet Disclosure Issues

Chapter 21 walks you through ten common disclosure notes to the financial statements. In this section, I introduce you to the four techniques of disclosure. Ready to shake hands and say hello? Time to get going!

The four techniques are parenthetical explanations, notes, cross-referencing, and supporting schedules. I discuss each in turn:

✔ **Parenthetical explanations:** In this technique, you explain something right on the balance sheet itself. An excellent example on every corporate balance sheet is the disclosure of shares issued. I show this in the final section of this chapter, "Seeing Sections of the Balance Sheet."

✔ **Notes to the financial statements:** If more explanation is needed for an event that shows up on the balance sheet, and this happens all the time, a company gives the users of the financial statements the entire lowdown in explanatory notes. Notes show up after the financial statements in the same order as the accounts relating to the notes show up on the balance sheet.

Debt obligations, lease contracts, pension arrangements, and the 411 on stock option plans are four items for which GAAP requires disclosure in the financial statements. These commitments are of a long-term nature, are often for a material amount, and are very important to the overall health of a business.

✔ **Cross-references:** Companies have to show direct relationships between asset and liability accounts. This requirement is to point out that although a great-looking asset may reflect on the balance sheet, it has a corresponding dark cloud looming over it in the form of a liability.

Contra-accounts and adjunct accounts also cross-reference assets and liabilities. Contra-accounts, which carry a balance contrary to the normal account balance (see Chapter 4), reduce asset, liability, and equity accounts. Your biggie example is accumulated depreciation.

On the flip side, adjunct accounts increase assets, liabilities, and equity. Your biggie example of an adjunct account is premium on bonds payable (see Chapter 15).

✔ **Supporting schedules:** If the user needs more information and it will be easier to understand if the description goes beyond a mere narrative, use a schedule. This technique is a great way to show a comparative analysis of accounts or show the ins and outs of fixed assets. Figure 6-3 shows an extremely simple accounting for equipment.

In general, don't use supporting schedules to satisfy GAAP requirements. The supporting schedules aren't part of the financial statements.

Beginning balance January 1, 2013	$ 125,000
2013 Additions	65,000
Equipment sold/retired in 2013	(50,000)
Equipment balance December 31, 2013	140,000
2013 Accumulated depreciation	(25,000)
Book value of assets at December 31, 2013	$ 115,000

Figure 6-3:
Equipment
schedule.

Seeing Sections of the Balance Sheet

Ta-da! You're at the end of this chapter showing an overview of balance sheet accounts. It's time to organize all these asset, liability, and equity accounts into a formal, proper financial statement.

Figures 6-4 and 6-5 show a fully developed balance sheet for a corporation. Your two signs that it's a corporation are the name and the equity section containing retained earnings, paid-in capital, and stock accounts.

Also take note of the date of the balance sheet. The facts and figures shown on this financial statement are as of December 31, 2012, showing the financial position of a business from the day the business started operations to that specific date. Enjoy!

Blue and Green Incorporated
Balance Sheet
December 31, 2012

Assets:		
Current assets		
Cash		$ 485,661
Short-term investments		16,000
Accounts receivable	53,000	
Less allowance for uncollectible accounts	(3,200)	49,800
Notes receivable - current		13,500
Inventory		225,000
Prepaid expenses		7,500
Total current assets		797,461
Long-term assets		
Notes receivable - long-term		32,000
Property, plant, and equipment:		
Land		115,000
Building		325,000
Machinery and equipment		23,400
Furniture and fixtures		43,000
Capital leases		6,000
Leasehold improvements		8,000
Less accumulated depreciation and amortization		(67,245)
Total property, plant, and equipment		453,155
Intangible assets (shown net of amortization)		
Patents		8,300
Trademarks		5,000
Total intangible assets		13,300
Total assets		**$ 1,295,916**

Figure 6-4:
Classified
balance
sheet –
assets.

Liabilities & Equity

 Current Liabilities

Accounts payable	$ 34,203	
Current maturities of long-term debt	6,365	
Accrued salaries and wages	14,500	
State tax payable	1,680	
Advances from customers	5,000	
Payroll taxes withheld and accrued	2,300	
Accrued expenses	8,500	
Total Current Liabilities		72,548
Long-term Liabilities		
Note payable	20,000	
Total long-term liabilities		20,000
Total Liabilities		$ 92,548

Stockholders' Equity

 Capital Stock:

Preferred stock, 5%, $15 par value, cumulative, 10,000 shares authorized, issued, and outstanding	$ 150,000	
Common stock, $75 par value, 5,000 shares authorized, 4,000 shares issued at December 31, 2012	300,000	
Additional paid-in capital	110,000	
Retained earnings	661,897	
Accumulated other comprehensive income (loss):		
Net unrealized loss on available for sale investments	(7,500)	
Unrealized loss from foreign currency translation	3,971	
Less: Treasury stock	(15,000)	
Total stockholders' equity		1,203,368
Total Liabilities & Equity		$ 1,295,916

Figure 6-5:
Classified balance sheet — liabilities and equity

Chapter 7

Follow the Money! Studying Cash Flow

....

....

*I*ntermediate accounting covers financial accounting topics, which are all about the accrual method. Under the accrual method, you record revenue when it is earned and realizable, and record expenses as they are incurred, regardless of whether they were actually paid. The missing piece when using the accrual method of accounting is the effect on business operations when cash changes hands.

For the users of the financial statements to get more of a total picture on the health of the business, cash payments and receipts have to be reconciled with accrual transactions. You accomplish this by preparing a statement of cash flows.

When you took the required accounting classes before you started intermediate accounting, you may have read a cursory review of the statement of cash flows in the same chapter that discussed the balance sheet and income statement. Oddly enough, in your intermediate accounting textbook, the author may use the same approach. In most instances, however, you will find an entire chapter devoted solely to cash flows that provides a more in-depth discussion and overview.

This chapter helps you get a grip on the important topic of cash flows. You find out about the three different sections of the statement of cash flows — operating, investing, and financing — and what type of accounting information you record in each. You also look at the two methods for preparing the statement of cash flows: the direct and indirect methods (although this may change in the future). And you learn how to use the information on the statement of cash flows for decision making.

The FASB prefers the direct method and is working toward vastly limiting the approved use of the indirect method.

Understanding the Purpose of the Statement of Cash Flows

Simply put, the statement of cash flows gives the user information about the cash receipts and cash payments of the business during the accounting period. Whereas cash sources come from many different origins, such as customer payments, loans, and sales of assets and equity, the ways a company uses cash most likely directly trace back to costs. For example, buying equipment, paying invoices, and payroll.

Don't confuse costs with expenses. In the world of accrual accounting, they're not the same. For example, if a company buys a fixed asset with cash, the price it pays or promises to pay for the fixed asset is a *cost.* Over the useful life of the asset, the company depreciates it. Depreciation is the process of reclassifying the cost of buying the asset as an *expense* of doing business — see Chapter 12 for more on that. In this process, the resource the company uses to purchase the fixed asset moves from the balance sheet (cost) to the income statement (expense).

Knowing how a company manages its cash is useful to the *external* users of the financial statement, who aren't privy to the day-to-day operations of the business. In other words, the company may be reporting net income period after period, but it doesn't necessarily mean the company is rolling in cash. And if a company has cash flow problems, there's a good possibility that the business won't be able to give the external users what they want: a return on their investment.

Besides potential investors, potential lenders are highly interested in whether the company has cash management under control. Lenders want to make sure the company can pay back both the principal portion of any loan plus any interest the lender charges for use of the money.

As with the income statement, which I discuss in Chapter 5, the statement of cash flows is for a certain period, such as the 12-month period ending December 31, 2013.

When you start your required tax classes, keep in mind that a statement of cash flows isn't required when using the tax basis of accounting. Also check out Chapter 17 for info on accounting for income taxes.

Formatting the Cash Flow Sections

The statement of cash flows has the following three sections classifying all cash receipts and payments:

- **Operating:** The sources and uses of cash in the operating section come from revenue, expenses, gains, losses, and other costs.

- **Investing:** This section shows sources and uses of cash from debt and equity purchases and sales, purchases of property plant and equipment, and collection of principal on debt.

- **Financing:** You report activities such as long-term liability (paying or securing loans beyond a period of 12 months from the balance sheet date) and equity items (sale or repurchase of company stock and payment of dividends) in the financing section.

From your previous accounting classes, you may find some or most of these terms familiar. If not, or if you recognize a term but are drawing a blank on its exact intermediate accounting meaning, don't fret. This chapter gets you well on your way to being totally up-to-speed on cash flow lingo.

Working our way from top to bottom of the statement of cash flows, first I satisfy your curiosity about the operating section.

Figuring cash operation results

If you pull out your trusty generally accepted accounting principles (GAAP) guide (see Chapter 1 if you don't know what I'm talking about), you see that the description for what you include in the operating section is simply transactions that don't show up in the investing or financing section. Well, that clears it up — not! Don't let this make your head spin. Start by associating the operating section with the income statement, and then worry about including any other items not recorded as investing or financing activities.

Accounts receivable, accounts payable, and inventory are the reasons for the major differences when preparing the operating section of the statement of cash flows. Have a look at these topics in more details in Chapters 9, 14, and 10, respectively.

Consider two examples of operating cash sources (generally, income statement items):

When talking about the statement of cash flows, some accountants refer to cash sources and uses, and some refer to inflows and outflows. Don't let that confuse you. Sources and inflows mean the same thing, as do uses and outflows.

- ✔ **Cash receipts from the sale of goods or services:** This category is either the cash that customers pay the company at point of contact or what the company collects at a later date from existing accounts receivable. For example, say I go into a discount department store and buy a new cordless vacuum cleaner. It costs $125, and I plunk over the cost of the purchase plus sales tax in cash. The store records this as a cash source.

- ✔ **Cash investment income:** This amount includes interest the business earns from bank accounts or on loans it makes to others, or dividends it receives on equity securities such as stock it owns in other companies.

Not quite as much fun as receiving cash, here are typical operating activity cash uses:

- ✔ **Payments for inventory:** Goods the business holds for resale to customers; see Chapter 10 for more.

- ✔ **Payroll:** Net wage payments made to employees. *Net payroll* is the gross amount minus all deductions required by law or authorized by the employee.

- ✔ **Governmental:** Paid to local, state, and federal government for income, employment, and sales tax; Chapter 17 includes a discussion on this topic.

- ✔ **Cash to lenders:** Reflecting the interest portion of loans payable by the company; see Chapter 15 to read more.

- ✔ **Other expenses:** Including cash payments to any other entities or vendors for business expenses.

Showing cash investing transactions

Investing transactions involve the purchase and sale of noncurrent assets — this is a topic of Part III. *Noncurrent assets* are assets that the company anticipates owning for more than one year past the date of the balance sheet (such as office furniture).

The following are three typical examples of investing cash sources and uses. First up, cash sources:

✔ **Selling property, plant, and equipment (PP&E):** This example includes the cash proceeds from any PP&E the corporation owns and sells, such as cars, buildings, or equipment.

✔ **Sale of debt or equity securities of other entities:** If the company sells stock it owns in other corporations, the cash received goes in the investing section. Ditto if the company sells bonds or other type of debt it owns, which another company has issued, and receives cash for the sale.

✔ **Cash collected for the principal amount of loans receivable:** Bet you didn't have to think twice about this one! When the business loans money to individuals or other businesses, and the debtor makes payments, the principal portion of the payment is an investing activity.

The interest portion of the loan payment goes in the operating section.

The following are your investing cash uses, which mimic the investing cash sources, but from the other side of the equation:

✔ To purchase PP&E

✔ To purchase another company's debt or equity securities

✔ To loan money to other businesses or individuals

Accounting for financing activities

Well, if at this point your head is spinning like a top, take consolation in the fact that you've made it to the last section: financing activities! On the statement of cash flows, financing activities show long-term liabilities and equity. The good news is that financing activities are the flip side of investing activities, so if you have a handle on investing activities, you'll be able to whiz through financing activities.

To keep things quick and dirty (read: nice and simple), for this section, I show two typical financing cash sources and uses. Cash sources include the following:

✔ **Notes or bonds payable:** This source includes receiving cash for debt the company issues, lasting beyond a period of 12 months from the balance sheet date.

✔ **Equity items**: This category includes selling your own company stock. Read more about equity items in Chapter 16.

Financing activity cash uses include the following:

- ✔ **Dividends:** Cash payments made to shareholders of record based on how many shares of stock they own.

- ✔ **Redeemed debt and reacquired company stock:** Any principal payments a company makes on bonds or loans are a financing activity. Ditto for *treasury stock* transactions, which are shares of corporate stock that the issuing corporation previously sold and has since reacquired.

Principal payments on capital lease obligations are also financing activities.

Capital leases take place when the renter (lessee) assumes just about all the benefits and liabilities of ownership of the leased asset; jump over to Chapter 18 to read more.

Recognizing Methods for Preparing the Statement of Cash Flows

In the past, when teaching my financial and intermediate accounting classes, my lecture about preparing the statement of cash flows always kicked off with a discussion about how many companies preferred to use a method for preparing the statement of cash flows that differed from the Financial Accounting Standards Board (FASB) method. Chapter 1 discusses this in more detail.

Currently, companies use two different methods: *direct* and *indirect*. FASB prefers the direct method because it feels it gives the user more standardized info to more accurately compare companies. However, most companies use the indirect method because compiling the information is less expensive than using the direct method.

With recent accounting standards events involving the FASB and the International Accounting Standards Board (IASB), using two different methods will eventually be a thing of the past in this extravaganza. See Chapter 1 for more information about the FASB and the IASB.

Regardless of this possible change, I want to give you a brief overview of the indirect method, with more emphasis on the direct method.

Whether using the direct or indirect method, you need information from three different sources:

- ✔ **Income statement:** The financial document reflecting a company's revenue, gains, losses, and expenses. More information about income statement accounts and preparation comes in Chapters 5 and 20.

- ✔ **Balance sheet:** The financial document showing a company's assets, liabilities, and equity. More information about balance sheet accounts and preparation crops up in Parts III, IV, and IV.

- ✔ **General ledger:** The record of all financial transactions that take place within the company during a particular accounting cycle. Use the general ledger to ferret out the beginning balances for accounts receivable, accounts payable, and inventory (just to name three potential accounts you may be using to prepare the statement of cash flows). See Chapter 4 for the 411 on this source of accounting information.

And don't forget about the trial balance which lists all accounting in the chart of accounts and their balance at the date of the report. Although a trial balance is useful, it doesn't prove that a company records all transactions correctly.

Without further ado, let's move in a bit closer and look at preparing the statement of cash flows.

Using the direct method

As I said in the previous section, if the FASB/IASB proposed changes take effect, the direct method for preparing the statement of cash flows will be required, eliminating the choice of using the indirect method, which is the topic of the next section of this chapter. Unfortunately, many of my students find the direct method more confusing than the indirect. However, if you keep in mind the primary purpose of the statement of cash flows, which is to give the users of the financial statements relevant data about cash a business brings in and pays out during a financial period, you should be able to stay more focused with the whole preparation procedure.

Here are a few important direct method basics, to build upon the material in your intermediate accounting textbook:

✔ You show cash received and paid, not net income or loss as shown on the income statement. Why? Because the income statement shows both cash and noncash transactions, and the users of the statement of cash flows want to know about only cash transactions. A biggie noncash transaction is depreciation — see Chapter 12 for more.

✔ To figure cash receipts from customers, you adjust accrual-based sales revenue by the change in accounts receivable (A/R) during the period. If A/R goes up, you decrease sales revenue. If A/R goes down during the period, it's an addition to sales revenue.

For example, if during July 2013 the company has sales revenue of $200,000 and a $20,000 decrease to accounts receivable, total cash received from customers is $220,000 ($200,000 + $20,000).

✔ To figure cash payments to suppliers during the period, you use the income statement account, the cost of goods sold (COGS), and the balance sheet accounts, inventory and accounts payable (A/P).

This process involves two steps. First, you adjust the COGS by adding an increase or subtracting a decrease in the inventory account balance during the month. The resulting figure is further adjusted by subtracting an increase or adding back a decrease in the accounts payable account balance during the financial period.

Figure 7-1 illustrates these steps. For this computation, COGS is $100,000, inventory shows an increase of $10,000, and A/P shows an increase of $5,000 during the financial period.

Figure 7-1: Computing cash payments to suppliers.	Cost of goods sold	$ 100,000
	Plus inventory increase	10,000
	Less accounts payable increase	(5,000)
	Cash payments to suppliers	$ 105,000

You can walk through the process of preparing a statement of cash flows using the direct method at the end of this chapter in the last section of this chapter "A Sample Statement of Cash Flows." Using a portion of the very abbreviated financial statement information from Figure 7-1, Figure 7-2 shows the operating section of the statement of cash flows.

Figure 7-2:
Operating
activity
section
using the
direct
method:
Partial
statement of
cash flows.

Cash flows from operating activities:

Cash received from customers	$ 220,000
Cash payments to suppliers	105,000
Net cash provided by operating activities	$ 115,000

Starting indirectly with net income

When preparing the statement of cash flows using the indirect method, the operating section starts with net income from the income statement, which you adjust for any noncash items hitting the income statement. Your three biggies are depreciation, amortization (both of which are noncash transactions), and gain or loss on the disposal of assets. See Chapters 12, 13, and 5 for more on depreciation, amortization, and gain or loss on the disposal of assets, respectively.

Using the same facts from the direct method section of this chapter, and adding a few extra needed facts for this example, I show the operating activity section using the indirect method in Figure 7-3.

For Figure 7-3, net income is $95,000, depreciation on PP&E is $4,250, and cash received when selling some equipment results in a gain of $750. Note that the bottom-line net cash provided by operating activities is (and has to be) the same whether you use the direct or the indirect method.

Gains and losses from the sale of assets usually require adjustments on the statement of cash flows because the gain or loss shown on the income statement for the sale rarely, if ever, equals the cash a company receives for the transaction.

Statement of Cash Flows

Indirect Method

For the Year Ending 12/31/2013

Figure 7-3:
Operating
activity
section
using the
indirect
method:
Partial
statement of
cash flows.

Cash Flows from Operating Activities:	
Net Income	95,000
Add (deduct items) not affecting cash:	
Depreciation expense	4,250
Gain on sale of equipment	750
Decrease in accounts receivable	20,000
Increase in accounts payable	(5,000)
Net cash provided by operating activities	115,000

Any differences when using the direct versus the indirect method show up only in the operating section. The investing and financing sections are prepared the same using either method.

Using the Statement of Cash Flows

Users of the financial statements can do all sorts of relevant analysis. You learn about ten methods of ratio analysis in Chapter 22. In this section, you take a closer look at the three primary ways to use information on the statement of cash flows: to figure liquidity, gauge flexibility, and show free cash flow.

Figuring financial liquidity

A business is considered to be *liquid* if it can cover current debt with current assets. In other words, can a company pay off its current liabilities without going to outside sources (such as a bank) to borrow money? A common example of a *current liability* is *accounts payable,* which is money the company owes its vendors for goods and services it purchases during the normal course of business and anticipates paying back in the short term. Visit Chapter 14 for more on current liability.

The ratio to figure financial liquidity is the *current cash debt coverage ratio*. The formula for this ratio is net cash provided by operating activities (Sound familiar? If not, check out the previous section in this chapter, "Using the direct method") divided by average current liabilities. Using net cash provided by operating activities from Figure 7-3, and assuming average current liabilities of $112,000, the ratio is 1.027, rounded ($115,000 ÷ $112,000).

Current debt coverage for this example is close to 1:1, which is generally considered good. Financiers agree this usually indicates that the company can pay current obligations without going to outside borrowing sources.

 Anytime one of your intermediate accounting homework or exam questions asks for an average figure, you find the average by adding the beginning and ending balances together and dividing by 2. If accounts payable at January 1 is $215,000 and $175,000 at January 31, the average accounts payable is $195,000 ([$215,000 + $175,000] ÷ 2).

Analyzing financial flexibility

The *cash debt coverage ratio* gives interested users of the financial statements the scoop on the company's financial flexibility. Divide net cash provided by operating activities by average total liabilities for this computation. *Total liabilities* include the whole ball of yarn, debt wise — in other words, current liabilities, discussed in Chapter 14, and long-term obligations, a topic of Chapter 15.

If it seems a little unclear, perhaps an example is due. Here's a typical homework question:

"If ABC, Inc., has average total liabilities of $200,000 and net cash provided by operating activities of $230,000, what is ABC's cash debt coverage ratio? Based on this result, do you think ABC has financial flexibility?"

First, to figure the cash debt coverage ratio, divide $230,000 by $200,000, which equals 1.15. Well, ladies and gentleman, this isn't good news! In the world of financial flexibility, the higher the ratio, the better. This ratio is very low, indicating to most financial users the chance the company will have to resort to outside borrowing to meet obligations (at least sometime in the near future) is quite high.

Showing free cash flow

Investors are very interested in *free cash flow,* which is the net cash provided by operating activities minus capital expenditures and dividends. You figure free cash flow by subtracting money spent for *capital expenditures,* which is money to purchase or improve assets, and money paid out in dividends from net cash provided by operating activities.

Free cash flow is important to investors because, in the long run, it can have a major effect on whether the company can continue as a going concern (which means the company anticipates being in operation for at least the next 12 months). It also has a bearing on whether investors can anticipate being paid dividends in the future and on the stability and possible increase of the market price of the stock. This consideration is important if the investor is planning to sell the stock in the near future at a price equal to or above what he originally paid for it.

Figure 7-4 illustrates a free cash flow calculation using our old familiar net cash provided by an operating activities figure of $115,000 and assuming capital expenditures of $45,700 and dividends of $25,000. In this calculation, free cash flow is a positive amount, which is always a good thing.

However, many users would not consider the $44,300 to be a substantial amount. One pending debt payment could eat it up entirely, leaving no free cash for other uses.

Net cash provided by operating activities	$ 115,000
Less: Capital expenditures	(45,700)
Dividends	(25,000)
Free cash flow	$ 44,300

Figure 7-4: Calculating free cash flow.

Any ratio by itself is rather meaningless unless you have some point of comparison, such as an industry average or a competitor. Thus, even though the three cash ratios I discuss in this section of the chapter provide information regarding a company's liquidity, they're not frequently used because of the lack of comparison points.

Converting from accrual to cash

No discussion about cash flows is complete without walking through the steps to convert revenue and expenses kept on the accrual basis to cash. At some point, your intermediate accounting instructor may ask you to do this to test your knowledge. The following illustration is my handy cheat sheet for converting accrual-based revenue and expenses to cash receipts and payments.

The nifty thing about this cheat sheet is that it's a twofer! After you memorize and understand it, just reverse pluses and minuses to convert cash books to accrual. For example, you subtract beginning accounts receivable from accrual-based revenue earned. See the following illustration.

Accrual based revenue earned
+ beginning accounts receivable
– ending accounts receivable
– beginning unearned revenues – for example, *customer deposits,* which is money paid by the customer for goods or services the company has not yet delivered; see Chapter 14.
+ ending unearned revenues
= Cash receipts

Accrual based operating expenses
– beginning prepaid expenses – for example, inventory; see Chapter 10
+ ending prepaid expenses
+ beginning payables
– ending payables
= Cash payments

A Sample Statement of Cash Flows

Now let's explore a full-blown statement of cash flows prepared using the direct method (see Figure 7-5).

As with a statement of cash flows you prepare for a "real" business, the figures shown flow from the income statement (see Chapter 5) and the balance sheet (check out Chapters 4 and 6).

The increase in cash of $379,879 is the sum of net cash provided by operating activities, net cash used for investing activities, and net cash used for financing activities ($769,879 – $187,500 – $202,500).

When you prepare a statement of cash flows using the direct method, you also have to include a section reconciling accrual net income to cash provided by operating activities. This additional section, which comes at the end of the direct method statement of cash flows, is identical to the cash flows from operating activities section of the indirect method statement of cash flows.

Statement of Cash Flows
Direct Method
For the Year Ending 12/31/2013

Cash Flows from Operating Activities:

Cash received from customers	994,891
Cash paid to suppliers	134,028
Employee compensation	36,363
Other operating expenses paid	26,316
Interest paid	11,475
Taxes paid	16,830
Net cash provided by operating activities	769,879

Cash Flows from Investing Activities:

Proceeds from sale of equipment	37,500
Purchase of land	(225,000)
Net cash used for investing activities	(187,500)

Cash Flows from Financing Activities:

New long-term borrowing	135,000
Payment of long-term debt	(105,000)
Purchase of treasury stock	(57,500)
Payment of dividends	(175,000)
Net cash used for financing activities	(202,500)

Increase (decrease) in cash	379,879
Cash balance, January 1, 2012	105,782
Cash balance, December 31, 2012	485,661

Reconciliation of Net Income and Net Cash Provided by Operating Activities:

Net Income	665,754
Add (deduct items) not affecting cash:	
Depreciation expense	78,500
Gain on sale of equipment	52,500
Increase in accounts receivable	(56,000)
Increase in accounts payable	29,125
Net cash provided by operating activities	769,879

Figure 7-5:
A direct method statement of cash flows.

Chapter 8

Time Is Money: Looking at the Time Value of Money

In This Chapter
▶ Looking at simple and compound interest
▶ Understanding the difference between single payments and annuities
▶ Figuring future and present values
▶ Delving into more complicated time value topics

1 don't know about you, but making money through the magic of interest is just about my favorite way to earn. Sure, I like to work, but something about making money without active effort is pretty darn appealing.

This chapter looks at the time value of money from the perspective of both the investor and the creditor. I walk you through simple and complex interest and show you how to value the money you're holding in your hand now to see what it will be worth in the future. I also look at annuities — which are series of payments — and how to value them. Finally, the chapter wraps up with a more advanced discussion about deferred annuities and long-term bonds.

Taking an Interest in Interest

At this stage of your life, you've probably earned money to buy a car or a computer or enhance your wardrobe by earning income. And although working at a job isn't always a good time, some jobs are definitely less glamorous than others (which can actually be great motivation to do well in school!).

Investment rule: The Rule of 72

The Rule of 72 is a simple way to get a rough estimate on how long it takes for an investment to double with a fixed rate of interest. Here's how it works: If you're getting a fixed rate of 3 percent on an investment of $5,000, divide 72 by 3 to figure out how long it will take your investment to grow to $10,000. In this example, the time is 24 years (72 ÷ 3).

It's pretty much a fact of life that, unless you win the lottery or your Aunt Dottie leaves you a windfall in her will, in order to bring in money, you have to earn it by working. Making money with a job is *nonpassive* or *earned* income — that is, it takes action on your part.

However, there's also *passive* income, such as interest. *Interest* is revenue you earn from money on deposit. You take the earned income left over after you pay your bills, deposit it into a savings or money market account (or any other type of investment), and, while you're sleeping, walking on the beach, or working hard at your job, your invested money is making more money for you — you hope.

 I use the terms *passive* and *nonpassive* income at their most basic here, merely denoting the difference between sweating over the fry cooker at the fast food restaurant and earning cash from interest income. The two terms have slightly different "true" financial or tax accounting meanings, but we don't need to worry about that right now.

 Stocks are equity investments. For example, you may buy shares of AT&T common stock. Bonds are debt investments issued when a municipality sells bonds to the public to build a new school or hospital. More about stocks in Chapter 16 and bonds in Chapter 15.

Applying Earning Concepts

Well, now that I've piqued your interest in making money while you sleep, it's time to find out exactly how this works. What's the difference between simple and compound interest, anyway? It's important to have at least a basic understanding of how a company or bank determines the interest rate you earn on your money on deposit.

Basically, the two major criteria to setting interest rates are the riskiness of the investment and what rate is commonly being paid. For example, if you have a good credit score, you'll receive a more favorable interest rate when borrowing money to make a purchase than someone who has horrible credit. Or if your bank needs to beef up its money on deposit, it may pay a higher interest rate than the competition, to attract new customers.

The actual interest computations made by banks and other lending institutions are much more complicated, so we leave those to your finance classes.

Simple interest

You figure simple interest on the *principal,* which is the amount of money borrowed or on deposit using a basic formula: Principal × Rate × Time (Interest = $p \times r \times t$). Your intermediate accounting textbook may substitute n for time—the n stands for number of periods (time).

Let's say your brother wants to buy a used car for $5,000 and has only $2,000 for the down payment. He hits you up for a loan for the remaining $3,000. If the length of the loan is five months and he's paying you simple interest of 3.5 percent per month to borrow the additional $3,000, your interest income equals $525. Check out this calculation in Figure 8-1.

Simple interest is used only for loans and investments of less than one year. If the time is longer than one year, compound interest applies instead.

Figure 8-1:
Calculating
simple
interest.

Interest = p × r × t

= $3,000 × .035 × 5

= $525

Compound interest

Hold on to your hats! Now that you understand the basic calculation for simple interest, it's time to familiarize yourself with how to figure compound interest, which really shows the time value of money. You figure compound interest on both the amount of principal and any interest earned but not withdrawn. For example, let's say that your brother decides not to replace his old car and instead invests the $2,000 proposed down payment, earning 3.5 percent interest. Using the theory of compound interest, he earns interest each month on the amount of principal and interest the bank pays him for his money on deposit — in other words, the accumulated balance.

Any lending institution that's required to abide by federal law, such as a bank, must state its interest rates annually and as compound rather than simple interest. Figure 8-2 shows the time value of the investment.

		Interest	Accumulated Balance
Year 1	$2,000.00 × 3.5%	$70.00	$2,070.00 (2,000 + 70)
Year 2	$2,070.00 × 3.5%	$72.45	$2,142.45 (2,070 + 72.45)
Year 3	$2,142.45 × 3.5%	$74.99	$2,217.44 (2,142.45 + 74.99)

Figure 8-2: Calculating compound interest.

As you can see, the calculations in Figure 8-2 are a bit more involved than when figuring simple interest. Luckily, banks and other financial institutions that perform these calculations regularly have software for the job.

Your intermediate accounting textbook provides five interest tables to help you compute the time value of money. Two tables deal with a single sum; three address annuities, which is a series of payments. Itching to get started working with the time value of money? In the next two sections, you find out how to use the five tables.

If you don't want to have to crack open your huge intermediate accounting textbook every time you want to check out these interest tables, you'll be glad to know that you can also find them online. Do a search using the key phrase "present and future value tables" to find a plethora of options. You can also use a financial calculator or an Excel function on your computer.

Your intermediate accounting textbook also shows the formulas the tables are built on. You can just use those formulas, if you want, although I find the tables much easier to work with.

Calculating Single Sums

No, this section isn't about how to get a date. But it does give you some tips on how to do some simple calculations. Single-sum problems involve a single amount of money that you either have on hand now or want to have in the future. You use these two tables to figure single sums:

✔ **Future value of 1:** This table shows how much a single sum on deposit will grow when invested for a specific period of time at a particular interest rate. For example, you deposit $500 in the bank today and want to know how much you'll have two years from now.

✔ **Present value of 1:** The flipside of future value, this table tells you how much you'll have to save today to have a certain amount at your disposal in the future. For example, you want to have $2,000 saved for a down payment on a new car in three years — how much do you need to put away today to reach that goal?

Future value of a single sum

Suppose that a company with an extra $100,000 lying around is trying to decide between investing the money at 4 percent for five years and using the extra money to expand the business. It sure would help if they know how much the $100,000 would grow if they invested it.

Future value table to the rescue! Using this table, the company can calculate exactly what the $100,000 will grow to using the three variables of principal ($100,000), time (five years), and rate (4 percent). Figure 8-3 shows a partial future value of 1 table.

Periods	2%	3%	4%	5%
1	1.02000	1.03000	1.04000	1.05000
2	1.04040	1.06090	1.08160	1.10250
3	1.06121	1.09273	1.12486	1.15763
4	1.08243	1.12551	1.16986	1.21551
5	1.10408	1.15927	1.21665	1.27628

Figure 8-3: Partial future value of 1 table.

For this calculation, you find the number at the intersection of 4 percent and five periods, which is 1.21665. Multiply $100,000 times 1.21665 to get the future value of a single sum of $100,000. The future value of that single sum is $121,665 ($100,000 × 1.21665).

The company now has valuable information. If it reckons that using the $100,000 to expand the business won't increase the bottom line over the next five years by at least $21,665 ($121,665 – $100,000), investing the money at 4 percent is probably the wiser option.

Choosing between single sum tables

Would you use the future value table or present value table to figure a car payment of $4,000 that will be required in two years? Well, as you're looking into the future, you're trying to come up with a contemporaneous amount — so you use the present value of 1 table in Figure 8-4. Assuming that your rate of return is 5 percent, you need to save $3,628.12 ($4,000 × .90703) today to have $4,000 two years from now.

Future value of a single sum

As you saw in the last section, computing the future value of a sum results in a larger amount than what you started with. The opposite is true when figuring the present value of a single dollar amount. In this case, you start with a smaller figure that, through the magic of compound interest, grows into a larger amount. So let's say that a company wants to figure out how much it needs to invest today at 5 percent to have $200,000 three years from now. Figure 8-4 is a partial present value of a single sum table.

	Periods	2%	3%	4%	5%
Figure 8-4: Partial present value of 1 table.	1	098039	.97087	.96154	.95238
	2	.96117	.94260	.92456	.90703
	3	.94232	.91514	.88900	.86384

For this calculation, you find the factor at the intersection of 5 percent and three periods, which is .86384. Multiply $200,000 times .86384 to see how much the company has to invest today to have $200,000 in the future. The answer to that weighty question is $172,768 ($200,000 × .86384).

Calculating Annuities

We just talked about performing calculations to compute the time value of money using only one payment. Now let's make it interesting by calculating multiple payments. Annuities are a series of payments paid or received over a period of time. A typical example is rent payments made to a property owner. Annuities also include bond payments — companies issue bonds when they want to raise money. Bonds are debt (see Chapter 15 for more about bonds), which means that the company eventually has to pay back the bond investor.

Annui-whaties?

To be classified as an annuity, a constant amount of money has to be paid or received over a fixed period of time. The first annuity I ever received was the allowance my dad paid me every Saturday when I was a kid. Adult annuities can get a bit more complex than that, but the principal is basically the same. Two basic types of annuities exist: *ordinary annuities* and *annuities due*.

- ✔ **Ordinary annuity:** This annuity requires payments at the end of each previously determined financial period. For example, a bond may require payments to the investor at the end of every six months (for example, June 30), until maturity date (see Chapter 15 for more info about bonds).

- ✔ **Annuity due:** Got you on the flip-flop! Payments are due at the beginning of each period (for example, January 1). A good example of this is rent you for an apartment. The landlord normally expects payment in hand on the first of each month.

Bet you never saw this coming: Just as with single sums (discussed earlier in this chapter), other important calculations involve the future and present value of an annuity.

Future value of an annuity

To recap, the amount of an annuity and the interval between receiving and paying the annuity always has to be the same. Then you compound interest once during each interval. Thus, the *future value* of an annuity means that you compute the sum of all payments plus the accumulated compound interest on the payments. In this section, you first find out how to calculate the future value of an ordinary annuity. Then you do the same for an annuity due. Ready to get started? Get out that calculator and proceed to the next section.

Future value of an ordinary annuity

Let's say that you plan to deposit $1,500 at the end of each six-month period for the next two years, earning 8 percent interest annually. First, this is indeed an annuity because you are depositing the same amount ($1,500) over a constant period of time (every six months). So how much will you have at the end of the two years? To figure this out, you use the future value of an ordinary annuity of 1 table (see Figure 8-5).

	Periods	2%	3%	4%	5%
Figure 8-5:	1	1.00000	1.00000	1.00000	1.00000
Partial					
future value	2	2.02000	2.03000	2.04000	3.15250
of an ordi-					
nary annuity	3	3.06040	3.09090	3.12160	3.15250
of 1 table.					
	4	4.12161	4.18363	4.24646	4.31013

In this example, your number of periods is four (remember, you're depositing the investment every six months, which is two times a year multiplied by two years). Similarly, your interest rate must be halved because the interest rate is in annual, not semiannual, terms (8% ÷ 2 = 4%).

Using Figure 8-5, going to the intersection of 4 percent for four periods gives you a factor of 4.24646. At the end of the two years, your money will grow to $6,369.69 ($1,500 × 4.24646). Total cash out of hand for you is $6,000 ($1,500 × 4), and interest income is $369.69 ($6,369.69 – $6,000).

Future value of an annuity due

Using the same principal, time, and rate information from the previous section, it's time to figure out the future value of an annuity due. Remember, with an annuity due, the payments start at the beginning of the six-month period instead of at the end.

So guess what? The amount of interest you earn on the investment will be higher. You can thank the time value of money, as your investment is accruing interest six months sooner than with an ordinary annuity. Time to work through the numbers.

You still use the future value of an ordinary annuity of 1, but you increase the factor by 1 plus the interest rate. So your factor for an annuity due is 4.41631 (4.24645 × 1.04). $1,500 × 4.41631 is $6,624.47, an increase of $254.78 ($6,624.47 – $6,369.69). Not a lot of money, but consider the implications for businesses that conduct transactions in the millions of dollars.

Present value of an annuity

Now you approach the issue from a different standpoint. The present value of an annuity shows you the single sum you need to invest at compound interest now in order to provide a series of payments back to you in the future. Sound like the type of information you want to have to plan your retirement?

To mix this up a little bit, I present typical homework and test questions that you may encounter in your intermediate accounting class to illustrate how to figure out the present value of an ordinary annuity and an annuity due.

Present value of an ordinary annuity

Just to refresh your memory, don't forget that, with an ordinary annuity, payment occurs at the end of each period instead of at the beginning. So imagine that your financial accounting instructor has the following question on the midterm — how do you calculate the correct answer?

"What is the present value of nine annual cash payments of $10,000, to be paid at the end of each year using an interest rate of 6 percent?" You know that this is an annuity because the amount of the payment and the interval between payments is the same year after year. And at this point, you probably have a hint that you have to use either a table or a financial calculator. But what table? Gasp! You use the present value of an ordinary annuity of 1 table.

At this point, you're probably a pro at reading the tables, so I include the only relevant line from the table for this illustration. Using the factor from Figure 8-6, your answer is $68,017 ($10,000 × 6.8017).

Figure 8-6:
Partial present value of an ordinary annuity of 1 table.

Period	6%
9	6.8017

Present value of an annuity due

Just like the future value of annuities due, the present value of an annuity due calculates annuities taking place sooner — that is, at the beginning instead of end of the period.

The following is a typical homework assignment or test question you may see in your intermediate accounting class:

"Penway, Inc., rents equipment for nine years, with annual rent payments of $15,000 to be made at the beginning of each year. Compounding interest at a rate of 6 percent, what is the present value of the lease obligation?"

Checking out Figure 8-5, you see that the factor is 6.8017. Just like with the future value of an annuity due, you have to consider an additional factor of 1 plus the interest rate. So you multiply 1.06 times 6.8017 to get the present value of an annuity due, which is 7.2098. Your answer to the question is $108,147.03 ($15,000 × 7.2098).

Your intermediate accounting textbook may contain a table for the present value of an annuity due of 1. If it does, you don't have to go through the extra work of computing the annuity due factor. In that table, at the intersection of nine periods and 6 percent, you'll find the same 7.2098.

More Complex Annuities

If your head is spinning after looking at the different tables and ways to consider the time value of money, don't feel bad — you're not alone! But before you finish this chapter and move on to another intermediate accounting subject, you need to quickly review two more advanced annuity topics: deferred annuities and long-term bond valuation. First up, deferred annuities.

What happens to an annuity deferred?

Deferred annuities are a type of annuity contract that delays payments to the investor until the investor elects to receive them. When the investor is in savings mode, he makes payments into some sort of investment account. The investment grows and compounds in a *tax-deferred manner,* and the investor pays no taxes on its growth until he decides to convert the investment into an annuity and start receiving regular payments.

You need to understand how to figure the future and present value of a deferred annuity for your intermediate accounting class. The good news is that you use the same method to figure the future value of a deferred annuity as when you calculate the future value of an ordinary annuity; see the section earlier in this chapter titled "Future value of an annuity."

Future value of a deferred annuity

In 2013, Penway, Inc., starts planning for a major expansion in 2019. At the end of 2016, 2017, and 2018, Penway reckons that it will be able to invest $50,000 each year, earning 5 percent annually. How much money will Penway have to play with when it starts its expansion in 2019?

In this example, you have to ignore the first three years (2013, 2014, and 2015) because Penway has no plans to put aside any money during those years. You figure the value accumulated by using the standard formula for a future value of an ordinary annuity.

Checking out Figure 8-5, you see that three years at 5 percent gives you a factor of 3.15250. Multiplying that factor by the amount saved per year of $50,000 gives you the future value of the deferred annuity, which is $157,625.

Present value of a deferred annuity

The *present value of a deferred annuity* tells you how much you need to invest today to achieve your desired savings result in the future. To accomplish this, you use just one different table: the present value of an ordinary annuity of 1.

Let's put this to work and make it personal! Suppose that you're 18 years old. As an incentive to stay in school and get good grades, your Aunt Dottie says she'll give you $3,000 a year for three years starting five years from now (after your proposed graduation date). Given an annual interest rate of 5 percent and the total periods (which is seven — four years deferred plus three annual payments), you want to know the present value of the four payments.

Looking at the present value of an ordinary annuity of 1 table in your intermediate accounting textbook or online, you can see that the factor at the intersection of seven periods and 5 percent is 5.78637. Using the same table, you see that the factor at the intersection of four (deferred) periods and 5 percent is 3.54595. Figure 8-7 shows the calculation.

1.	Annual payment from Dottie		$ 3,000
2.	Present value of an ordinary annuity of 1 for seven total periods (four deferred plus the three annual payments)	5.78637	
3.	Less the present value of an ordinary annuity for the four deferred periods	(3.54595)	× 2.24042
4.	Present value of Aunt Dottie's payments ($3,000 times 2.24042)		$ 6,721.26

Figure 8-7:
Figuring the present value of annual payments.

Long-term bond valuation

I devote a whole section in Chapter 15 to the topic of bonds. So for the time value discussion regarding valuation of *long-term bonds,* which is debt outstanding for more than 12 months, I want you to primarily remember the fact that bonds have two different cash flows: interest and principal.

✔ **Interest:** The amount of income (interest payments) the investor receives over the life of the bond

✔ **Principal:** The face value of the bond that's paid back when the bond matures

For a quick-and-dirty computation of the present value of the two cash flows, imagine that Penway, Inc., issues $200,000 of 5 percent bonds on January 1 that are due in three years and pay interest annually in December. To figure the present value of the principal amount of $200,000, multiply $200,000 by .86384 (the factor at the intersection of three periods and 5 percent in Figure 8-4); you have $172,768.

Then to find the present value of the annual interest payments of $10,000 ($200,000 × 5%), you go to the present value of an ordinary annuity of 1 table. The factor at the intersection of three periods and 5 percent is 2.72325. And $10,000 × 2.72325 is $27,232. Add the two figures together ($172,768 + 27,232), and ta-da! You have the face amount of $200,000, which is the present value of the bonds.

It works out this way because the bonds were issued for face value and it's assumed that the current market rate for similar bonds is also 5 percent. I offer this simple example of long-term bond valuation as an introduction to the topic. In Chapter 15, you get into more complicated accounting when the bond is issued for a *discount* (less than face value) or a *premium* (more than face value).

Part III
Homing in on Current and Noncurrent Assets

The 5th Wave   By Rich Tennant

ACCOUNTANTS LUNCH

"So once I add the floating volume rate to my accumulated reserve assets and divide by the annualized ratio, I'll realize a profit. It still looks like a $6 tip on an $85 lunch."

In this part . . .

You explore the three types of current assets: cash, receivables, and inventory. Cash is always a fun topic. What isn't there to like about cash?

In addition to what you probably consider to be "regular" types of cash accounts, like checking accounts, Chapter 9 discusses cash equivalents, which are current assets that lack the liquidity of cash. This chapter also discusses accounts and notes receivable. Accounts receivable generally originate with customer transactions. You find out about accounting for the different types of debt hanging out on the balance sheet as notes receivable.

Chapter 10 discusses inventory. You find out about the different types of inventory and the costs associated with them. Inventory cost flow assumptions, which is how the cost of inventory moves from the balance sheet to the income statement, is also explored. Finally, I give you the skinny on how to estimate inventory, handle retail inventory transactions, and dispose of obsolete inventory.

You also delve into two types of noncurrent assets: tangible and intangible. Tangible assets include property, plant, and equipment, which have a physical presence. Intangible assets don't have a physical existence and include patents, copyrights, and goodwill.

I discuss issues related to tangible assets in Chapters 11 and 12. Chapter 11 is all about buying, selling, and valuing tangible assets. Then in Chapter 12, you determine how to use depreciation to move the cost of tangible assets from the balance sheet to the income statement.

Chapter 13 gives you the skinny on the two different types of intangible assets and further breaks down the first type into five different categories (the second type is just goodwill). You also find out how to use amortization and impairment to move the cost of intangible assets from the balance sheet to the income statement. Wrapping up Chapter 13 is a discussion on research and development costs, which are costs a company incurs to investigate new business processes or products. Although they're not an intangible asset, they often pave the way for intangibles such as patents.

Chapter 9

Assessing Cash and Receivables

. . . .

. . . .

*P*art III of this book covers current assets, which means assets that either are cash or are easily convertible to cash. Chapter 10 discusses inventory, and this chapter walks you through cash and receivables. In addition, you can find a great overview of the balance sheet, which shows cash and receivables, in Chapter 6.

In this chapter, you read about the different types of cash and cash-equivalent accounts a business may have. Included in this category are your garden-variety *operating cash account,* which a company uses to pay its day-to-day expenses, and the more exotic *sweep accounts,* which are income-bearing accounts a company uses in the short term to earn income from excess funds sitting in other bank accounts.

You also find out about cash equivalents, which are current assets, just not as liquid as straight-out cash sitting in a checking account. Finally, you look at how to account for and present on the balance sheet transactions that affect *accounts receivable,* which is money a customer owes a business, and short-term *notes receivable,* which is debt someone owes you that's coming due within 12 months of the balance sheet date.

Keep Your Eye on the Money: Managing Cash

Ah, cash! Gotta love it, but sometimes it's just hard to hang on to. We've all been in the position of evaluating the relative merits of making a purchase that we don't really need (but want, darn it!) versus watching our checking or saving balance stay steady.

A major part of the task of keeping the home fires lit at most businesses is effective cash management. In other words, the company needs an overall rationale for collecting, holding, and disbursing cash. In the next few sections of this chapter, you look at different types of business cash accounts and the methods businesses use to tame that wild cash beast.

Recognizing different cash accounts

I want to emphasize that the definition of cash goes beyond paper bills and coinage. Any sort of account that's backed by cash is deemed a cash account. For example, when you go to the college bookstore and write a check to pay for your honking big intermediate accounting textbook (1,600 pages, yikes!), your check is the same as cash. When you sign it, you attest to the fact that you have funds in your checking account, allowing this check to immediately clear — that is, those funds are withdrawable upon demand.

Depending on the size of the business, it may organize and manage its revenue and bill paying in one or more types of cash accounts. For example, a retail business probably has separate operating and *merchant accounts* (an account where credit card transactions deposit). A large service business may have separate operating and payroll accounts. Some companies have cash accounts for which they earn interest income.

Because this chapter is front and center in the part of this book about current assets, it goes without saying that cash is a current asset (and yet I just said it!) and is your most liquid of all current assets. However, it's also important that you understand the business purpose for different types of cash accounts. Here they are, along with a brief description:

- ✔ **Operating checking account:** A business usually earmarks a particular checking account, which it calls the operating account, to handle business activities such as depositing revenue and paying bills.

- ✔ **Payroll checking account:** Many midsize and large companies (some small ones, too!) have a checking account that they use only to pay employees. They figure up the total dollar amount of checks or transfers to pay employees and transfer that amount from the operating account to cover the payroll checks.

✔ **Merchant account:** If a business allows customers to pay by credit card, it probably has a dedicated merchant account into which they deposit only funds from the *merchant provider*, or the company enabling the business ability to process customer credit cards. Normally, companies use withdrawals from this account to cover bill-paying withdrawals.

✔ **Petty cash account:** Most companies have a cash box to pay for daily *de minimis* expenses. This account is also known as an *imprest account* because it always carries the same balance. By this, I mean that anytime the cash box is checked, it should have cash or receipts equaling the petty cash fund amount. So if the fund is $300, cash and receipts in the box have to equal $300, too.

✔ **Sweep account:** A sweep account is a way for the company to automatically earn investment income. Each evening, any extra cash in the company's' operating account is gathered up and transferred (swept) into investment accounts.

Money from many different companies is pooled into a bigger pot, thereby providing the advantage of a higher rate of return. Then as the company needs the money to clear checks and withdrawals, the money is swept back into the operating account.

The definition of cash includes coinage and currency in hand and on deposit in checking and savings accounts. It also includes near-cash assets, such as undeposited checks (checks received and in the process of being deposited) or deposits in transit (checks that have been deposited but have not yet shown up on the bank statement).

Walking through cash equivalents

In the accounting world of cash, cash equivalents are close but no cigar! Now, the basic premise of *cash equivalents* is that they're just a hair away from being available for withdrawal on demand. They're short term, readily convertible to cash; if they have a maturity date, it's so close to that date that the chance of them devaluing is negligible.

A "close" maturity date for a cash equivalent is three months or less.

Examples of cash equivalents are Treasury bills, commercial paper, and money market funds. I discuss each in turn here.

✔ **Treasury bills:** These items are debt instruments the U.S. Department of Treasury issues that mature in less than one year.

Don't confuse Treasury bills with *treasury stock* which is when a company reacquires their own stock. See Chapter 16 for more information about treasury stock.

✔ **Commercial paper:** This term refers to notes receivable with no collateral to back up the debt. Commercial paper has a maturity date of less than 270 days. See the section "Recognizing Notes Receivable," later in this chapter, for more information on how to account for commercial paper.

✔ **Money market funds:** Money market accounts are similar to checking accounts, except they generally pay a higher interest rate on deposited funds than regular checking. However, they also usually require maintaining minimum balances.

Because of the minimum balance requirement, money market funds aren't considered readily available, which is why they classify as a cash equivalent instead of straight-out cash.

Businesses usually put any type of short-term investment into play to get some use out of temporarily idle cash. If "extra" money is sitting in the company checking account earning no interest, it's a smart move to make every attempt to invest it short term in an interest-bearing vehicle.

Controlling cash

The big deal about controlling cash for your intermediate accounting class is making sure the balance sheet presentation doesn't mislead users with the amount of cash available to meet day-to-day expenses. The major issue here is to properly identify *restricted cash,* which is cash that's spoken for. Restricted cash is set apart from other cash accounts.

Cash is an account that is inherently risky, because it's liquid and lacking proper controls and is subject to misappropriation by dishonest employees; but this is an auditing class topic.

In other words, the cash isn't available for immediate use. Examples are petty cash funds or funds transferred from the operating account into a payroll account in anticipation of cutting employee checks. The funds may still be there, but they are earmarked for another purpose.

De minimis amounts sitting in petty cash or a separate payroll account don't have to be separately stated. Following is an example when the restricted cash presentation comes into play:

A large manufacturing company receives an advance payment of $300,000 on June 1 from a customer for a piece of industrial machinery that takes five months to make. According to the customer contract, the manufacturer must transfer this deposit in a separate bank account and cannot use it until the customer receives the machinery.

The advance payment shows up as restricted cash on the manufacturer's books because it cannot be used until a future event (the shipment of equipment). After the customer accepts the machinery, the manufacturer will be able to use the cash in operations. Figure 9-1 shows proper balance sheet presentation.

Assets:

Current assets:

Figure 9-1: Cash and bank deposits:
Cash and
restricted Restricted deposit $ 300,000
cash.
Unrestricted   475,800 $ 775,800

Recording and Valuing Accounts Receivable

Accounts receivable (A/R) is the amount of money a customer owes the business for merchandise it purchases from a company or services a company renders. Just about all types of businesses can and probably do have accounts receivable.

Any accounts receivable involve three important facts: recognition, valuation, and disposition. Recognition involves booking the A/R for the exchange price of the goods/services between the customer and the vendor, minus any discounts.

Making sure accounts receivable reflect properly (valuation) on the balance sheet involves the vexing subject of estimating how much the company reckons it won't be able to collect from its customers. Disposition is what happens ultimately to get the receivable off the books.

The next couple sections discuss recognition and valuation. I save disposition for later in this chapter in the section "Disposing of Receivables."

The origin of accounts receivable

Your intermediate accounting textbook talks about four types of receivables: current (the scope of this chapter), noncurrent, trade, and nontrade. At this point in your glorious accounting course work, you realize that anytime you see the term *current,* it means that whatever is going on will come to fruition within 12 months of the date of the balance sheet. And, of course, noncurrent is the opposite — the receivable will exist beyond 12 months.

But what about trade and nontrade receivables? *Trade receivables* are what customers owe the business for the goods or services they receive from the company. Examples of *nontrade receivables* are advances made to officers or employees of the company, investment income receivable, and insurance claims that haven't been paid.

This accounting event involves two basics: Cash doesn't exchange hands at the time of the transaction, and the amount of the receivable starts at the invoice or contracted amount. However, as a seasoned accounting scholar, you also know that nothing in financial accounting is ever quite that simple! Stirring up the pot with accounts receivable are discounts and those darn deadbeat customers.

Discounting customer balances

It's not unusual for the list price of the goods available for sale or the total amount of the invoice to not be what the customer eventually ends up paying. The amount the customer pays may be subject to a trade or cash discount. I discuss each in turn:

- ✔ **Trade:** With a trade discount, the company sells its products for less than list price. The easiest way to explain this is to imagine a catalog of goods a manufacturer has for sale. In this catalog, a certain model number of washing machine lists for $350.

  A buyer at a chain of appliance stores puts in an order for 500 washing machines. The manufacturer offers a trade discount of 20 percent, reducing the price per washer by $70 ($350 × 20%). The manufacturer books the revenue and accounts receivable at $140,000 [$280 (350 − $70) × 500].

- ✔ **Sales discounts:** If the customer accelerates payment, it's allowed a certain amount of discount. You're probably familiar with this basic financial accounting issue.

  Just to recap, companies usually present their cash discounts in a manner such as 2/10, n/30, which means the customer takes a 2 percent discount if paying within ten days; otherwise, the entire amount in due in 30 days. Using the $140,000 accounts receivable amount from earlier, if the washing machine customer is given terms of 2/10, net 30, the discount for early payment is $2,800 ($140,000 × .02).

Walking through the gross and net cash discount methods

Companies can use either the gross or net methods to book receivables, although, for simplicity's sake, most use the gross method.

Using a sales figure of $100,000 and terms of 2/10, net 30, the following figure shows how both play out.

Gross Method		Net Method	
To record the $100,000 sale			
Accounts receivable	100,000	Accounts receivable	98,000
Sales		Sales	98,000
	100,000		
To record payment within the 10 days			
Cash	98,000	Cash	98,000
Sales discount	2,000	Accounts receivable	98,000
Accounts receivable			
	100,000		

If a company is using the net method and the customer doesn't end up taking the discount, the amount of discount passed up gets credited (added to) the Sales Discount Forfeited account.

Estimating uncollectible accounts

It's a sad fact of life that businesses extending credit to their customers will probably have at least one or more deadbeat customer who just won't pay the bills. Under generally accepted accounting principles (GAAP — see Chapter 1), you have to make a valuation adjustment for uncollectible accounts.

GAAP requires that businesses extending credit to customers use the *allowance method*, which means they estimate uncollectible accounts. Companies use a few different types of methods, usually based on their past experience with bad debt.

For example, imagine that a company that's been in business for five years has found that 2 percent of all credit sales will be uncollectible. Nothing in the current period causes the company to question the correctness of this percentage for the contemporaneous financial period, so it again uses this method and percentage. Here's an example of how this works:

Sales on account are $250,000, so the estimate for uncollectible accounts is $5,000 ($250,000 × .02). The journal entry (see Chapter 4) to record this is to debit bad debt expense, an income statement account (see Chapter 5), and credit allowance for uncollectible accounts, a balance sheet contra-asset account for $5,000 each.

Figure 9-2 shows the journal entries. Figure 9-3 shows balance sheet presentation. This figure builds upon Figure 9-1 and assumes gross accounts receivable is $75,500.

When you determine that a particular customer's account is uncollectible (maybe the customer died and left no estate or closed up shop), your next step is to remove the balance from both allowance for uncollectible accounts and the customer accounts receivable balance. After all, this is no longer a mystery — you know that the customer won't be coughing up the cash.

For example, Parmelee Supplies owes you $1,000. You send a past-due notice that the post office returns as undeliverable, with no forwarding address. After following up, you have no success at locating Parmelee. The journal entry is to debit allowance for uncollectible accounts for $1,000 and credit A/R – Parmelee Supplies for $1,000.

Figure 9-2:
Journalizing
the
allowance
method.

To record estimate of uncollectable:

Bad debt expense	5,000	
Allowance for doubtful accounts		5,000

Assets:

Current assets:

Cash and bank deposits:

Restricted deposit	$ 300,000	
Unrestricted	475,800	$ 775,800

Figure 9-3:
The
allowance
method.

Accounts receivable	75,500	
Less: Allowance for doubtful accounts	(5,000)	70,500
Total current assets		$ 846,300

Taking the easy way out with direct write-off

Smaller, closely held companies sometimes opt to use the direct write-off method instead of the allowance method for their uncollectibles. It's easier and, if the financial statements aren't being distributed publicly, an okay method to use.

With the direct method, you totally cut out figuring estimates by simply reporting A/R at gross. Then when an account is deemed to be uncollectible, you debit bad debt and credit the customer's A/R account. Using the Parmelee example, from earlier, the journal entry is to debit bad debt expense and credit A/R – Parmelee Supplies for $1,000 each.

Recognizing Notes Receivable

For the current asset section of the balance sheet, a note receivable is a *short-term* (coming due within 12 months of the balance sheet date) debt someone owes you. In many cases, this current asset arises from a trade receivable.

For example, a customer has cash flow problems that keep it from paying for purchases. So the customer asks the vendor for extended terms in the form of a formal written document, in place of the more informal agreement to pay for the goods or services per the terms of the invoice.

A note receivable has three major components:

 ✔ **Principal:** The amount the debtor owes the lender

 ✔ **Rate:** The amount of interest the debtor pays on the principal

 ✔ **Time:** The period in which the debtor has to pay back the note

As with A/R, any note receivable (N/R) involves three important considerations: recognition, valuation, and disposition. Recognition involves booking the N/R at face value or other than face value.

Making sure the note receivable reflects properly (valuation) on the balance sheet involves the vexing subject of estimating plus impairment. Disposition is what happens ultimately to get the receivable off the books; I discuss this in the "Disposing of Receivables" section of this chapter.

Face value! Impairment! If it's making your head spin a bit, don't despair. The next few sections of this chapter walk you through accounting for face value and impairment.

A note receivable reflects only in the current asset part of the balance sheet because the debt you anticipate will be paid back within 12 months of the balance sheet date. Any portion of the note receivable that extends past that 12-month period gets put in the long-term asset section of the balance sheet.

Issuing at face value

The easiest type of note to account for, the present value of the notes, is the same as its *face value,* which is the amount stated on the note. This fact is true because the *effective* (or market) interest rate and the *stated* (what's printed on the face of the note receivable) interest rates are the same.

Market is what the interest rate is for a note of similar risk.

Easy-peasy to account for. Now consider that one company loans another $5,000 at an effective and stated rate of 10 percent due in three years. The journal entry for the lender to record issuance of the note is to debit notes receivable and credit cash for $5,000.

Then each year, the lender records interest revenue at $500 ($5,000 × .10). When the debtor pays at the end of the three years, the lender records a debit to cash and a credit to notes receivable for $5,000.

Issuing at other than face value

Your intermediate accounting textbook talks about three situations in which a company may issue a note receivable for other than face value: zero interest bearing, interest bearing, and notes for other than cash. They can be wild and wooly situations! Let's work through each.

Zero-interest-bearing notes

These types of notes issue for the present value of the cash the lender gives to the debtor. Chapter 8 talks about the present value of 1 and an annuity of 1, so I don't belabor the point here. Just keep in mind that the future value of $1 is assumed to be worth more than the present value of $1.

With that caveat in mind, let's say Joseph Inc. lends Michael Company $20,000, with payment due in five years. Joseph figures that the present value of the $20,000 is $13,612. The difference between $20,000 and $13,612 of $6,388 is the discount on notes receivable. Figure 9-4 shows how to journalize this transaction.

How did Joseph get the present value of $13,612? You don't have to compute this for your intermediate accounting classwork on notes receivable. However, for inquiring minds, Joseph has an effective interest rate of 8 percent. Going to the present value of 1 table, the factor at the intersection of 8 percent and five periods is .6806. $20,000 × .6806 is $13,612.

Figure 9-4:
Journalizing
a zero-rate-
interest-
bearing
note.

Notes receivable	20,000
Discounts on notes receivable	6,388
Cash	13,612

The discount on notes receivable account is a contra-asset account. It follows the note receivable, amortized over the five-year life. It moves from the balance sheet to the income statement via interest revenue using the effective-interest method. Figure 9-5 gives you a bird's-eye view on how this works, assuming that the effective interest rate is 8%.

Schedule of Note Discount Amortization

Effective Interest Method at 8%

	Interest Revenue	Discount Amortized	Carrying Amount
Date of Issue			$13,612
End of year 1	$1,089**	$1,089	14,701
End of year 2	1,176	1,176	15,877
End of year 3	1,270	1,270	17,147
End of year 4	1,372	1,372	18,519
End of year 5	1,481	1,481	20,000
	$6,388	$6,388	

Figure 9-5:
Discount
amortization
schedule,
zero-rate-
interest-
bearing
note.

** $13,612 × .08 = $1,089. $13,612 + $1,089 = $14,701.

Cash doesn't factor into this schedule because Joseph receives no cash until the end of the fifth year.

Journalize the first year by debiting discounts on notes receivable for $1,089 and crediting interest revenue for the same amount. For the second year, you debit discounts on notes receivable and credit interest revenue for $1,176; in year three, you use $1,270, and so on for the remaining two years.

Interest-bearing notes

The concept from the prior section is somewhat the same for interest-bearing notes, except that the market and stated interest rates quite often are different. Time to walk through an example.

Going back to the $20,000 and effective interest rate of 8 percent example from the "Zero-interest-bearing notes" section earlier, the note receivable has a stated interest rate of 6 percent. At the stated rate, interest is $1,200 per year ($20,000 × .06). Michael pays interest to Joseph at the end of each year.

We know the present value of the principal is $13,612. However, you also need to figure out the present value of the interest portion of the note. Use the present value of an annuity of 1 table for the interest because it's a series of payments.

The factor at the intersection of 8 percent and five years in the present value of an annuity of 1 table is 3.9927. The present value of the interest is $4,791 ($1,200 × 3.9927). Add the two present value figures to get the carrying value of the note, which is $18,403 ($13,612 + $4,791). Subtract $18,403 from the face value of the note receivable to get the discount of $1,597 ($20,000 – $18,403).

Figure 9-6 shows how to journalize this transaction.

I'm sure you knew it was coming — Figure 9-7 shows the schedule for this transaction with a 6 percent note discounted at 8 percent.

Bringing it home with the journal entry to record payment at the end of each year, journalize the first year by debiting cash for $1,200, discounts on notes receivable for $272, and crediting interest revenue for $1,472. For the second year, you debit cash for $1,200 discounts on notes receivable for $294 and credit interest revenue for $1,494, and so on for the remaining three years.

	Cash	Interest Revenue	Discount Amortized	Carrying Amount
Date of Issue				$18,403
End of year 1	$1,200	$1,472**	$272	18,675
End of year 2	1,200	1,494	294	18,969
End of year 3	1,200	1,518	318	19,287
End of year 4	1,200	1,542	342	19,630
End of year 5	1,200	1,570	370	20,000
	$6,000	$7,597	$1,596	

Figure 9-6: Recording discounted note receivable.

** $18,403 × .08 = $1,472. $1,472 − $1,200 = 272. $18,403 + $272 = $18,675.

Note receivable	20,000	
Accumulated depreciation	1,000	
Discount on note receivable	($20,000 − $17,000)	3,000
Equipment		14,000
Gain on disposal of equipment		4,000

Figure 9-7: Discount amortization schedule — interest-bearing note.

Notes received for property, goods, or services

Sometimes companies exchange notes for value other than cash. In that case, use the stated interest rate unless one of the three circumstances exists:

- ✔ There's no stated interest rate.
- ✔ The stated interest rate is unreasonable. For example, it's not in line with what's fair for the marketplace.
- ✔ The face amount of the note differs materially from the cash price of the property, good, or service.

Deciding on an interest rate using imputation

As a more advanced financial accounting topic, if you can't determine the fair value of property, goods, or services, and the note receivable has no ready market, you have to approximate an applicable interest rate by imputing the interest rate. Do this by using the prevailing rates for similar note receivables or by using info from issuers with similar credit ratings. Any information on this topic that's wider in scope isn't a tested objective for your intermediate accounting class.

If one of these three rears its ugly head, use the fair market value of the property, good, or service subject to the note transaction to approximate the present value of the note receivable.

Going back to the Joseph (lender) and Michael (debtor) transaction, imagine that Joseph sells equipment to Michael for $20,000 on a note with no stated interest rate. The equipment has a fair market value of $17,000 and a basis of $13,000 (cost of $14,000 and accumulated depreciation of $1,000) on Joseph's books. Figure 9-8 shows how to journalize this transaction.

Note receivable	20,000	
Accumulated depreciation	1,000	
Discount on note receivable	($20,000 – $17,000)	3,000
Equipment		14,000
Gain on disposal of equipment		4,000

Figure 9-8: Recording note received for equipment.

Valuing notes on the balance sheet

As with accounts receivable, which shows on the balance sheet net (see Figure 9-3), short-term notes receivable also report at their net realizable value. The valuation account for notes receivable is — ta-da! — allowance for doubtful accounts (just as with A/R). Companies use the same methods I discuss in the "Estimating uncollectible accounts" section of this chapter for notes and accounts receivable.

Building on the facts in Figures 9-3 and 9-8, Figure 9-9 shows balance sheet presentation and assumes uncollectibles of $200.

Notes receivable on crutches!

One thorny issue with notes receivable is *impairment,* which means the debtor probably won't pony up all the cash owed on the note. When this happens, the lender has to measure and report the impairment as a loss on the income statement.

For your intermediate accounting class, just keep in mind that first the creditor figures its investment in the note (principal plus interest receivable). Deducting the *expected future cash flows,* what the company reckons the debtor will pay (discounted at the loan's effective interest rate) from the investment in the note equals the lender's impairment loss.

Cash and bank deposits		$ 775,800
Accounts receivable	75,500	
Less: Allowance for doubtful accounts	(5,000)	70,500
Note receivable	20,000	
Less: Discounts on note receivable	(3,000)	
Less: Allowance for doubtful accounts	(200)	16,800
Total current assets		$ 863,100

Figure 9-9: Showing the allowance method for notes receivable.

Disposing of Receivables

Instead of waiting for the customer or debtor to pay, a company may opt to "sell" a receivable to another company at a discount. Cash flow is a major factor in these sorts of instances. If a company finds that it lacks funds to make payroll or cut a check to pay some other type of expense, the company may prefer to accept a lesser amount for a receivable transaction than try to get a working capital (short-term) loan.

A company can structure disposing of receivables in a variety of ways. The most prevalent are pledging, assignment, and factoring.

You may remember these terms from previous accounting classes but don't quite remember the difference in the three. Never fear! Here's a thumbnail sketch of all three:

- ✔ **Pledging:** Nope, you're not applying for fraternity membership. Pledging takes place when the company uses a receivable as security for a loan for which the company is the debtor. When this situation occurs, the company discloses it in the balance sheet parenthetically — as in, "Accounts receivable ($500,000 of which has been pledged as collateral for bank loans)" — or as a note disclosure; see Chapter 21 for more info on note disclosures.

- ✔ **Assignment:** A formal transfer of the debt takes place from one company to another. Often this process is invisible to the debtor. The debtor merrily continues to make payments to the original company, none the wiser. Assigned accounts stay on the balance sheet of the original issuer, with disclosure similar to pledging.

- ✔ **Factoring:** Factoring takes place when there's an outright sale of the receivable to a new owner. Notification goes to the debtor that payments are henceforth to be made to the new owner of the debt.

Sales transactions can be either recourse, which means the seller guarantees payment to the purchaser in case the debtor doesn't pay, or nonrecourse, which means the seller has no further obligation for collectability.

Current assets are cash or any asset that the company anticipates converting to cash within a 12-month period from the date of the balance sheet. List current assets in order of liquidity on the balance sheet. Because cash is the most liquid (duh, it's cash!), it shows up on the balance sheet first. Other common current assets are marketable securities, accounts receivable, inventory, prepaid assets, and deferred tax assets.

Chapter 10

Inventory Cost Flow Assumptions

. . . .

In This Chapter

▶ Taking a big-picture look at inventory management

▶ Understanding the difference between merchandising and manufacturing inventory

▶ Looking at inventory valuation methods

▶ Dealing with special inventory costs

▶ Calculating the value of ending inventory

▶ Handling stale inventory

. . . .

*F*or manufacturing and merchandising businesses, inventory is probably the most significant current asset. Accounting for inventory isn't as simple as just placing orders for merchandise, recording the value at cost, and reducing inventory balances by sales. Accountants also have to consider different *cost flow assumptions* and *ending inventory valuation issues.*

Adding to the confusion is the fact that there are different types of inventory. Some people think inventory is only the merchandise available for sale in a store. I discuss that kind of inventory (called *retail* or *merchandise inventory*) in this chapter, but I also introduce you to other kinds of *product inventory* manufacturers use. These categories include direct materials, work in process, and finished goods.

You also find out in this chapter about two methods your client may use to keep track of merchandise inventory (*perpetual* and *periodic*), as well as the four methods businesses may use to value ending inventory.

Why are some goods excluded from inventory even though they're on company premises, and how do you handle inventory that's no longer sellable? How do you figure the difference between inventory accounted for at its original cost and inventory at its current market price? Stick with me — I reveal all.

Looking into Inventory Management

Inventory management is a business process that strives for the efficient and effective flow of materials into and out of existing inventory. For many businesses, inventory is the largest current asset — in terms of both dollars and the amount of business square footage it occupies. Costs of carrying inventory are high, so a company doesn't want to have too much inventory on hand. But the company also doesn't want to risk running out of needed inventory and perhaps jeopardizing a sale to a potential customer.

Controlling inventory

Successful inventory management requires a strategy to control operational costs stemming from the total value of the inventory product, as well as the cash flow or debt burden due to the cumulative value of the inventory. *Inventory operational costs* include storage space, costs to safeguard the inventory, and payroll for warehouse employees.

For retail shops, a big inventory concern is that the item may fall out of fashion before the shop is able to rotate it to the selling space. In addition, the business owner may have to pay the same amount of rent per square foot for the back area that holds excess inventory as it does for the front selling area, the profit center.

A business also has to worry about the amount of money it spends or debt it incurs by purchasing the inventory. Although inventory is a current asset, it may not be easily converted to cash. As an example, a company still needs ready cash to handle payroll and long-term debt. If it doesn't have that cash, the company may have to look to outside for short-term financing, which is expensive and, if recurring, indicates either that the company is poorly managed or that the product isn't selling as expected.

Controlling inventory involves three major keys to success: wait time, amount on hand, and record keeping. *Wait time* is the amount of time a customer is willing to wait between placing an order and satisfying that order. Ideally, the timeline between the two allows the company to utilize a *just-in-time* inventory method. In other words, the company can reorder depleted inventory items after the customer places the order, thus keeping the items in inventory for a brief period.

The second major key is maintaining an effective stock level, or amount on hand. Closely associated with just-in-time inventory management, effective stock level management minimizes the risk that production will be interrupted due to a lack of essential parts in the supply inventory. Based on past experience, a company keeps adequate inventory for items that are used often or that are difficult to obtain quickly.

Finally, without good record keeping, a company can't know when it's running out of a certain item. A company has to keep up-to-date records showing physical stock balances. Successful methods include tracking items into inventory and recording items that were sold or incorporated into a product.

Recognizing different inventoried goods

Three types of businesses operate: service, manufacturing, and merchandising. Breathe a sigh of relief, because you have to worry about only two (manufacturing and merchandising) in this chapter. Service businesses don't provide a tangible good and normally don't have any type of appreciable inventory.

Service companies provide more of a knowledge-based work service — think dentists, family physicians, or accountants. However, if a service company keeps a large amount of office supplies or other products on hand, they may take it to the balance sheet as inventory instead of immediately expensing the purchase.

Manufacturing companies make products that *merchandising companies* sell. For example, Hewlett-Packard is a manufacturer of many different products, including printers; any retail outlet that sells those items is the merchandising company.

Merchandisers can be retail and wholesale. Wholesalers act as the middleman between the manufacturing company and the retailer. The retailer sells to the end-user customer. For more about this, see the section toward the end of this chapter titled "Retailing inventory."

In a nutshell, that's the difference among service, manufacturing, and merchandising type businesses — pretty straightforward. The next section looks at special types of inventoried goods, including goods in transit, consigned goods, and special sales agreements.

Who owns goods in transit?

Inventory in transit is a big issue for both revenue and inventory valuation. Who owns goods that are neither here nor there? It's a hot button as well if the company is undergoing a *financial statement audit,* when certified public accountants check to see if reports prepared by managers of companies fairly present the company's financial position.

Two key terms spell out who owns goods in transit: FOB shipping point and FOB destination. *FOB* stands for either free on board or freight on board. *FOB shipping point* means that the sale to the customer occurs at the shipping point, or when the goods leave the seller's loading dock. *FOB destination* indicates that the sale occurs only when the goods arrive at their destination, the buyer's receiving dock.

Goods shipped to a destination point are included in the seller's inventory until the buyer receives and accepts the goods. So the value of the inventory remains as a current asset; it doesn't migrate to the income statement as a cost of goods sold and revenue.

Consigned goods

Consigned goods are goods that a company offers for sale but that it doesn't officially own. The company offering the goods for sale (the *consignee*) is acting as a middleman between the owner of the goods (the *consignor*) and the customer. The consignee is charged with safeguarding the consigned goods within its control, but legal title of the goods remains with the consignor.

In accounting for this type of extravaganza, make sure you include in your inventory any inventory for which your company is a consignor. Under no circumstances should the consignee include consigned goods as part of its inventory!

Special sales agreements

Inventory can be subject to sales transactions a bit outside the norm of a customer walking up to a cash register in a department store and exchanging cash for store merchandise. Three such sales transactions are sales with buyback agreements, sales with a high rate of return, and sales on installment.

I discuss these special sales agreements thoroughly in Chapter 20. If you want the complete scoop, hustle on over to that chapter. For now, I give you merely a thumbnail sketch of each:

- **Sales with buyback:** The seller agrees to "buy back" the merchandise from the customer sometime in the future.

- **Sales with a high rate of return:** Customers are afforded a liberal return policy for a full or partial refund.

- **Sales on installment:** Purchases are made but not fully paid for at point of sale or delivery. Instead, they are paid for over time, in installments.

Merchandising versus manufacturing inventories

Accounting for merchandising inventories is pretty easy. The merchandiser buys goods from the manufacturing company and records the goods in inventory at cost. When the items are sold, the cost moves over to the income statement as cost of goods sold (see Chapter 5).

A manufacturing company has more hubbub going on with its inventory because manufacturers have three different types of inventory:

Raw materials inventory: Let's say the company makes ladies' blouses. This inventory includes the raw materials to make a blouse, such as fabric, buttons, and thread. Remember, the material has to directly relate to the product, and

this type of inventory includes only raw materials not yet put into the production process.

Work in process inventory: This inventory category includes all raw materials in various stages of completion. Besides the cost of the raw materials, it also includes the cost of direct labor and overhead. Figure the value of this inventory based on how far each item has been processed.

Finished goods: This type of inventory includes items that are completely finished and ready for sale to customers but that have not yet been purchased. It includes all the material, labor, and overhead cost associated with each item.

You may be wondering how to handle drop-shipping, or when a business sells a product shipped directly from the manufacturer. In most cases, the business taking the customer's order doesn't own the merchandise and thus can't record it as inventory.

Walking through inventory costs

Two types of business costs are directly related to inventory: product and period. As you can probably guess from their names, one directly ties to inventory and can span financial periods; the other is expensed when it occurs. Want to take a guess?

Okay, your mini pop quiz is over! Read on for the definition of product versus period business costs:

- **Product costs:** Any costs that relate to manufacturing an item for sale are product costs. Product costs include *direct material,* reflecting all the raw materials you use to make a product, and *direct labor,* which includes only what you pay your workers who are directly involved in making the items and overhead. *Overhead* includes all manufacturing costs except those you include as direct material or labor — one example is factory utilities.

- **Period costs:** These costs, although necessary for a business to keep the doors open, don't directly tie back to any specific item of inventory. Examples are general and administrative expenses such as office salaries and postage expense.

Let's get physical: Taking the physical inventory

The remainder of this chapter discusses various financial accounting methods for managing and booking the value of the inventory asset account. However, there's one immutable fact about inventory: Regardless of what allowable method a company uses to represent inventory and the related cost of goods sold on the financial statements, a physical inventory must be taken by a real, live human being to confirm inventory levels. That's right, no matter how fancy the computer system, company staff or professional inventory takers hired by the company have to count the actual items of inventory wall to wall.

The purpose of the physical inventory is to make sure that inventory reflected on the balance sheet actually exists and that the balance sheet includes all inventory the company owns. Some occurrences just have to be double-checked by a human hand: Among them are missing inventory due to theft by employees, customers, or outsiders, and damaged inventory that's no longer sellable.

Discovering Inventory Carrying Valuation Methods

This section of the chapter discusses how to value ending inventory. You may be thinking it's a no-brainer — you just value inventory at whatever the original cost happened to be for whatever is left in inventory at the end of the financial period, right? Well, to a certain extent, yes. You find out more about valuing inventory at cost in the "Using Lower of Cost or Market" section of this chapter.

This section gives you the scoop on how to use a systematic cost flow assumption to determine which items that the company previously purchased remain in inventory at the end of the financial period (and come up with a dollar amount for both cost of goods sold and ending inventory).

I go over three different cost flow assumptions GAAP allows: specific identification; weighted average; and first in, first out (FIFO). I also review last in, first out (LIFO), which is not codified in GAAP but is a tax concept that Internal Revenue Code (IRC) 472 addresses.

The application of GAAP for LIFO is based on income statement rules – not financial accounting pronouncements. Although GAAP cites LIFO as an acceptable inventory method, it does not give rules for implementing it. So IRC defines financial accounting treatment.

Ready to get started? Get out your handy pocket calculator so you can follow along with the calculations!

Cost flow assumption doesn't mean the company has to select the method that most closely shows the physical movement (purchase and sale) of the inventoried goods.

Specific identification

Use the *specific identification* method when the inventory items are easily differentiated. Good examples of companies that can use this method are car dealerships and ritzy jewelry stores with one-of-a-kind creations. It's relatively easy to trace back the exact cost of each individual item in inventory because each item is special and unique or is equipped with a serial number that can be traced back to its purchase price.

For example, a used car dealership can quickly identify how much it cost to originally purchase vehicles on the lot by matching the description of the car or the vehicle identification number (VIN) to the purchase invoice.

So if the dealership pays the auto auction $1,500 for a used Buick, inventory goes up by $1,500. When a customer buys the Buick, the dealership's accounting department increases cost of goods sold for $1,500 and decreases inventory for the same amount; the dealership then reduces ending inventory by that same $1,500.

You figure ending inventory for the balance sheet (see Chapter 6) by adding the total of all payments made to the particular vendors from whom the company purchased the inventoried goods.

Weighted average

When a company uses the *weighted average* method, inventory and the cost of goods sold are based on the average cost of all units purchased during the period. This method is generally used when inventory is substantially the same, such as with grains, fuel, and metal.

So if the company sells steel rods, the total cost of all the rods available for sale is divided by the total number of steel rods in inventory. Then the company multiplies that figure by the number of steel rods remaining in inventory at the end of the accounting period to get the ending inventory dollar amount.

Weighted average ending inventory and cost of goods sold

Let's look at figuring out how to use the weighted average method. Don't worry – it's not going to involve you hauling at that bathroom scale!

Carter Hauling has 9,725 steel rods with a total cost of $35,325. Using weighted average, the cost per rod is $3.63 ($35,325 ÷ 9,725). Carter sells 6,000 rods in June. Those 6,000 rods sold times an average cost of $3.63 equals a cost of goods sold of $21,780. Value the 3,725 rods remaining in ending inventory (9,725 – 6,000) at $13,545 ($35,325 – $21,780).

First in, first out (FIFO)

Using the FIFO method, the company assumes that the oldest items in its inventory are the ones first sold. So the items remaining in ending inventory are always assumed to be the most recent purchase additions to inventory, regardless of whether they actually are.

Consider buying milk in a grocery store. The cartons with the most current expiration date are pushed ahead of the cartons that have more time before they go bad. The oldest cartons of milk may not always actually be the first ones sold (because some people dig around looking for later expiration dates), but the business is basing its numbers on the oldest cartons being sold first.

Consider an example. Figure 10-1 shows bags of potato chips in beginning inventory and purchases for Norfolk Mini-Mart from July 1 to the end of the calendar year (no purchases were made in December).

Figure 10-1 shows that 600 bags of chips were sold, leaving 775 bags in inventory. Your next step is to figure out the cost of goods sold and value ending inventory using the FIFO cost flow assumption.

Using FIFO, you start at the top of the list because the bags of chips in beginning inventory are first in. Then you follow with the chips purchased on July 15, the chips purchased on August 5, and 50 of the 450 chips purchased on September 6. As you can see from Figure 10-2, the cost of goods sold (COGS) is $695 and ending inventory is $838 ($1,533 – $695).

Date of Purchase	Number	Cost per Unit	Total Cost
July 1 (beginning inventory)	200	$ 1.00	$ 200
July 15	250	1.20	300
August 5	100	1.50	150
September 6	450	0.90	405
October 3	325	1.30	423
November 21	50	1.10	55
Total available for sale	1,375		$ 1,533
Chips sold	600		
Chips remaining in December 31 inventory	775		

Figure 10-1: Norfolk Mini-Mart potato chip purchases and sales.

FIFO

Date of Purchase	Number	Cost per Unit	Total Cost
July 1 (beginning inventory)	200	$ 1.00	$ 200
July 15	250	1.20	300
August 5	100	1.50	150
September 6	50	0.90	45
Total	600		$ 695

Figure 10-2: COGS and ending inventory under the FIFO cost flow assumption.

Last in, first out

With this method, the company assumes that its newest items (the ones most recently purchased) are the first ones sold. Going back to Carter Hauling in the "Weighted average" section of this chapter, imagine a big stack of steel rods in a building supply store. If a customer wants to buy a single steel rod, for convenience, he takes one off the top. As customers purchase the steel rods, new rod purchases are added on top of the old ones instead of redistributing the old rods so they move to the top of the pile. Therefore, the newest rods are consistently sold to customers first.

Many manufacturing companies use LIFO because it more closely matches revenue to expenses than FIFO does. Why? The cost of the item being sold has been incurred closer to the sale in terms of time, so there's a better match of dollar-to-dollar value.

Now you can use the same facts and circumstances from Figure 10-1 to calculate COGS and value ending inventory using the LIFO cost flow assumption. Using LIFO, you start at the bottom of the list because the company assumes that the last bags of chips it purchased are the first ones sold. The relevant purchases are the chips purchased on November 21, the chips on October 3, and 225 of the chips purchased on September 6. As you can see from Figure 10-3, cost of goods sold is $680 and ending inventory is $853 ($1,533 – $680).

Depending on whether Norfolk Mini-Mart uses FIFO or LIFO, ending inventory for the same facts and circumstances differs by $15 ($695 – $680). Although this difference isn't dramatic, consider what a difference the accounting method makes if the company has sales in the thousands or millions of units!

LIFO

Date of Purchase		Number	Cost per Unit	Total Cost
November 21		50	$ 1.10	$ 55
October 3		325	1.30	423
September 6		225	0.90	203
	Total	600		$ 680

Figure 10-3: COGS and ending inventory under the LIFO cost flow assumption.

The accounting inventory methods shown in this example assume that the inventory is valued at cost rather than market, which is the price the company can charge when it sells its merchandise. See the later section in this chapter titled "Using Lower of Cost or Market" for more information.

LIFO is a big no-no for International Financial Reporting Standards (IFRS).

Handling Special LIFO Issues

Figuring COGS and valuing ending inventory using all the cost flow assumptions is pretty easy when you get the hang of it. Plus, larger companies have software tailored to the task, which makes the undertaking of a physical inventory the heavy lifting chore for the accounting department.

I discuss taking a physical inventory later in this chapter in the "Retailing inventory" section.

However, a monkey wrench is thrown into the whole thing because many companies use LIFO for tax and financial statement purposes and another method (FIFO, specific identification, weighted average) for internal reporting.

Managerial accounting classes discuss internal reporting, but one example is measuring the performance of different company segments to see which one is operating the most efficiently.

The pros and cons of LIFO

The LIFO method offers two major advantages related to satisfying the matching principle and paying taxes.

- ✔ **Matching revenue to expenses:** Remember that LIFO more closely matches revenue and expenses. The business purchases the inventory closer to the date of sale than under FIFO, which more closely matches revenue to expenses. This fact is a definite plus because financial accounting loves the matching principle (see Chapter 2).

- ✔ **Reducing taxable income:** In times of rising prices and stable inventory levels, LIFO also has a major tax effect. Higher purchase prices give the company a higher COGS with LIFO versus FIFO. A higher COGS reduces net and taxable income (see Chapter 17). Of course, if the company is operating in a time of deflation rather than inflation, the effect is the opposite.

Companies that use the LIFO method have two major disadvantages as well: reduced net income and understated current assets:

- ✓ **Reducing net income:** The flipside of the second advantage is that, in times of rising prices, LIFO shows less net income than FIFO. Although the company pays less in taxes, it also appears to be making less money, which investors and creditors don't want to see.

- ✓ **Understating current assets:** Compared to other inventory methods, LIFO shows a lesser dollar amount sitting in the inventory account because inventory is valued using the oldest costs. This fact wreaks havoc with any ratio analysis that uses current assets. See Chapter 22 for more info about financial statement ratio analysis.

LIFO reserves

LIFO reserves are the difference between the inventory carrying value that a company reports if using LIFO and the inventory carrying value with another method that the company uses for managerial or financial accounting purposes, such as FIFO. For example, Carter Hauling's ending inventory on December 31, 2013, is $275,000 using FIFO and $225,000 using LIFO. The LIFO reserve is $50,000 ($275,000 – $225,000).

Now let's say that Carter's LIFO reserve on December 31, 2012, was $15,000. The journal entry to adjust LIFO reserve at year-end 2013 debits cost of goods sold and credits LIFO reserve for $35,000 ($50,000 – $15,000). This change in LIFO reserve from one period to the next is called the *LIFO effect.*

The chart of accounts name for the contra-inventory account that holds the difference between LIFO and another method can simply be LIFO reserve, although your textbook probably calls the account "allowance to reduce inventory to LIFO."

When a company uses the LIFO method, it may have to include a LIFO reserve amount in its notes to the financial statement. This reserve amount gives the dollar difference between ending inventory when using FIFO and LIFO. I discuss notes to the financial statements in Chapter 21.

LIFO Liquidation

Everything must go! Well, that's sort of what happens when LIFO liquidation takes place. Breaking it down to the lowest common denominator, *LIFO liquidation* occurs when a company sells more inventory than it purchases in the current period. In this case, older inventory costs that are probably lower than current replacement costs are matched with current sales. This fact causes the cost of goods sold to record as artificially low and inflates net income.

The authors of your intermediate accounting textbook probably discuss layers in conjunction with LIFO liquidation. When inventory levels rise (that is, inventory doesn't move as quickly as anticipated) these "layers" the author refers to are just the additional valuation of inventory that's eventually moved to cost of goods sold when inventory quantities drop.

Using Lower of Cost or Market

I mention using the lower of cost or market in previous sections of this chapter, and you may have been wondering when the heck you were going to get more info on the topic. Time to dive in now!

Using the *lower of cost or market* means comparing the market value of each item in ending inventory with its cost and then using the lower of the two as its inventory value.

The difference between cost and market value

Cost is how much the company pays for the item if it buys the item or, if the company is the manufacturer, how much it costs to make the item. The *market value* of an item is usually its replacement cost. However, this assumption has one caveat: Market can't go above the item's net realizable value (ceiling) or below the item's floor.

Floor? Ceiling? What the heck does this mean and how does it affect the carrying value of inventory? You ask and I deliver:

- ✔ **Net realizable value (NRV):** The NRV is the expected selling price of an item minus any selling costs or costs to complete the item (for example, the cost to reclassify in process inventory to finished goods inventory).

- ✔ **Floor:** The floor is the NRV minus a normal profit on the item.

Still a little fuzzy on this concept? Here's an example of how it works:

ABC, Inc., has unfinished goods sitting in work-in-process inventory with a sales value of $25,000 and an estimated cost to complete of $3,200. ABC has a normal profit on these items of 35 percent. Figure 10-4 shows how to figure NRV and the floor.

Inventory	$ 25,000
Less: Estimated cost to complete	3,200
Net realizable value	21,800
Less: Allowance for normal profit	8,750 ($ 25,000 × .35)
NRV less a normal profit	$ 13,050

So ABC's market can't be higher than $21,800 or lower than $13,050.

Figure 10-4:
Calculating NRV and floor.

Different application methods

You can apply lower of cost or market (LCM) to the entire inventory, or you can cherry-pick between inventory items. The general rule is to apply LCM on an item-by-item basis because this method is the most conservative; see Chapter 2 for more information about the financial statement restraint of conservatism.

Consider an example of applying LCM. Figure 10-5 shows how to calculate LCM for four different inventory items, and Figure 10-6 shows alternative applications of LCM. Checking out Figure 10-6, you can see that, if you apply LCM by item, your ending inventory is $2,630; if you apply LCM for the inventory as a whole, your ending inventory is $2,790.

Item	Historic Cost	Replacement Cost	Ceiling	Floor	Market
A	800	890	975	960	960
B	1500	1200	1300	900	1200
C	210	185	150	120	150
D	900	360	720	480	480

Figure 10-5:
Calculating LCM.

Figuring Lower-of-Cost-or-Market

Item	Cost	Market	By Item	By Total Inventory
A	800	960	800	
B	1500	1200	1200	
C	210	150	150	
D	900	480	480	
Total	3410	2790	2630	2790

Figure 10-6:
Applying
LCM per
item and
by total
inventory.

Estimating Inventory

Earlier in this chapter, in the sidebar "Let's get physical: Taking the physical inventory," I explain that, regardless of the cost flow assumption or valuation method a company uses to record inventory on the balance sheet, the company must take a physical inventory. The regularity of this physical inventory varies based on company policy and the type of business.

However, sometimes it's just not feasible to take a physical inventory. After all, closing down a mom-and-pop grocery store every time a set of financial statements is prepared to take a count of inventory will have a strong negative impact on sales. To work around this problem, companies use methods to come up with as good a guess as possible to approximate actual inventory.

Using the gross profit method

One estimation method that's pretty easy to use is the gross profit method. Now, you know what *gross profit* is, right? It's the difference between net sales and cost of goods sold (COGS). Putting this in very basic terms with round numbers, if net sales are $100,000 and COGS is $75,000, gross profit is $25,000 and, stated as a percentage of selling price, the gross profit percentage 25 percent ($25,000 ÷ $100,000).

Now you can use that same 25 percent gross profit percentage to estimate ending inventory using another set of facts and circumstances. In addition to the 25 percent gross profit percentage, you need to know that there are goods available for sale at cost, totaling $155,000, and that sales at selling price equal $125,000. Whip these figures around, and Figure 10-7 gives you approximate inventory at cost.

Goods available for sale at cost		$ 155,000
Sales at sales price	$ 125,000	
Less gross profit at 25%	31,250	
Sales at cost		93,750
Approximate inventory at cost		$ 61,250

Figure 10-7: Applying the gross profit method.

Evaluating the gross profit method

The gross profit method is certainly more accurate than throwing a dart at a number board, but it's only an estimate to be used until the physical inventory can be taken. Often inventory taking is a once-a-year extravaganza, so the gross profit percentage in use is based on past performance. Using stale sales and COGS figures may not provide truly reliable figures.

However, GAAP allows the gross profit method for *interim statements,* which are financial statements for less than one year, such as monthly or quarterly statements, as long as the company discloses the use of this method. See Chapter 21 for more info about disclosure notes to the financial statements.

Retailing inventory

Accounting for merchandise inventory has its frustrating moments, but it's easier than accounting for manufacturing inventory. A merchandising company such as a retail store has only one class of inventory to keep track of: goods the business purchases from various manufacturers for resale.

Here's the basic flow of inventory for a retailer:

A cookware sales associate at a major department store notices and informs the manager of the department that the department is running low on a certain style of frying pan. The manager follows the department store's purchasing process, with the end result that the department receives a shipment of frying pans from its vendor.

This transaction is a purchase (cost), but it's not an expense until the department store sells the frying pans. So the business records the entire shipment of frying pans on the balance sheet as an addition to both inventory and accounts payable (see Chapter 14), since the department store has payment terms with this vendor and money hasn't yet changed hands for this transaction.

Say that, in August, the store sells a fancy-pants frying pan to a customer for $95 that cost the company $47 to purchase from the vendor. Sales revenue increases by $95, cost of goods sold increases by $47, and inventory decreases by $47. Matching revenue to the expense portion of its purchase, the effect increases net income by $48 ($95 – $47).

Seems like pretty basic stuff. The retailer buys inventory and sells it, reducing inventory and increasing COGS. Alas, like many intermediate accounting topics, it's not quite that simple. In the next section of this chapter, you read about how to determine ending inventory by using the retail inventory method.

Getting up to speed with the retail inventory method

I have a lot of clients who are retail businesses. Some are art galleries and other types of specialty shops that use the specific identification method to value their ending inventory. However, retailers selling many different types of merchandise find the specific identification method impossible to use.

Stepping up to handle the task, the *retail inventory method* uses a cost ratio to convert the ending inventory from retail to cost. This explanation may sound a bit like gobbledygook. To un-gook this for you, consider an example for ABC, Inc.

To put the retailing inventory method into action, ABC, Inc., needs to have a handle on the following three items:

- ✔ Total cost and retail value of merchandise purchased for resale. For this example, total cost is $50,000 and retail value is $88,000.

- ✔ Total cost and retail value of goods available for sale. Going back to Accounting 101, beginning inventory plus purchases equals goods available for sale. For this example, beginning inventory at cost is $25,000 and at retail is $32,000.

- ✔ Total sales for the period. For this example, total sales are $97,000.

Then goods available for sale at cost is divided by goods available for sale at retail. Multiply sales by the resulting percentage to come up with ending inventory at cost. Figure 10-8 shows how to use these facts to figure ending inventory at cost under the retail inventory method.

	Cost	Retail
Beginning inventory	$ 25,000	$ 32,000
Purchases	50,000	88,000
Goods available for sale	$ 75,000	120,000
Deduct sales from retail		97,000
Ending inventory at retail		$ 23,000

Figure 10-8:
Calculating
ending retail
inventory at
cost.

$75,000 / $120,000 = 62.5%.

Ending inventory at cost is $14,375 ($23,000 × .625)

Watching for falling — and rising — prices!

You may get quite a thrill when you're out shopping and you see something fantastic on the discount rack. When you see it, you probably think, "Ching-ching, I just scored!" However, have you ever thought about what markups or markdowns mean to the retailer? Well, wonder no longer — here's how to handle markups and markdowns from an accounting point of view.

First, some important definitions:

- **Original retail price:** The price at which a company offers items for sale.

- **Markup:** The difference between the cost of the item and the original retail price (what the item is selling for). For example, Penway Manufacturing may pay $1.00 for an item and sell it for $2.00. (Retailers refer to a 100 percent increase between cost and sales price as *keystoning*.)

- **Additional markup:** Increasing the price of an item above its original retail price. Due to demand, Penway increases the retail price from $2.00 to $2.25.

- **Markup cancellation:** Moving the price back down from the additional markup but not decreasing the price below the original selling price. The Penway item price can't reduce to less than $2.00; if the price goes below $2.00, it's a markdown.

- **Markdown:** Reducing the price of an item below its original selling price. If Penway reduces the price of the item to $1.25, the markdown is 75 cents.

✔ **Markdown cancellation:** Increasing the item price after a markdown, not increasing the price above the original selling price. A good example of this is a sale for a specific period of time. The price of the item goes back to $2.00. If it goes above $2.00, it's an additional markup.

✔ **Purchase returns:** A contra-purchases account that reflects goods returned by customers after purchase.

Now that you have a handle on the lexicon of retail markups and markdowns, lay all those ugly snakes in a straight line and calculate ending inventory for Penway Manufacturing using the retail and cost account balances I provide in Figure 10-9. Test yourself by not looking at Figure 10-10 until you are done!

Ready? After considering the information in Figure 10-9, what figure do you get for inventory at cost under conventional retail? Go to Figure 10-10 and check your answer!

	Cost	Retail
Beginning inventory	$ 35,000	$ 50,000
Purchases	57,500	94,100
Less: Purchase returns	(2,200)	(3,900)
Add: Markups		12,000
Less: Markups cancellation		$ 1,700
Freight in	2,500	
Available	92,800	153,900
Less: Markdowns		9,800
Add: Markdowns cancellation		3,000
Less: Sales		125,000
Add: Sales returns		3,000
Inventory at retail		294,700
Cost/retail ratio		60.3%
Inventory at cost under conventional retail		$ 177,701

Figure 10-9:
Inventory account balances

Sales	$ 125,000	Purchases – cost	$ 57,500
Sales returns	3,000	Purchases – sales price	94,100
Markups	12,000	Purchase returns – cost	2,200
Markup cancellations	1,700	Purchase returns – sales price	3,900
Markdowns	9,800	Beginning inventory – cost	35,000
Markdown cancellations	3,000	Beginning inventory – sales price	50,000
Freight-in	2,500		

Figure 10-10: Ending inventory at cost under conventional retail.

Using perpetual and periodic inventory methods

Now I want to talk about how retail shops normally track inventory. Two major types of inventory systems exist: *perpetual* and *periodic*.

Perpetual system

Larger retailers have electronic cash registers (ECRs). If you've ever used the self-checkout, you've used one. The checkout features a glass window with a red beam of light. You run the bar code of a product over the red beam, and the price of the item automatically records as a sale for which you are charged and the business records revenue.

If the business also uses a *point-of-sale system,* which means transactions at the register automatically update all accounting records, the inventory count is updated constantly, or *perpetually,* as the ECR records the item sold. This means that the cost of the item sold is taken out of the asset inventory account and moved to cost of goods sold.

With point-of-sale inventory, transactions taking place at the cash register update all purchase, inventory, COGS, and sales information throughout the system in real time as the transactions occur. Let's say you go into Target and buy a birthday card for a friend.

As you check out, the point-of-sale software is updating the greeting card department records to show that one less birthday card is available for sale. The software is also updating COGS, showing the cost for the card, and it's updating revenue to reflect the retail price (what you just paid) for the birthday card.

Periodic system

Instead of this incessant updating of accounting records taking place when using the perpetual system, when using the periodic system, the physical inventory is taken periodically. The resulting figure is used to adjust the balance sheet inventory asset account.

Retail shops that use periodic inventory usually take inventory at their particular year-end. However, inventory can be taken more often, such as quarterly or at the end of every heavy sales season (such as Valentine's Day, Mother's Day, and the December holidays).

Here's how the periodic system works:

The business takes *ending inventory* and comes up with a dollar amount for all unsold inventory as of the last day of the accounting period. Next, the company's accounting department subtracts ending inventory totals from the beginning inventory after adding in all inventory purchases made during the period.

The resulting number is *cost of goods sold* (COGS). The balance sheet inventory account is reduced and the income statement expense account COGS is increased by that number to match revenue with expenses.

Using the periodic system, cost of goods sold can be determined with accuracy approaching 100 percent only after the physical inventory is taken.

Disposing of obsolete inventory

Obsolete items include components for products the company no longer makes or items it can no longer sell. For example, a computer manufacturer may no longer need certain processors for its new line of computers. Damaged items are those that are no longer in saleable condition. Maybe they were dropped and no longer work or they were run over by mistake with a forklift. (Well, we hope it was by mistake.)

Whatever the reason, any obsolete or damaged inventory should be noted and usually reduced in valuation to its *net realizable value*. This term refers to the item's expected selling price minus the cost to sell it.

Obviously, smashed items probably have a net realizable value of $0 and need to be scrapped (removed from the ending inventory).

The company may be able to sell obsolete items at a deep discount — for instance, for their parts. The inventory value of those items then is reduced to reflect the anticipated discounted selling price plus shipping to the liquidator, if applicable.

Chapter 11

Buying and Selling Property, Plant, and Equipment (PP&E)

In This Chapter

▷ Getting familiar with different types of tangible assets

▷ Assigning costs to the balance sheet

▷ Determining the cost of self-constructed assets

▷ Preparing the asset section of a balance sheet

▷ Placing a value on PP&E

▷ Getting rid of old PP&E

---

*N*ow that you've read about current assets, it's time to move on to noncurrent assets, which are assets with a life of more than one year. Your biggie noncurrent assets are tangible and intangible assets. This chapter talks about *tangible* assets, which you can touch and feel — they have a physical presence.

Tangible assets, also called *fixed* assets, include property, plant, and equipment (PP&E). I cover intangible assets, which lack a physical presence such as patents, in Chapter 13.

Companies don't always acquire tangible assets just using cash or credit — they also use other means, such as self-construction or trading one tangible asset for another. You've probably done this in the past yourself when purchasing a new car and using your old one as a trade-in.

This chapter covers how you go about accounting for and valuing the various noncash and credit costs to acquire the assets. Costs relating to tangible assets don't stop at purchase — they continue into maintenance, so this chapter also discusses how to account for any costs to repair, improve, or reinstall the tangible asset subsequent to purchase.

And when the time comes for a tangible asset to be put out to pasture, this chapter walks you through how to get sold, junked, or donated tangible assets off the books.

Defining Types of Property, Plant, and Equipment

This chapter covers the same fixed assets you find discussions on in your intermediate accounting textbook. Specifically, it looks at various types of PP&E: land, building, equipment, and self-constructed assets.

Land

Land, also called *real property*, is the earth on which the company's office buildings or manufacturing facilities sit. The cost of the land plus any improvements the company has to make to the land to use it for business operations reflects on the balance sheet at historic cost.

Four types of costs relate to the purchase of land:

1. **Contract price:** The purchase price for the land.

2. **Closing costs:** Expenses to change the title of the land from buyer to seller. These costs include real estate broker commissions, legal fees, and title insurance.

3. **Survey costs:** Basically, the fee for a land surveyor to give you a professional opinion on where the boundaries of the property are.

4. **Land improvements:** Expenses the company incurs to get the land ready for use, which include clearing the land, if necessary, to build the manufacturing plant or adding sidewalks and fences to an existing property.

Because it's not considered to be "used up" like other PP&E, land is never depreciated.

If a company buys land as an investment, you record it in the investment section of the balance sheet instead of using PP&E. Wondering whether it goes in the current or long-term section? Well, that classification depends on how long the company plans to own the land. If the company anticipates selling it within 12 months of the balance sheet date, it's a current asset. Otherwise, record it as a long-term asset.

Buildings

This category includes the company-owned structures in which the company conducts business operations. It includes office buildings, manufacturing facilities, and retail shops. If the business owns off-site storage facilities or warehouses, these assets go in the building category, too. Like land, buildings are also known as real property assets.

Unlike land, buildings are depreciable (see Chapter 12). Also, when preparing a balance sheet for your intermediate accounting class, make sure you list land and buildings separately — it's a requirement of generally accepted accounting principles (GAAP).

Then breathe a sigh of relief! You presumably aren't a real property valuation expert, so your intermediate accounting textbook breaks out the value of land versus building for you, when applicable.

The cost of buildings includes all costs you can tie to either the purchase or construction of the building. If the company purchases a building, its cost includes the purchase price plus all closing costs and professional fees, just to name a few possible expenses. An example of professional fees is the fee for the attorney who negotiates the purchase or surveying costs.

If the company constructs the building, costs include material, labor, building permits, and any professional fees, such as fees for site engineers or architects. I talk more about self-constructed assets later in this chapter in the section "Self-constructed assets." Also on the agenda later in the chapter is interest expense the company incurs during construction.

If a company purchases land with a teardown structure, the cost of removing the dumpy old building (minus salvage value) is a land cost, not a building cost. Your intermediate accounting textbook may call this the "net razing cost."

Equipment

This category is quite broad, consisting of any equipment a company uses to make the products it sells to customers. For example, a company that makes cookies includes as equipment cost all the mixers, ovens, and packaging machines they need to turn the flour, sugar, and spices into delicious cookies ready to ship to grocery stores.

A merchandising company doesn't make product; it purchases product from manufacturers. However, the merchandising company includes in this category any office computer equipment it owns and forklifts or mechanized ladders to move inventory around. Retail shops also usually categorize their cash registers as equipment.

The cost of equipment generally includes the purchase price, sales tax, transportation, and insurance while in transit. It also includes setup costs or the cost to modify the equipment so that it looks or works exactly like the company wants it to. Setup also may include painting the company logo on the side of the equipment.

Self-constructed assets

So far in this chapter, you've probably been thinking "Easy enough!" This material is the stuff of basic accounting, which you covered in your prerequisites to your intermediate accounting class. But now it's time to roll up your sleeves a bit and discuss a more advanced tangible assets topic: self-constructed assets.

As I discuss in the previous section of this chapter, a company doesn't always buy an existing building in which to set up shop. Sometimes a company builds a factory or office building to its precise specifications and needs. Ditto for equipment. If the manufacturing process is unique, the business may have to construct some of its processing equipment.

The cost of self-constructed assets includes direct labor and material and overhead costs. It also generally includes interest on funds borrowed for the construction. Here's some info about each of the four costs:

- ✔ **Direct labor:** This expense includes only what the company pays to workers who are directly involved in constructing the assets.

- ✔ **Direct materials:** These materials are the building materials, supplies, and other items a company buys to make the self-constructed assets.

  The cost for direct labor and materials is usually a no-brainer; the company has material and supply invoices and worker payroll information to substantiate the costs that directly tie to the self-constructed assets.

- ✔ **Overhead costs:** Also known as indirect costs, overhead includes all costs tied to making the self-constructed assets, except those you include in direct materials and direct labor. It also includes indirect labor and materials.

  An example of *indirect labor* is a supervisor who oversees the construction of more than one asset. *Indirect materials* are nails or other fasteners that the company buys in bulk and uses for many different projects.

Head's up for overhead!

Normally, companies take overhead costs to the various self-constructed assets in a *pro rata* fashion. In other words, the company comes up with a reasonable method for allocating the costs among the different self-constructed assets and general company operations.

What rationale a business uses for allocation isn't an intermediate accounting issue — it's more of an on-the-job learning process. Therefore, your homework and test questions on this topic give you any allocation dollar amounts you need to answer the question.

If allocated overhead is higher than the cost an outside vendor would charge for the same work, the excess goes to period losses (income statement) and isn't capitalized as a cost of the asset.

✔ **Interest:** Depending on the type of assets, a company may not have spare cash to pay for direct labor, material, and overhead costs.

If the company borrows money to pay for costs related to constructing the asset, GAAP (see Chapter 1) states that actual interest expense incurred during construction is *capitalized* — that is, added to the basis of the asset instead of used as an expense on the income statement.

The capitalization period for interest begins when purchases for the assets have already been made, when the company has started gearing up to get the self-constructed asset process going, or when the interest cost is being incurred. The capitalization period ends when the asset is substantially finished and ready for use.

Profit or loss on self-constructed assets isn't reported until the asset is sold. Even though Joe's didn't take the discount, you still have to reduce the cost of materials and supplies by the amount of discount lost.

PP&E also includes furniture and fixtures, examples of which are desks, chairs, and filing cabinets. Add to these three common examples any other furniture items you see in an office setting: credenzas, conference tables, area rugs — the list goes on and on. Fixtures include glass display cases and floor or wall display racks. Mannequins are also considered fixtures and, depending on their quality, can be a high-dollar item on the balance sheet.

PP&E's related account, depreciation, has a whole chapter devoted to it in this book. Depreciation is how you move the cost of using the PP&E from the balance sheet (see Chapter 6) to the income statement (see Chapter 5). To get the complete lowdown on depreciation, check out Chapter 12.

Now that you've walked through the categories of PP&E, Figure 11-1 shows how they show up on the balance sheet.

Costing out the self-constructed asset

So that you look like an accounting genius in your intermediate accounting class, here's a typical test question regarding self-constructed assets. Consider the following circumstances:

Joe's Cookie Cutters, Inc., wants to streamline its cookie-making production line by using a unique cookie-cutting tool. Manufacturers are willing to fabricate the machine, but Joe's thinks their prices are too high. Joe's decides to make the machine and incurs the following costs:

Direct material and supplies for $100,000. The various vendors offer Joe's a 2% cash discount, which the company fails to utilize.

Direct labor of $190,000.

Allocated costs of $2,000

Interest on funds used during construction of $6,700.

Joe's figures it made a profit of $25,000 by self-constructing instead of buying the machine from a manufacturer.

Installing the cookie-cutter machine on the factory floor cost $3,000.

Okay, before you look at the answer, try to figure out for yourself the total cost of the self-constructed cookie cutter. Ready?

Now check out the answer. How'd you do?

Direct materials and supplies at 98%	98,000
Direct labor	190,000
Allocated costs	2,000
Interest	6,700
Installation	3,000
Total cost	299,700

Property, plant and equipment:

Land	$ 75,000
Building	263,000
Machinery and equipment	112,000
Furniture and fixtures	75,842
less accumulated depreciation	(67,245.00)
Total property, plant and equipment	458,597

Figure 11-1:
Fixed-asset portion of the balance sheet.

Valuing PP&E

If money doesn't change hands when a company purchases PP&E, special issues can arise when valuing PP&E on the balance sheet. For example, imagine that a shareholder acquires company stock for land and buildings that the shareholder owns personally. Or say that same shareholder trades a personally owned tangible asset for a company-owned tangible asset.

What do you do? Hiding in the school break room isn't an option! Never fear, this chapter answers those questions — plus gives you the skinny on accounting for deferred payment and those pesky lump-sum purchases. First up, paying after the fact.

Deferring a payment

If a company signs a note for the asset purchase that extends 12 months past the balance sheet date, the company has to account for the assets using present value. Present value raises its ugly head in a few different parts of this chapter. Since I discuss this topic in Chapter 8, I just briefly touch on present value calculations in this chapter.

Don't worry, the info you get here will be enough to understand the whole deferral extravaganza for this chapter. If you want more information, flip back and forth between this section and Chapter 8.

Going back to the Joe's Cookie Cutter example from earlier, imagine that Joe's purchases the machine instead of self-constructing it, for a cost of $324,700. Joe's doesn't just have $324,700 lying around, so the company issues a two-year note to the manufacturer for the purchase.

The note is zero interest bearing and the prevailing market rate for the same type of note is 10 percent. Joe's will make two annual payments for $162,350 at year-end (see Chapter 15 for more information about notes payable).

On the date of purchase, Joe's records the note payable for $324,700 and has to divvy up the $324,700 between equipment and discount on note payable using the present value of the note. Going to the appropriate present value of an ordinary annuity table (see Chapter 8), the factor at the intersection of 2 years and 10 percent is 1.7355.

Equipment books for $281,758 ($162,350 × 1.7335) and discount on note payable is $42,942 ($324,700 – $281,758). At the end of the year, Joe's records interest expense and reduces the discount on note payable by $28,176 ($281,758 × the market rate of 10%). Figure 11-2 shows how the journal entries look for the purchase and payment at the end of first year.

Equipment	281,758	
Discount on notes payable	42,942	
Notes payable		324,700
Date of first payment		
Interest expense	28,176	
Notes payable	162,350	
Cash		162,350
Discount on notes payable		28,176

Figure 11-2:
Journal entries, end of first year.

Issuing stock

If a company swaps stock for PP&E, you can't just use the *par value* (arbitrary value listing on the face of the stock certificate) of the stock as the cash-equivalent exchange rate for the PP&E. Par most likely doesn't reflect the market value of the stock. For more on accounting for common and preferred stock transactions, see Chapter 16.

If the stock trades on an open marketplace such as the New York Stock Exchange, using the trading value of the stock as the cash equivalent is probably a safe bet. For example, say that Joe's Cookie Cutters, Inc., is a publicly traded company with actively traded common stock valued at $25 a share.

As Joe's anticipates expanding operations due to its spanking new cookie-cutter machine, it buys the plot of land adjacent to the existing factory. After a meeting of the minds with the owner of the land, Joe's swaps 4,000 shares of no-par common stock for the land. The resulting journal entry is to debit land for $100,000 and credit common stock for $100,000.

If Joe's stock is not actively traded on an open marketplace, use the fair market value of the land, which is $80,000, as the cash equivalent. The resulting journal entry is to debit land for $80,000 and credit common stock for $80,000. Joe's issues 3,200 ($80,000 ÷ $25) shares of stock to the owner of the land.

This example ignores stock with a par value. If the stock has a par value, the calculation must account for additional paid-in capital, which is the excess of what shareholders pay to buy stock over the stock's par value. I discuss this topic in Chapter 16.

Buying in bulk: Lumping purchases

Adding intrigue to the mix, sometimes a company buys a bunch of different assets for a lump-sum price. A good example is a real estate transaction that includes all existing equipment within the four walls of the building. The purchaser has to allocate purchase price among land, building, and equipment.

Three valuation approaches are useful for lump-sum purchase allocation:

1. **Market approach:** Uses the price of similar assets in an open marketplace

2. **Income approach:** Uses expected future cash flows from the assets.

3. **Cost approach:** Uses the current replacement cost of the assets.

The company uses the valuation approach that most fairly represents the value of the assets and the transaction.

Walking through an example, imagine that Joe's $100,000 land purchase includes a small outbuilding and a forklift. Similar forklifts have a price tag of $1,500, the outbuilding costs $14,500, and the land has a fair value of $98,000. The total value of the purchased assets is $114,000 ($1,500 + $14,500 + $98,000). Figure 11-3 shows how the purchase price of $100,000 is allocated among land, building, and equipment.

Figure 11-3:
Allocation
of purchase
price.

Equipment	$ 1,500 / $114,000 × $100,000 = $ 1,316
Building	$ 14,500 / $114,000 × $100,000 = $12,719
Land	$ 98,000 / $114,000 × $100,000 = $85,965

Exchanging assets

Last but not least in our thrilling discussion of valuing PP&E, it's time to talk about accounting for transactions that involve exchanging one tangible asset for another. This situation arises a lot when trading in an old business vehicle for a new one — an occurrence you've probably encountered in your personal life.

Key to these types of transactions is the *fair value,* which is what the asset would fetch in an *open marketplace,* in other words — a transaction between unpressured parties. Chapter 3 digs into *fair value accounting,* valuing assets and liabilities on the balance sheet at their current worth rather than historic cost (what you paid/incurred for it) and the concept of commercial substance. *Commercial substance* comes into play if the asset exchange affects future cash flows.

For example, if a business trades in an old delivery truck for a new one, the new delivery truck most likely has a longer useful life. This extended useful life affects future cash flows. GAAP is picky about accounting for these types of transactions, so make sure you follow these guidelines:

- ✔ **Commercial substance exists:** Recognize gains or (loss) on the exchange contemporaneously.

- ✔ **No commercial substance, no cash changing hands:** Defer gains and recognize losses contemporaneously.

- ✔ **No commercial substance and cash received:** Recognize gain and loss contemporaneously.

If the cash received in an exchange that lacks commercial substance is less than 25 percent of the fair value of the exchange, only a partial gain is recognized.

GAAP and International Financial Reporting Standards (IFRS) are similar in their treatment of exchanges of nonmonetary assets. Chapter 1 introduces both.

Make sense? Well, maybe not. Time for a typical homework assignment involving an asset exchange with a gain on exchange and commercial substance. Here are the facts surrounding this transaction:

- ✔ ABC Manufacturing trades in two old delivery vans and coughs up $15,000 cash for a large delivery truck.

- ✔ The fair value of the two old delivery trucks is $55,000. Their book value is $42,000 (cost of $75,000 minus accumulated depreciation of $33,000).

- ✔ The fair value of the two old delivery trucks is more clearly evident than the fair value of the larger delivery truck that is the subject of the exchange.

Figure 11-4 shows how to figure gain for this transaction.

Fair value of delivery vans		$ 55,000
Cost of delivery vans	$ 75,000	
Less accumulated depreciation	33,000	(42,000)
Gain on disposal of delivery vans		$ 13,000

Figure 11-4: Computation of gain on disposal of delivery trucks.

Figure 11-5 gives you the lowdown on the journal entries. The $70,000 value for the delivery truck comes from adding the delivery vans' fair value of $55,000 plus the $15,000 cash.

Trading in one similar asset for another is typically considered a like-kind exchange and new depreciable basis is reduced by the unrecognized gain on disposal.

Delivery truck	70,000	
Accumulated depreciation – delivery vans	33,000	
Delivery vans		75,000
Gain on disposal		13,000
Cash		15,000

Figure 11-5: Recording nonmonetary exchange transaction.

Assigning Costs to PP&E

Regardless of their fair market value, most tangible assets go on the balance sheet at their original historic cost. So if the company buys a building for $300,000 in 2004 and in 2013 its fair market value is $450,000, the value of the asset on the balance sheet stays at $300,000. This is also known as the asset's *book value*. And if the asset is subject to depreciation (see Chapter 12) the historic cost minus the depreciation is known as net book value.

Capitalizing costs

With your accounting prerequisites for intermediate accounting, you're probably familiar with the concept of capitalizing costs. But just as a refresher, I want to briefly review the basics of capitalizing PP&E.

When a tangible asset is capitalized, the purchase initially goes on the balance sheet as a fixed asset. Through the wonderful process of depreciation, the cost of the tangible asset eventually moves from the balance sheet to the income statement.

Common sense also has to come into play. Most companies have a capitalization policy that sets a dollar limit for items to be capitalized instead of expensed. For example, items that cost less than $100 are automatically expensed to the income statement.

Recording repairs and maintenance expenses

Sad but true, costs related to PP&E don't stop at the purchase point. After getting plant assets up and running, repair and maintenance (R&M) expenses will eventually follow.

R&M expenses are inevitable — that is, unless the company has an extremely neurotic replacement policy and replaces serviceable equipment instead of fixing it! But I've never seen this happen in real life.

The pressing question here is when the cost of R&M should go on the balance sheet versus the income statement. Just off the top of your head, you may think that it's the nature of the beast for R&M to always go to the income statement. After all, it's an expense, right?

Well, kinda sorta. It all depends on the type of the R&M and how materially it affects the asset. To add the cost of the R&M to the balance sheet instead of expensing it on the income statement, one of the following conditions apply:

1. **The useful life of the asset increases.** For example, a company may totally rebuild the motor for a piece of equipment on an assembly line.

2. **The number of units the asset produces must increase.** Before the repair, the company expects the equipment to tap out at another 1,000 units. After the repair, the old gal has new life, and the company estimates that another 5,000 units will come shooting out of the machine.

3. **The quality of the units the asset produces must increase.** Prior to the repair, the assembled units had all sorts of quality control problems that the repairs subsequently eliminated.

This situation is one of those weird "opposite world" issues between GAAP and tax. Companies like to capitalize as many costs as possible to beef up the bottom line, but they also like to expense as many costs as possible to reduce taxable income. Sigh! The life of an accountant is never easy — but it sure is a good challenge.

Many maintenance costs, such as oiling machines or changing the toner in a copier, are obviously income statement expenses and are not capitalized.

Capitalized costs follow the asset to which they relate. The cost increases the book value of the asset and is subject to depreciation over the course of the remaining useful life.

Improving and replacing PP&E

Improving is the process of substituting a better asset for the one that's already in place. *Replacing* means the company swaps out the old asset for another one that's similar in nature.

Going back to the three conditions in the "Recording repairs and maintenance expenses" section of this chapter, if the improvement or replacement increases the future service potential of the asset, capitalize the cost. You can handle this in three ways: using the substitution approach, using the new cost, or using the accumulated depreciation account.

- **Substitution approach:** If the company has *net book value* (cost basis minus accumulated depreciation) figures for the asset readily available, it's easy to use the substitution approach. In this case, the company removes the cost of the old asset and replaces it with the cost of the new asset.

- **Capitalization of the new cost:** This approach leaves the old asset on the books and adds the cost of the new asset as well. Many times this isn't any big deal because the net book value of the old asset is *de minimis*, or immaterial.

- **Charge to accumulated depreciation:** If the process extends the useful life of the existing asset, the cost of the improvement goes to accumulated depreciation.

Now that you've gotten those explanations out of the way, it's time to see how this looks in black and white. For example, ABC, Inc. pays $135,000 to replace some plant assets. The net book value of the assets is $10,000 (cost of $125,000 minus $115,000 accumulated depreciation).

Figure 11-6 shows how to journalize this transaction using the substitution approach.

Plant assets - new	135,000
Accumulated depreciation – old plant assets	115,000
Loss on disposal of old plant assets	10,000
Plant assets – old	125,000
Cash	135,000

Figure 11-6: Substitution approach for replacing PP&E.

Now, imagine that ABC, Inc., combined a bunch of plant assets on the balance sheet and doesn't know the exact net book value of the plant assets being replaced. In that case, the only journal entry needed is to debit plant assets and credit cash for $135,000.

Finally, ABC, Inc., decides to pay $50,000 to beef up the old plant assets, which extends their useful life. In that case, the journal entry is to debit accumulated depreciation and credit cash for $50,000.

Reinstalling equipment

If a company moves into a new building or expands square footage in the old building, which necessitates rearranging the equipment, the cost is usually capitalized. For your intermediate accounting class, keep three facts in the back of your mind:

1. If the original cost of installation is known, account for the reinstall using the substitution approach.

2. If the original cost is unknown and the cost of the new install is material, capitalize the new cost.

3. If the original cost is unknown and the cost of the new install is immaterial, just expense it.

Selling and Other Dispositions of Plant Assets

In the normal course of doing business, a company rids itself of unneeded fixed assets. Different ways they may do this include selling the asset, trading it in on a new fixed asset, junking it, or doing involuntary conversion. *Junking* an asset means it's totally worn out and thrown away. *Involuntary conversion* can occur when the asset is destroyed in a fire or stolen.

Whatever the circumstance, you need to make sure the company has completely removed the cost of the asset and its accumulated depreciation from the balance sheet. Additionally, if the company made or lost any money with the transaction, that amount has to be recorded on the income statement.

Recording sales

To calculate gain or loss on the sale of a fixed asset, book value of the asset is figured up to the date of sale. So if the sale took place on October 1, the company must calculate depreciation from January 1 through September 30. The asset has to be completely removed from the balance sheet so that the cost of the asset is reduced to zero and so is the accumulated depreciation.

For example, say that a business sells equipment with a net book value of $5,000 (cost is $20,000 and accumulated depreciation is $15,000) for $8,000 on December 31. Gain on sale is $3,000 ($8,000 sales price minus $5,000 book).

This amount is recorded on the books by debiting cash for $8,000, debiting accumulated depreciation for $15,000, crediting the income statement account gain on disposal of asset for $3,000, and crediting the asset account for $20,000.

The same general routine applies for junking assets, although the effect to the income statement is called loss on abandonment.

Dealing with involuntary conversions

If an involuntary conversion takes place, the company has to record the difference between insurance proceeds and the asset's net book value as gain or loss on disposal of the asset. Using the example from the earlier section "Recording sales," section, suppose that, instead of selling the equipment, a thief breaks into the business during the night and steals it.

The company reports the thief to its insurance provider, which, after subtracting the deductible, cuts the company a check for $4,000. Figure 11-7 shows the journal entry to record this transaction.

Figure 11-7:
Recording loss on involuntary conversion.

Cash	4,000	
Accumulated depreciation – plant asset	15,000	
Loss on disposal of asset	1,000	
Plant assets		20,000

Chapter 12

Recognizing Depreciation, Impairments, and Depletion

....

In This Chapter

▶ Getting familiar with how depreciation affects the financial statements

▶ Considering the differences between costs and expenses

▶ Calculating depreciation

▶ Reducing the cost of natural resources with depletion

▶ Accounting for assets that are no longer useful

▶ Looking at the difference between tax and GAAP depreciation

....

This chapter is an introduction to a company's *tangible* assets — assets that you can touch and feel, that have a physical presence. Tangible assets, also called *fixed* assets, include property, plant, and equipment (PP&E). *Natural resources* are another type of asset, which includes items such as oil, gas, and timber; we look at those assets in this chapter as well.

The chapter walks you through the types of costs that go on the balance sheet when the company initially buys or leases these assets. It also talks about the various *depreciation methods* accountants use to move the cost of tangible assets from the balance sheet to the income statement. Specifically, I cover the straight-line, declining-balance, sum-of-the-years' digits, and units-of-production methods.

Natural resources aren't depreciated; instead, you use depletion. Depletion, while using more complex calculations is essentially the same as depreciation — it's a way to move the cost of natural resources from the balance sheet to the income statement.

This chapter shows you how to figure a base for depletion, come up with the unit rate of depletion, and determine the amount of depletion charged to each financial period.

Sadly, some assets don't hold their value. In some instances, you have to account for this devaluation (impairment) on the balance sheet. Don't worry! This chapter gives you the complete scoop on the types of impairment and shows you how to accurately measure and report them on the financial statements.

Understanding How Depreciation Affects All Financial Statements

Depreciation is the systematic method accountants use to move the cost of buying tangible assets from the balance sheet onto the income statement as an expense. Depreciation expense is one of those accounting transactions that has an effect on all three financial statements.

Of course, depreciation affects the income statement, because it's considered an expense. It also affects the balance sheet because that's where the book value of tangible assets shows up. *Book value* is the difference between the cost of the asset and how much depreciation has occurred on that particular asset.

Accumulated depreciation is the account you'll be looking for on the balance sheet. It's a contra-asset account that stores the accumulated depreciation expense charged against an asset from date of purchase to date of the balance sheet.

And because depreciation is a noncash transaction, it's a big deal when preparing the statement of cash flow (see Chapter 7 for more on the statement of cash flow, and you can find information on the income statement in Chapters 5 and 20). Many chapters in this book discuss balance sheet accounts, but the chapter you're most interested in for depreciation info (besides this one!) is Chapter 11.

Distinguishing Costs and Expenses: What's the Difference?

What's a cost and what's an expense? Consider an example. Let's assume Penway Manufacturing, Inc., makes toasters and needs to buy some new metal fabrication machines to form the outer shell of the toaster. When the company buys the machines, the price Penway pays or promises to pay is a cost. Then as Penway uses the machines, it reclassifies the cost of buying the fabrication machines as an expense of doing business. So the resources Penway uses to purchase the machines move from the balance sheet (cost) to the income statement (expense).

Under GAAP, every transaction you record has to satisfy the matching principle (see Chapter 2). This means you associate all relevant expenses the business incurs to revenue earned and realizable during the accounting period. If a company buys a long-lived tangible asset that it reckons will be in use for more than 12 months past the balance sheet date, it must allocate the cost of the asset (in other words, depreciate the asset) to financial periods beyond the current one.

Tangible assets are those you can touch and feel, such as desks, vehicles, and equipment. Intangible assets such as patents and copyrights don't have a physical presence.

Companies have to record all asset purchases on the balance sheet at their original cost, along with all the ordinary and necessary costs to get the asset ready to use. For example, these costs may include the asset's purchase price, sales tax, freight-in, and assembly of the machine on the factory floor. (Freight-in is the buyer's cost to get the machine from the seller to the buyer.)

When moving the cost of an asset from the balance sheet to the income statement, you have to answer the following three questions:

1. What is the depreciable base of the asset? The *depreciable base* is the original cost of the asset minus any salvage value. *Salvage value* is how much the company estimates it'll get when it disposes of the asset — for example, when the company sells it.

   Suppose a company buys a piece of machinery for $10,000. It expects to use the machinery for three years until it's obsolete and then sell it for $3,000. Depreciable base is $7,000 ($10,000 – $3,000).

2. What is the asset's useful life? Well, you know it's more than one year, or else you wouldn't be depreciating it. But how much more than a year? Here's an example of an accounting estimate (see Chapter 19 for more).

   Companies use various ways to estimate useful life. One method is prior experience with the same type of asset. In any event, all your intermediate accounting assignments and test questions provide useful life, so you won't have to estimate.

3. Which cost allocation (depreciation) method is best for the asset? Again, deciding which of the allowable methods under GAAP to use is an estimate the company makes. Keep reading — the next section talks more about allowable depreciation methods.

   Companies use various ways to decide which method to use to allocate balance sheet costs to income statement expenses. One way is the business purpose of the asset in question. If it's a piece of factory machinery, the units-of-production method (see the next section in this chapter for more info) may be more appropriate. In any event, all your intermediate accounting assignments and test questions provide a useful life.

The depreciation cost allocation method the business uses is a matter of choice, as long as the method is appropriate for the asset. For financial accounting, the method meets the standard of appropriateness if the company uses the method that most closely matches revenue to expense or the method that's common in that industry.

Choosing Among Depreciation Methods

Depreciation is the method of allocating costs to the appropriate period. Although accountants have to follow GAAP for financial statement reporting purposes, they have different allowable methods to consider. This section takes you on a tour of some of the methods available to companies.

Depreciation isn't part of the whole equation for figuring the fair market value, which is the amount of money the company may fetch when it sells any of the assets.

Your intermediate accounting textbook discusses a few different methods of depreciation. Three are based on time: straight-line, declining-balance, and sum-of-the-years' digits. The last, units-of-production, is based on actual physical usage of the fixed asset. Here's a brief explanation of each:

- ✔ **Straight-line:** This method spreads the cost of the fixed asset evenly over its useful life.

- ✔ **Declining-balance:** An accelerated method of depreciation, it results in higher depreciation expense in the earlier years of ownership.

- ✔ **Sum-of-the-years' digits:** Compute depreciation expense by adding all years of the fixed asset's expected useful life and factoring in which year you are currently in, as compared to the total number of years.

- ✔ **Units-of-production:** The total estimated number of units the fixed asset will produce over its expected useful life, as compared to the number of units produced in the current accounting period, is used to calculate depreciation expense.

Psssst — just a quick word on two special methods: group and composite. Using one depreciation rate across the board, a company uses the group method when the assets are similar and have a similar expected life. And, bet you didn't see this coming, companies use the composite method when assets are dissimilar and have different lives. These methods aren't allowed for tax and are used in only very special circumstances for GAAP.

Generally, International Financial Reporting Standards (IFRS; see Chapter 1) and GAAP account for deprecation similarly. International Accounting Standard (IAS) 16 states that companies must review the method of depreciation periodically; if the previous estimate changes, the method must also be changed.

Walking the straight-line method

When using the straight-line method, the salvage value reduces the depreciable base. Going back to Penway's toaster fabrication machine, which I discussed in an earlier section of this chapter, Penway purchases the machine for $30,000. Salvage value is $3,000. The cost of the machine ($30,000) minus its salvage value ($3,000) gives you a depreciable base of $27,000.

The expected useful life is 5 years. So depreciation expense for the toaster machine is $27,000 ÷ 5, or $5,400 depreciation expense per year for each of the five years. Book value at the end of year 5 is the salvage value of $3,000.

Accelerating by using the declining-balance method

Don't deduct salvage value when figuring the depreciable base for the declining balance method. But do limit depreciation so that, at the end of the day, the asset's net book value is the same as its estimated salvage value. I know, it's not easy to imagine without an example. Have a look at Figure 12-1.

You compute cost and salvage value for the asset the same as with the straight-line method. For your rate, you use a multiple of the straight-line rate.

Going back to the Penway example, the straight-line rate is 20 percent. How did I figure that? Well, because the toaster-making machine has a useful life of five years, shown as a percentage, the straight-line rate is 1/5, or 20 percent per year.

In this example, I want you to use the double declining-balance method. The multiplier is 2, so the double-declining rate is 40 percent (20% × 2).

Figure 12-1 shows how to figure double-declining balance depreciation for the Penway machine.

	Net Book Value	Factor	Depreciation Expense	Accumulated Depreciation	Ending Net Book Value
2012	$ 30,000	0.4	$ 12,000	$ 12,000	$ 18,000
2013	18,000	0.4	7,200	19,200	10,800
2014	10,800	0.4	4,320	23,520	6,480
2015	6,480	0.4	2,592	26,112	3,888
2016	3,888	0	888	27,000	3,000

Figure 12-1: Double-declining balance depreciation.

Remember, the last year is limited to salvage value, that's why depreciation is limited to $888.

Using the units-of-production method

Units-of-production is an *activity method* because you compute depreciation on actual physical use, making it a fantastic method for computing factory machinery depreciation.

Here's how it works while using the toaster-making machine:

In addition to knowing the cost basis and estimating the salvage value, you need to estimate how many outer shells the machine can produce prior to retirement. The best estimate for Mr. Toaster-Maker is 60,000 units. Taking cost minus salvage value gives you $27,000. Divide $27,000 by your antici-pated usage of 60,000 units ($27,000 ÷ 60,000), which equals $0.45. This is your unit-of-production depreciation rate.

To compute depreciation expense year after year, you multiply the actual number of units the machine makes during the year by the depreciation rate. In 2012, this is 10,100 units, so depreciation expense is $4,545 (10,100 × $0.45). For 2013 through 2016, the same calculation applies.

Now work through one more year. In 2013, actual units are 15,300. Depreciation is $6,885 (15,300 × $0.45). Accumulated depreciation is $11,430 ($4,545 + $6,885) and book value is $18,570 ($30,000 – $11,430).

Calculating sum-of-the-years' digits

With this method, you come up with a depreciation fraction using the number of years of useful life. Penway's machine has a useful life of five years. Add (5 + 4 + 3 + 2 + 1 = 15) to get your denominator for the rate fraction. In year 1, your multiplier is 5/15 (1/3); in year 2, the multiplier is 4/15; and so on.

Again, you subtract the estimated salvage value from the cost ($30,000 – $3,000 = $27,000). The first year, the depreciation expense is $9,000 ($27,000 ÷ 3). In the second year, the depreciation expense is $7,200 ([$27,000 × 4] ÷ 15). For year 3, the depreciation expense is $5,400 ([$27,000 × 3] ÷ 15).

Year 4 is $3,600 ([$27,000 × 2] ‖ 15). Year 5 is $1,800 ($27,000 ÷ 15).

Checking the math, you know you can't depreciate past salvage value, so adding all five years of depreciation expense equals $27,000. Yippee, 100 percent correct!

Understanding special depreciation issues

Your intermediate accounting textbook probably highlights two special issues that happen quite often in the business world: figuring partial-year depreciation and accounting for changes in the depreciation rate.

I discuss each in turn:

- ✔ **Partial-year depreciation:** Rare indeed is the day a company buys an asset on the first day of the financial period. So what to do when a company buys an asset on September 1 (or any other day), when the financial year starts on January 1? You prorate the depreciation expense among the accounting periods involved.

  If the asset has a useful life of five years, the first year of depreciation is prorated using the fraction 4/12 (four months remain in the year, September through December). Any leftover depreciation is taken in year 6. Consider the toaster machine while using the straight-line method. Depreciation expense in year 1 is now $1,800 ($5,400 × 4/12). For years 2 through 5, depreciation expense remains $5,400. In year 6, you finish up by expensing the remaining $3,600 ($5,400 × 8/12).

- ✔ **Accounting for rate changes:** The cost of the depreciable asset is the only part of this equation that isn't an estimate. Until the whole asset spiel plays out, you don't know how accurately you estimated the asset's salvage value or useful life.

  For example, let's say that, at the end of year 3 of the estimated life of Penway's toaster-making machine, you reckon you'll be able to use the asset for another four years past the original estimate of five years. This gives you a new estimated life of nine years, of which three have already elapsed. What do you do?

  I talk about this more in Chapter 19. But for now, here's a simple example of how to handle this estimating situation when using the straight-line method:

Tax versus book depreciation

This book isn't about taxation, so I don't want to belabor this point. Just make sure you understand that tax depreciation methods are, for the most part, different from GAAP depreciation methods. For example, businesses can use the straight-line method for some assets for tax as well as GAAP.

Tax depreciation rules and rates are set as part of Internal Revenue Code (IRC), not GAAP. The Modified Asset Cost Recovery System (MACRS) is the method you'll most likely see on business tax returns. Special tax deprecation methods

also allow businesses to expense some tangible assets at time of purchase instead of depreciating them over their useful lives.

For more information about accounting for income taxes, see Chapter 17. You can also find out more about income tax depreciation methods at the Internal Revenue Service website, `www.irs.gov`. In the search box in the upper-right side of the home page, enter "Publication 946" to bring up links for the publication that discusses how to depreciate property.

From your cost ($27,000), subtract three years' depreciation ($5,400 × 3), to get a book value of $10,800.

The useful life remaining for your new estimate is 6 years (9 − 3). Straight-line depreciation per year is now $1,800 ($10,800 ÷ 6), for the remaining new useful life of six years.

Under IFRS, if an entity changes the method of depreciation when the previously expected pattern changes, the change is accounted for as a change in estimate, prospectively only.

Impairing Assets

An *impairment loss* takes place when a company makes the judgment call that the carrying value of an asset on the company balance sheet is less than *fair value*, which is what an unpressured person would pay for the asset in an open marketplace (see Chapter 3). If the impairment loss isn't recoverable, under U.S. GAAP, the company has to adjust the books to reflect this lessening in value.

Be careful not to confuse asset impairments with the lower of cost or market method for valuing inventory (see Chapter 10). They are two different accounting events.

Now, you may be wondering about the criteria for measuring recoverability. Good question! In a nutshell, it means the asset's carrying value isn't recoverable from its undiscounted cash flows. Now, that's clear, is it not? Not! Before I elaborate on the recovery aspect of impairments, I want to give you the straight skinny on the circumstances that can lead to impairment.

Recognizing impairments

When the carrying value of an asset or *group of assets,* such as an operating segment, is more than its fair value, the company may have an impairment event on its hands. U.S. GAAP in Accounting Standards Codification (ASC) 360-10-35 provides guidance to financial accountants on the type of events and circumstances to look for, as the first step in determining whether assets have to be evaluated for recovery (there's that term again — but don't worry, I discuss it in the next section) and subsequent impairment loss.

Every GAAP guide discusses six biggies. However, this list doesn't include all the events that can trigger the need to test for impairment:

- **Market downturn:** The market or market price of a long-lived asset experiences a significant downturn. For example, the company is holding a piece of raw land to develop whose fair value is currently less than cost.

- **Change in use of asset:** An event such as a natural disaster causes an adverse change in the manner in which a long-lived asset is used or changes its condition.

- **Change in business or legal climate:** A lawsuit or other adverse change in the general business or legal climate affects the value of the asset. Maybe a factory has been deemed unsafe and can't be used for production until improvements are made.

- **Premature disposal of asset:** The company plans to dump an asset significantly before the end of its previously estimated useful life.

- **Escalating costs:** Costs to build or acquire an asset start to pile up and are significantly more than the company originally estimates.

- **Souring investments:** History of operating or cash flow losses demonstrates that the company will experience continuing losses from using the asset.

Although this chapter talks about depreciation of tangible assets, and they can definitely be impaired, other assets are subject to impairment, too. For example, goodwill and other intangibles, such as patents and copyrights (see Chapter 13), can also lose value and have to be adjusted on the balance sheet.

If a company has goodwill, which comes into play during business combinations when one business purchases another for a price greater than the fair market value of the net assets acquired during the sale, there's an annual requirement to test it for impairment. See Chapter 13 for more info about goodwill.

Walking through the recovery test

Okay, an event occurs that causes you to determine whether an asset's carrying amount is less than fair value. Your next step is to see whether the asset can eventually bounce back from this loss in value. You tackle this weighty evaluation by using the recoverability test.

The first step of the recovery test is to compute the future net cash flows from both the use and eventual disposition of the asset. Then you compare this figure to the assets carrying value on the balance sheet to see whether you need to book an impairment loss.

If the carrying value is less than future net cash flows, you take no action. If the future net cash flows are less than the carrying value, it's time to spring into action!

Measuring impairments

Imagine that Penway invested in a whole production line of toaster fabricators with a current book value of $300,000. Because of innovations in the process of manufacturing toaster makers, the company anticipates a change in the use of this $300,000 group of assets.

Penway reckons that future cash flow from the machines and their eventual sale is $250,000. In this case, Penway recognizes an impairment loss of $50,000 ($300,000 – $250,000).

The impairment loss of $50,000 is recorded as part of income (loss) from continuing operations (see Chapter 5). The journal entry to book the impairment is to debit the income statement account Loss on Impairment, and credit the machine's associated accumulated depreciation account for $50,000.

If you have a group of assets, after figuring the impairment loss, you allocate the loss across the group of assets based on each asset's carrying value. For example, if an asset's carrying value is 10 percent of the total asset group's carrying value, then you allocate that asset as 10 percent of the impairment loss.

If both intangible and tangible assets are being tested for impairment, the order of testing is as follows: first, intangibles other than goodwill; second, tangibles such as property, plant, and equipment; and third, goodwill.

Evaluate impairment at the lowest level possible for assets or groups of assets. For example, a parent corporation could measures a group of buses they purchase in the same year to see if there is any impairment loss of a bus company subsidiary. For example, if the price of newly purchased busses is less than those carried in the balance sheet by the subsidiary, there may be impairment loss.

Restoring impairment loss

This next bit may come as a surprise: If circumstances reverse, you don't automatically restore the impairment loss. Whether you restore the loss hinges on whether the company plans to dispose of the asset.

You don't depreciate assets that aren't put to use: you treat them like inventory (see Chapter 10) and adjust the carrying value up or down, based on the lower of cost or *net realizable value,* or how much the company anticipates it will get for the asset when it disposes of it in the future (minus all disposal costs).

Companies can write up an asset for disposal in future periods as long as the carrying value of the asset after write-up is less than the preimpairment carrying value.

Table 12-1 is a quick reference for accounting for impairment loss and the yea-or-nay on restoring impairment loss.

Table 12-1	Rules when accounting for impairment loss
Assets Held for Use	**Assets Held for Disposal**
Compute impairment loss at the excess of carrying value over fair value.	Compute impairment loss as the excess of carrying value over net realizable value.
Use the new cost basis for the depreciate base.	No depreciation.
Do not restore.	Yes. When the circumstances warrant it, you can restore impairment loss.

IFRS allows write-ups for recovery of impairment loss (up to the original amount before impairment) for all affected assets.

Explaining Depletion

Well, you've been through a lot of Ds in this chapter: depreciation, accumulated depreciation, declining balance, and the devaluing of assets through impairment loss. Hold on to your hats, because you need to work through one more D — depletion — before you can finish this chapter with an A+.

Instead of, or in addition to, owning tangible assets, a company may purchase or own rights to certain natural resources. *Depletion* is the way companies allocate the cost of natural resources to financial periods. As with depreciation, depletion gives the owner of the resources a way to account for the reduction in the natural resource reserves (after all, natural resources don't last forever!).

Understanding which assets can be depleted

I mention that natural resources are subject to depletion rather than depreciation. So what's the lowdown on the type of assets you classify as natural resources? Well, natural resources have two major characteristics:

- ✔ There is a complete consumption of the asset.
- ✔ Replacement of the asset takes place only by an act of nature.

Examples of natural or wasting resources are timber, coal, oil, precious metals such as gold and silver, and gemstones such as diamonds, rubies, and emeralds — oh my!

Figuring your base for depletion

To correctly figure the annual expense for the use of natural resources, you have to correctly allocate costs to the natural resource's depletion base.

Four factors affect depletion base: acquisition costs, exploration costs, development costs, and restoration costs. I discuss each in turn:

- **Acquisition costs:** The cost to purchase or lease the property rights to the land, which a company believes has natural resources. For example, cattle ranches in Wyoming may lease drilling rights to oil companies.

  Acquisition costs are held in an asset account. If the purchase pans out, they convert to exploration costs. If the investment is a bust (no diamonds, dang it!), the company writes off the costs as a loss.

- **Exploration costs:** The costs to dig around in the leased or owned property to find the natural resources — sometimes successfully, sometimes not. Typically, companies expense these costs as incurred.

- **Development costs:** The costs necessary to exploit the natural resources after exploration, such as drilling machinery and equipment. These costs are capitalized as part of the depletion base.

  If equipment used to develop the natural resources is multipurpose and used on other nondepletion projects, it may not be included in the depletion base and is depreciated instead.

- **Restoration costs:** The costs a company incurs to restore the land to its original state as or after all natural resources are exploited. These costs reduce the net amount the company expects to receive from the sale and, therefore, increase the depletion base.

Using salvage value and recoverable units

After you work through the costs and have a depletion base, you still have to come up with an estimate for salvage value and the total amount of recoverable units you feel the natural resources will provide. Coming up with these types of estimates isn't a function of accounting. Engineers, geologists, and other experts in the various fields provide this information.

Basically, depletion works like the units-of-production method I discuss in the "Choosing Among Depreciation Methods" section of this chapter. To get the unit depletion rate, you figure up all the costs, deduct salvage value, and divide that amount by the total estimated units available for the natural resource.

To bring this concept home, consider a complete example. Figure 12-2 shows the oil drilling costs Wyoming Land Company expects to incur with its latest well (Oil Well #509).

Depletion Base & Rate

Land acquisition costs		$ 1,500,000
Exploration costs		200,000
Development costs		1,275,000
Less: Estimated salvage value	$ 300,000	
Adjusted by restoration cost	(50,000)	(250,000)
Total Depletion Base		$ 2,725,000

Figure 12-2: Depletion base and rate.

Now, let's say that the experts Wyoming Land Company hired estimate that this well will provide 5,250,000 barrels of crude oil. The depletion rate per barrel is $0.519 ($2,725,000 ÷ 5,250,000 barrels).

Now you have to compute the depletion charge for each period, basing your figure on the actual number of barrels produced. For example, if in the first period production was 500,000 barrels, depletion charged to the period would be $259,500 (500,000 × $0.519).

The journal entry to record this extravaganza is to debit inventory and credit another asset account, Oil Well #509, for the $259,500. As barrels are sold, inventory reduces and the cost moves to the income statement account cost of goods sold.

If there are future additional costs or changes in the estimated units to be extracted, the depletion base and depletion rate are changed prospectively, which means they apply to current and future periods only. See Chapter 19 for more info about changes in estimates.

Chapter 13

Keeping Track of Other Noncurrent Assets

*P*art III of this book is all about assets, current and noncurrent. *Noncurrent assets* are assets with a life of longer than one year. Your biggie noncurrent assets are tangible and intangible assets. I discuss issues related to tangible assets, which have a physical presence, including property, plant, and equipment, in Chapters 11 and 12. Other examples of noncurrent assets are investments the company plans on holding for more than one year and deferred income tax assets (see Chapter 17).

This chapter talks about *intangible* assets. As you may derive from their name, these assets lack a physical presence. Some examples are patents, copyrights, and trademarks. *Goodwill* is another type of intangible asset that arises only in a *business combination* — an instance when one business wholly or partially buys another.

From an accounting point of view, working with intangible assets presents a unique set of challenges. In the following pages, I untangle all of them. I will walk you through how to move the cost of intangible assets from the balance sheet to the income statement using amortization, and I fill you in on what happens accounting-wise if intangible assets are deemed to no longer be useful.

I also touch on research and development costs, which are costs a company incurs to investigate new business processes or products. Although research and development isn't technically an intangible asset, the investments made often pave the way for intangibles such as patents, which earns this topic a mention in the chapter.

Can't Touch This: Investigating Intangible Assets

I tell my students to remember that they can touch, feel, and see tangible assets like property, plant, and equipment (PP&E). So the big difference between tangible and intangible assets is that intangible assets don't have a physical existence like PP&E. Another important point to remember is that intangible assets also aren't financial instruments, such as stocks, bonds, or accounts receivable, to name a few.

The value of PP&E lies in the use of the physical asset itself. The value of most intangible assets comes from the rights or privileges the company gets by being the owner of the intangible asset.

So what assets are considered intangibles? Two types of intangible assets exist. One occurs only in a business combination. The other type can arise during day-to-day operations of just about any business.

Identifying types of intangibles

You're probably somewhat familiar with intangibles from other accounting classes you've taken. However, your intermediate accounting textbook takes a slightly difference approach to the discussion by dividing the two types of intangibles into six different categories: marketing, customer, artistic, contract, technology, and goodwill.

A discussion of the first five follows. Goodwill gets its own section later in the chapter.

Marketing

These intangibles help promote the company's goods or services. Your biggie marketing-related intangible asset is a trademark. These assets are unique signs, symbols, or names the company uses to create a brand or unique image. For example, think "Kleenex" versus "facial tissue."

If a company buys the trademark from another company, it capitalizes the purchase price. If the company develops the trademark itself, all costs relating to its development are capitalized, except for research and development costs. (I talk about research and development later in this chapter in the section "Handling the Costs of Research and Development [R&D]).")

If the costs to develop the trademark are immaterial, just expense them. What is material versus immaterial? Well, it's all relative. What may be material for one company may be immaterial for another. For example, to a multinational company worth millions of dollars, $50,000 is probably immaterial. While the same amount is very material to a smaller company worth in the tens of thousands.

Customer

Your biggie customer-related intangible assets are customer lists and any other customer-related information. Every time you're the (un)lucky recipient of an unsolicited credit card offer, you've been a hapless victim of the buying and selling of customer-related information. As you can probably guess, this asset is extremely lucrative.

So how do you account for it if the company purchases a customer list from another company? For your intermediate accounting class, you first have to figure out the useful life of the customer-related asset. You also have to look into the future and decide whether your company will be able to sell the customer list to another company when it's done with it. In other words, does the list have residual value?

Artistic

My favorite intangible assets are artistic-related intangibles such as copyrights, which protect ownership rights. In other words, someone can't use the company's printed work (books, poems, and the like) or recorded work (musical score, song lyrics, movies, and so on) without permission. Any original piece of work is automatically copyrighted.

Capitalize the cost to acquire a copyright and also the cost to defend it if some nasty plagiarizer starts using the material without permission. Then allocate the costs of the copyrights to its useful life.

I explain how to move the cost of intangible assets from the balance sheet to the income statement later in this chapter in the section "Writing off intangibles with amortization."

Contract

Contract-related intangibles include franchise agreements, licenses, and permits. I discuss franchise agreements in Chapter 20. For now, keep in mind that a *franchise* is a business that perhaps started out as a one-location shop but grew to be so popular that the original owners allowed other individuals to open shops with the same concept in other locations.

The parties to a franchise are the *franchisor,* the party granting the business rights, and the *franchisee,* the individual purchasing the right to use the franchisor's business model.

Licenses and permits come into play when a government agency grants a private company operating rights, such as the use of city streets or designated areas for taxicab stands.

Expense the cost of acquiring a franchise over the life of the agreement. Expense annual franchise costs in the financial period in which the franchisee incurs them.

Licenses and permits are capitalized if the company can match the costs to obtain the operating right with the actual license or permit. Again, expense *de minimis,* or immaterial, costs when they occur.

If a company pays a minimum guarantee for the privilege associated with the license or permit, the amount of the guarantee records as an intangible asset and moves to the balance sheet over the life specified in the license agreement.

Technology

The biggie technology-related intangible is patents. A *patent* provides licensing for inventions or other unique processes and designs. Items that patents protect run the gamut from pharmaceuticals, to automobile circuitry, to unique machinery designs.

If a company purchases a patent from the inventor, the capitalized cost is the purchase price plus any costs incurred as part of the acquisition process, such as legal fees. Costs leading to patents developed in house aren't capitalized, but are shown immediately as expenses on the income statement. (See the section "Handling the Costs of Research and Development [R&D]," later in this chapter, for more info.)

Unlike goodwill, these first five categories of intangible assets are relevant to the day-to-day operations of just about any business.

Leasehold improvements, which are costs a company incurs when it leases its business location and updates the rental space with features it can't take along at the end of the lease, are also considered to be intangible assets. In this situation, balance sheets prepared in accordance with generally accepted accounting principles (GAAP) lump leasehold improvements with PP&E.

Accounting for goodwill

The second type of intangible asset, goodwill, emerges only during the purchase of a business for a price greater than the fair market value of the net assets acquired during the sale. For many assets, like cash, the fair market value (what an unpressured buyer would pay in an open marketplace — see Chapter 3 for more) of an asset matches book value. For other assets, such as property, plant, and equipment (which are discussed in Chapter 11), an independent appraisal shows fair value.

Net assets are total assets minus total liabilities. Figure 13-1 shows how ABC Corp., the purchaser, figures goodwill.

ABC Corp. buys XYZ Corp. for $350,000. The fair value of XYZ's net assets is $315,000. ABC Corp. acquires $35,000 ($350,000 – $315,000) of goodwill in the transaction. To record this transaction on ABC's books, debit each asset for fair value, credit each liability for fair value, and debit goodwill for $35,000.

XYZ. Corp. Net Assets

	Book Value	Fair Value
Cash	$ 25,000	$ 25,000
Accounts receivable	10,000	10,000
Inventory	53,000	110,000
PP&E, net of depreciation	225,000	205,000
Liabilities	35,000	(35,000)
Total Fair Value		$ 315,000

Figure 13-1: Determination of goodwill.

What if the opposite happens and the selling price is less than the fair value of net assets? Well, there's no such thing as negative goodwill. The purchaser records the difference as a gain. For example, if net assets are $150,000 and the purchase price is $100,000, record a gain on the purchaser's books for $50,000.

Valuing Intangibles

Companies use historic cost to value intangibles they purchase from another company. If cash isn't the payment method *du jour*, the cost of the intangible is the fair value of the noncash payment or the fair value of the intangible the company receives — whichever cost is more clearly evident.

However, as with PP&E, the cost of intangible assets eventually has to move from the balance sheet to the income statement. You accomplish this through amortization and impairment.

The treatment of purchased intangibles when cash doesn't change hands is pretty much the same as the treatment of tangible assets in the same circumstance. You probably don't need to go into this area for your intermediate accounting class, but curious minds can look for more in the section of Chapter 11 called "Valuing PP&E."

Writing off intangibles with amortization

Amortization mimics depreciation (see Chapter 12) because you use it to move the cost of intangible assets from the balance sheet to the income statement. Most intangibles are amortized on a straight-line basis using their expected useful life.

Intangible assets have either a limited life or an indefinite life. *Limited* means the intangible asset won't be useful forever. For example, the U.S. government grants patent protection for a period of 20 years. Unless the patent has become obsolete, that term is probably the expected useful life the business uses.

Indefinite means no factors affect how long the intangible asset will provide use to the company. You don't amortize indefinite life intangible assets.

To eventually move the cost off the balance sheet, test indefinite life intangibles at least annually for *impairment,* which means the carrying cost of the intangible is no longer recoverable. I discuss this topic in the next section of this chapter, "Impairing intangible assets."

The second class of intangibles, goodwill, is never amortized. Financial accountants test it yearly for impairment, which means they see whether any worthless goodwill needs to be written off.

To bring this all home, consider a common intermediate accounting homework assignment involving amortization. Here are your facts and circumstances for this assignment:

On October 1, 2012, Green Inc. purchases a patent from an inventor for $18,000. Green reckons the patent has a useful life of 10 years. Figure 13-2 shows how to account for this transaction and amortization expense on December 31, 2012.

Figure 13-2:
Journalizing purchase and amortization of a patent.

October 1, 2012:

| Patent | 18,000 | |
| Cash | | 18,000 |

To record cash purchase of patent

December 31, 2012:

| Amortization expense | 450 | |
| Patent | | 450 |

To record 3 months of amortization expense [($18,000/10 years) X 3/12]

Figure 13-3 shows a typical balance sheet intangible section. This section normally shows up on the balance sheet after PP&E. See Chapter 6 for more info about the balance sheet.

Intangible assets (shown net of amortization)

Figure 13-3:
Intangible asset section of the balance sheet.

Goodwill of acquired business	60,000	
Patents	27,500	
Trademarks	8,000	
Total intangible assets		35,500

Accumulated amortization is sometimes used. Most companies are permitted to take the credit directly to the intangible asset account.

Impairing intangible assets

An *impairment loss* takes place when a company makes a judgment call that the carrying value of an intangible asset on the company balance sheet is less than *fair value,* or what an unpressured person would pay for the asset in an open marketplace (see Chapter 3). Companies have to periodically test intangible assets to see whether there's potential for any loss due to impairment.

If the impairment loss isn't recoverable, under U.S. GAAP, the company has to adjust the books to reflect this lessening in value. The basic criteria for measuring recoverability centers on whether the asset's carrying value is recoverable from its undiscounted cash flows. If it isn't recoverable, the fair value test is used to compare the intangible asset's fair value to its carrying amount, to measure impairment.

 U.S. GAAP in Accounting Standards Codification (ASC) 360-10-35 gives financial accountants guidance on the types of events and circumstances to look for in determining whether assets have to be evaluated for recovery. For more information, see Chapter 12, which gives you the straight skinny on circumstances that might lead to impairment.

But remember, intangibles can be limited life, indefinite life, or goodwill. Each is impaired differently. Table 13-1 is a handy impairment test summary.

Table 13-1	Impairment Test Summary
Type of Intangible Asset	*Impairment Test*
Limited life	Perform the recovery test.
	If lacking recovery, test fair value. If fair value exceeds carrying amount, no further action is needed.
	Otherwise, record impairment loss for the difference between fair value and carrying value.
Indefinite life (except goodwill)	Test fair value. If fair value exceeds carrying amount, no further action is needed.
	Otherwise, record impairment loss for the difference between fair value and carrying value.
Goodwill	Test fair value. If fair value exceeds carrying amount, no further action is needed.
	Otherwise, compare fair value of goodwill to carrying value of goodwill. If fair value exceeds carrying amount, no further action is needed.
	Otherwise, record impairment loss.

Handling the Costs of Research and Development (R&D)

For accounting, *research expenses* are ones the company incurs in the discovery of new knowledge, with the hope that such knowledge will be useful in developing a new product or service. Businesses incur *development expenses* when applying research results to the design for the new product or service.

You probably think of drug companies when pondering R&D, since the process to develop, test, secure regulatory approval, and bring a drug to market are the classic R&D-related phases. However, R&D costs run rampant through U.S. corporations. Look at the income statement (see Chapter 5) of many publicly held corporations, and you'll most likely see R&D.

Identifying R&D

This topic may seem to be a no-brainer — and it is, as long as you remember the unique qualities that set R&D apart from other expenses. The major one is that R&D expenses don't include routine or periodic tweaking to existing services or products.

To qualify as research expense, the cost happens while seeking new knowledge — that is, where the outcome isn't certain. For example, a drug company may think that a certain combination of chemicals will cure the common cold, but until testing is complete, the outcome remains uncertain.

Do your homework: What isn't R&D

Here's your quick-and-dirty guide to expenses that you may think qualify as R&D but don't:

Start-up costs, which companies incur to organize a new business. They occur before the company opens its doors for business.

Initial year's operating losses that show up on the income statement.

Advertising costs, which are part of selling or marketing expense, not R&D, even if the advertising is for the new and improved process.

Computer software development, which is one of the industries that has specialized GAAP.

Development costs include those related to the design of new products or processes. A good example is the fabrication of a *prototype,* which is a mockup of an actual product to see if it works as expected.

Valuing R&D

Getting R&D on the books is pretty simple — companies have to expense all research and development at cost. Still, you need to be on the lookout for two special circumstances:

1. If the company reckons that it can reuse material or PP&E for another R&D or non-R&D project in the future, those specific costs should be capitalized.

2. Purchased intangible assets that a company uses for R&D go on the books at fair value, not cost.

Differing from GAAP, International Financial Reporting Standards (IFRS) require that some development costs be capitalized rather than expensed.

Part IV
Analyzing Debt and Equity

The 5th Wave   By Rich Tennant

"I'm not familiar with accounting terms. What do you think that means?"

In this part . . .

A company's balance sheet contains various asset, liability, and equity accounts. Part III discusses assets. In this part, you get into the other two pieces of the balance sheet pie: liabilities and equity. For your reading pleasure, this part of the book further breaks liabilities into current and noncurrent, giving each its own chapter.

Chapter 14 is all about the short-term claims payable by the company, or debts; in accountant-speak, they're *liabilities*. Current liabilities are one the company reckons it will pay within 12 months and help a business manage its day-to day operations.

Businesses use long-term debt obligations, such as mortgages and bonds, to acquire assets. Chapter 15 discusses accounting for long-term obligations under various debt scenarios. This chapter also gives you the lowdown on bonds payable, including ones a company issues at face, discount, and premium.

Finally, Chapter 16 discusses the equity section of the balance sheet, which shows the combined total of each owner's investment in the business. You read about corporate equity, represented by stock and additional paid-in capital. I also explain the difference in common, preferred, and treasury stock. You also find out about dividends and how to figure earnings per share, both simple and complex.

Chapter 14

Tracking Current Liabilities and Contingencies

. . . .

In This Chapter

▶ Understanding how a company raises cash

▶ Identifying current liabilities

▶ Discovering short-term debt

▶ Knowing when gain and loss contingencies are reportable

▶ Walking through the current liability section of the balance sheet

. . . .

*N*obody likes debt, but it's often an inevitable part of a company keeping its doors open for business. In this chapter, I cover current debt such as *accounts payable,* which is money a company owes its vendors for goods or services rendered. I also walk you through many other items of current liabilities that are necessary for the day-to-day operations of nearly any business.

You also read about gain and loss contingencies, events in the life of a business that haven't yet happened and may never end up happening. Because they're not always reportable items on financial statements, this chapter gives you the lowdown on when and how to include them.

Wondering about long-term debt? Check out Chapter 15. Because some aspects of current liability can also show up as noncurrent, I tie together these two chapters as need be so you understand the total picture of liabilities.

Getting Up to Speed with Current Liabilities

Liabilities are claims against the company by other businesses. *Current liabilities* are liabilities the company expects to satisfy within one year of the balance sheet date.

Examples of current liabilities are accounts payable and any other short-term debt, such as notes payable due within 12 months of the balance sheet date, dividends declared but not yet paid out to shareholders, and unearned *revenues* (which occur when a client pays the business for goods or services he hasn't yet received, like paying for an airline ticket for a future flight).

All or a portion of unearned revenues can also be noncurrent debt. It all depends on when the company anticipates being able to complete the customer order.

The rest of this section goes over all the other current liabilities you encounter in your intermediate accounting textbook. To make you a current liability star, I also provide typical journal entries you'll see in your homework assignments or on course tests.

Ready to get started? First up, accounts payable. In conjunction with accounts receivable (which is money customers owe the business — more on that in Chapter 9), accounts payable form the foundation for accrual accounting.

It's important to break out current liabilities from long-term liabilities so the user of the financial statements can easily use the reports to compute liquidity and solvency figures such as working capital (current assets minus current liabilities) or the current ratio (current assets divided by current liabilities).

These ratios and others (see Chapter 22) that give the user specific criteria for deciding how well the company is performing would lack usefulness if current and noncurrent items aren't broken out into separate categories.

Understanding accounts payable (A/P)

Accounts payable includes money a company owes it vendors for services and products that it has purchased in the normal course of business and anticipates paying back in the short term.

For example, the company may purchase inventory from a manufacturer or may buy office supplies from a local supply retail shop.

The terms *accounts payable* and *trade payables* are often used interchangeably. However, technically, trade payables generally refer to vendors from which a company buys business supplies and direct materials included in inventory (see Chapter 10). Accounts payable include all other short-term vendors.

On the flip side of sales discounts (see Chapter 9), many vendors selling on credit give a purchase discount to customers who pay their balance due early. For example, the terms of the purchase may call for full payment in 30 days but offer a discount of 2 percent if the customer pays the bill within 10 days. Your intermediate accounting textbook refers to this type of arrangement as 2/10, n/30.

Figure 14-1 walks you through the debiting and crediting for $3,000 of inventory purchased on account with discount terms of 2/10, n/30, and the subsequent payment.

Per GAAP, accounts payable (A/P) is always assumed to be a current liability. However, a transaction originally entered as A/P could eventually be reclassified as a long-term debt.

This situation may arise if the company can't pay the vendor and the vendor agrees to reclassify the short-term A/P to a long-term note (see Chapter 15).

To record November 15, 2013, purchase

Debit Inventory	3,000	
Credit Accounts payable		3,000

Figure 14-1: Inventory purchase on account and payment within discount period.

To record November 24, 2013, payment

Debit Accounts payable	3,000	
Credit Cash		2,940
Credit Purchase Discounts		60

Getting down to business with notes payable (N/P)

Transactions originally booking as A/P could eventually be reclassified as a short-term note payable. This situation may happen if the company can't pay the vendor and the vendor wants to formalize this open account via a *note payable,* which is a formal document showing an amount owed and a mutually acceptable interest rate and payback period. Notes payable showing up as current liabilities will be paid back within 12 months.

Vendors can issue notes that are interest or zero-interest bearing. If the note is interest bearing, the journal entries are easy-peasy.

For example, on November 1, 2013, Big Time Bank loans Green Inc. $50,000 for five months at 6 percent interest. Green Inc. records this short-term note by debiting cash and crediting short-term notes payable for $50,000.

When preparing the financial statements as of November 30, 2013, Green Inc. makes an adjusting journal entry (see Chapter 4) to record one month of interest in the amount of $250 ([$50,000 \times .06] \times \frac{1}{12}$).

You use $\frac{1}{12}$ because you're figuring interest for one month and there are 12 months in the year. Debit interest expense and credit interest payable for $250.

If the note is zero-interest bearing, the present value tables (discussed in Chapter 8) have to come into play. Without going into all the oohs and aahs of working it out with the present value tables (it isn't a tested objective for the current liability section of your intermediate accounting class), for this chapter, just assume that, using the appropriate present value factor, the discount on the note payable is $1,250.

To get this transaction on the books, debit cash for $50,000 and discount on notes payable for $1,250. The total amount of the short-term note payable is $51,250 ($50,000 + $1,250).

The discount on a zero-interest note payable shows the cost to the debtor of borrowing the money.

Accounting for the current portion of long-term debt

Remember back in the beginning of this chapter when I told you that, under GAAP, current and long-term liabilities have to show up separately on the balance sheet? Well, the same rule holds true for the *current portion of long-term debt,* which is due on demand or is due on demand within 12 months of the balance sheet date.

For example, if a company signs a 25-year mortgage in exchange for land and building and it's year five of the mortgage, the principal amount the company owes in the next 12 months goes on the balance sheet as a current liability. The rest of the mortgage payable is a long-term liability, a subject I discuss in Chapter 15.

Paying dividends

Dividends are distributions of company earnings to its shareholders. They can be cash or noncash (see Chapter 16). If a company declares a cash dividend on common stock, there's no messing around. These dividends have to be paid within one year, although normally they are paid in the much shorter term. Therefore, dividends payable are a current liability.

Returning advances and deposits

The cornerstone of revenue recognition under GAAP is the fact that you record revenue when it's earned and realizable. Deposits and advances in the world of business are slightly different — although the glue that ties the two events together is that these monies a company receives from the customer aren't earned.

Deposits are funds a company secures from its customers as a future guarantee against nonpayment or other type of damages. A typical personal example is a security deposit you pay to the landlord when leasing your college pad.

Advances are money a company receives from a customer before providing the agreed-upon goods or services. Businesses ask for advances in many different types of circumstances. A common reason is if special or expensive material has to be special-ordered for a job.

Because neither a deposit nor an advance is earned at point of receipt, you can't record it on the income statement as revenue or gain. So what does that leave you to do with the money?

Well, it's probably not a big mystery, as this chapter focuses on current liabilities. Yep, that's right — customer deposits or advances go on the books as a debit to cash and a credit to the deposit/advance current liability account.

Although deposits and advances are a topic for this chapter on current liabilities, they can classify as noncurrent if the time between the payment and the conclusion of the relationship is more than twelve months past the balance sheet date.

Earning revenue

It's just the nature of the beast that many businesses receive advance payments from customers under circumstances that aren't deposits or your typical "customer advance." Typical examples you see in accounting textbooks are for magazine subscriptions or season tickets to sporting events.

Unearned revenue takes place anytime a business enters into a relationship with a customer and the fulfillment of the customer/vendor contract is spread out over time. Magazine subscriptions are a popular example of this (un)earning revenue situation, so here you walk through how to handle a typical transaction.

Imagine that you pay $48 for an annual subscription, consisting of 12 issues, to your favorite magazine. Until the magazine publisher mails the 12th issue to you, your payment isn't 100 percent earned revenue for the publisher.

The publisher debits cash and credits unearned revenue for your payment of $48. Then each month after the publisher mails you an issue, it records earning that portion by debiting unearned revenue and crediting gross sales for $4 ($48 ÷ 12).

To record revenue, it has to be earned and realizable. Because the customer has already paid, the realizable part is a wrap. However, in the example given on this page, it's not yet earned.

Up, up, and away — but first, you have to pay!

With rare exceptions, I've never purchased an airline ticket so close to the date of travel that my bag is already packed. So to spice up this conversation about unearned revenues, ever wonder how the airlines account for tickets you purchase months in advance or what happens to tickets travelers purchase and subsequently don't use?

Well, there's a GAAP for that! Under GAAP, airlines have to account for flights paid for in advance as unearned revenue until the subject of the ticket is *uplifted* — that is, when the customer completes the flight as booked.

If a passenger fails to use a nonrefundable ticket, airlines can consider the revenue earned for the unused ticket the next day.

Similarly, exchangeable tickets that aren't used within a certain time period set by the airlines are moved from the balance sheet unearned revenue account to the income statement as gross receipts.

To figure a reasonable time period, the airline looks to historic data reflecting how long in the past it took passengers to reticket their exchangeable flights. This time period is normally between 6 and 24 months, depending on the airlines and their past experience.

Paying sales and income tax

Sales tax collected from customers and income tax payable are both short-term liabilities. The governmental regulatory agencies overseeing both keep a pretty tight leash on how long companies can take before remitting the taxes.

Sales tax

In most instances, companies have to collect sales tax only from the end user of the good or service. For example, when manufacturer Toaster Plus sells a bunch of toasters to retailer Best Brands Inc. for the purpose of resale to people like you, Toaster Plus doesn't assess or collect sales tax from Best Brands. Best Brands isn't the end user — you are.

Now, the sales tax a business collects isn't — *ching, ching* — a money machine because the company is only briefly holding these collected funds until it remits them to the proper state taxing authority. Normally, that tax authority is the state Department of Revenue.

The Department of Revenue doesn't want the retailer to have its grubby mitts on sales tax collected, which is revenue to the state, for any longer than state statutes allow. And the statutory timeline for remitting sales tax collections is pretty darn short.

So for the brief period of time between when customers remit the sales tax to the retailer and when the retailer remits the sales tax to the Department of Revenue, this money sits on the books as a current liability.

What throws a small monkey into this wrench is how retailers account for their sales tax collections. The logical way to do it is to record the sales revenue and sales tax payable separately.

Suppose you go into Best Brands to purchase that toaster for $35. Sales tax is 6 percent. You swipe you debit card, paying Best Brands a total of $37.10 ($35 for the toaster and $2.10 sales tax). Ignoring the inventory and cost of goods sold effect, Best Brands records this transaction as an increase to cash for $37.10, sales revenue of $35, and sales tax payable of $2.10.

A smaller retailer may consider this to be too much work, so it just takes the whole shebang to sales revenue. Periodically, it figures out how much it owes in sales tax and adjusts both the revenue and sales tax payable accounts.

For example, Mom and Pop Appliances has merchandise sales of $5,000 during the first half of November. On November 16, Mom wants to figure out how much sales tax the company owes to the Department of Revenue. Quick and dirty, if sales tax is 6 percent, she divides the $5,000 sales revenue figure by 1.06 to calculate sales revenue of $4,716.98.

Mom books a journal entry to move sales tax out of revenue in the amount of $283.02 ($5,000 – $4,716.98). To accomplish this, sales revenue is debited and sales tax payable is credited for the $283.02.

You may be surprised by the number of retailers who get themselves into hot water by using sales tax collections to pay operating expenses. I've seen this in action while conducting financial statement audits — the company always thinks it will be able to pay back the money. Sadly most companies that start doing this never catch up and eventually are subject to hefty fines by the applicable Department of Revenue.

Income tax

Income tax is a pretty crucial intermediate accounting topic. Therefore, I devote an entire chapter in this book to its accounting: Chapter 17. For this chapter about short-term liabilities, just remember that income taxes payable, be they local, state, or federal, record on the balance sheet as short-term liabilities.

Taking care of employees

It's the nature of the beast that most companies will have *accrued* payroll and related payroll taxes. In other words, a company owes these taxes but has not yet paid them. This topic is easy to understand if you think about the way you've been paid by an employer in the past.

Most companies have a built-in lag time between when employees earn their wages and when the paychecks are cut. For example, Green Inc. pays its employees on the 1st and 15th of every month, with 15 days of wages in arrears. This means that when the employees get their paycheck on July 15, it's for work they did from June 16 through June 30.

So to match expenses to revenue when preparing financial statements for the one-month period ending June 30, the gross wages earned but not yet paid as of June 30 have to be added to the balance sheet as a current liability.

In addition, you have to add any payroll taxes or benefits that will be deducted from the employee's paycheck when the check is finally cut.

The following are examples of employee payroll–related accruals:

- ✔ **Federal Insurance Contributions Act (FICA):** The Social Security portion of this tax provides old age, survivor, and disability benefits.

    For decades, the FICA rate was 6.2 percent on wages up to a certain wage base dollar amount. The Medicare portion had no base wage limit with a tax rate of 1.45 percent. Together, the rate is 7.65 percent for employees and a 7.65 percent match for the employer's portion.

    However, legislation subsequent to publication can always affect any type of payroll tax rates. Your intermediate accounting professor will have the current info should your contemporaneous rates not be the same as above.

- ✔ **Federal withholding tax:** The company calculates this tax using Circular E, based on the marital status and exemptions the employee lists on form W-4.

- ✔ **State and local withholding tax:** The business also deducts any tax for state or local jurisdictions that mandate tax collection.

- ✔ **Healthcare or other insurance premiums:** An employer may pay only a portion or all of the health insurance premium for employees and their family. The additional amount for health and other insurance, such as life insurance, is a deduction as well if the employee authorizes it.

✔ **401(k) and other retirement deductions:** Many employers have plans that allow employees to make benefit deductions on pretax dollars. *Pretax* means the deduction is made before the employee is assessed federal withholding tax, or FICA. So if your gross wage is $500 and you have $100 in pretax deductions, you pay tax on $400.

The employer business also has payroll tax expense based on the employees' gross wages. These items are recorded as short-term liabilities as well:

✔ **FICA:** The employer is obligated to match each employee's contribution dollar for dollar.

✔ **State Unemployment Tax Act (SUTA):** This tax percentage varies based on employers' unemployment claim experience, as well as each state's rates. There is a statutory taxable wage limit that varies by state.

✔ **Federal Unemployment Tax Act (FUTA):** The employer pays FUTA tax at 6.2 percent of the first $7,000 of wages each year. (A credit up to 5.4 percent is given to companies subject to and current on their SUTA payments). In times of catastrophic unemployment, FUTA kicks in to pay unemployment claims after SUTA is exhausted.

✔ **Employer benefits:** Additionally, the employer has an expense for the company portion of healthcare, 401(k) match, and any other benefit programs the company provides.

So that you can better understand this class of current liabilities, here's a typical payroll and payroll tax accrual question. It's quite similar to the questions in your financial accounting textbook:

Green Inc. owes its employees gross wages of $75,000. Employee FICA tax on this amount is $5,737.50, and employees have opted to have income tax withholdings of $3,680.

They also have health insurance for $3,000 and retirement contributions for $4,500 withheld from their paychecks. Total deductions are $16,917.50. Net payroll is the difference between the gross of $75,000 and the deductions of $16,917.50, which equals $58,082.50.

After a company runs payroll, how does it record gross wages, tax, and other deductions made from the employees' checks as short-term liabilities? Additionally, how does it record the related payroll tax expense?

Given in this example is the fact that federal unemployment tax totals $100 and state unemployment tax totals $465. The employer has no employer benefit expense.

Wondering how to answer this question via journal entries? I show you how in Figure 14-2.

Wages Expense	75,000.00	
Wages Payable (net)		58,082.50
FICA Tax Withheld (employee)		5,737.50
Income Taxes Withheld		3,680.00
Health Insurance		3,000.00
Retirement Contributions		4,500.00
To record accrued payroll		

Figure 14-2:
Journal
entry to
record
accrued
payroll and
taxes.

Payroll Tax Expense	6,302.50	
FICA Tax Withheld (employer match)		5,737.50
Federal Unemployment Taxes		100.00
State Unemployment Taxes		465.00
To record accrued payroll taxes		

Planning for Future Events

Other liabilities show up on the balance sheet to account for *loss contingencies,* which are liabilities that may crop up in the future. Some examples of contingencies are lawsuits that are still in litigation; *estimated warranties,* which reflect how much money a company may have to pay to repair or replace products sold to customers; and debt guarantees. To add more excitement to the mix, this chapter also discusses obligations that may exist for environmental asset retirements.

Ready to know the future? First, it's important to understand why gain contingencies pop up in a chapter about liabilities!

Contingencies are generally noncurrent liabilities. However, most intermediate accounting textbooks include them with current liabilities, so I follow the same treatment for this book.

Understanding Contingencies

Contingencies exist when a company has an existing circumstance as of the date of the financial statements that may cause a gain or loss in the future, depending on events that haven't yet happened and, indeed, may never happen. You just can't take a quick look into the crystal ball to decide what contingencies to book and for how much.

It seems somewhat of an oxymoron to discuss gains in a chapter about liabilities. Most intermediate accounting textbooks throw in a quick discussion about gain contingencies right before discussing loss contingencies, so I mimic them.

Gain contingencies

When you realize that some gain contingencies reduce liabilities, it makes more sense to include the info in a chapter about current liabilities. If you understand just the basic concept of these four gain contingencies, you'll ace any test question on the subject:

- ✔ Possible future sources of cash from the sale of assets or other sources, such as gifts.

- ✔ Ongoing tax examination that may result in adjustments in the company's favor, resulting in a tax refund. Woo-hoo!

- ✔ Ongoing litigation that may result in cash awards in the company's favor.

- ✔ Future tax loss carryforwards that may reduce income tax payable in the future. (See Chapter 17 for more information.)

A conservative approach to gain contingencies is the key. Except for tax loss carryforwards, companies don't record gain contingencies. They disclose them (see Chapter 21) only if there's a high possibility that they will indeed come to fruition.

Loss contingencies

Loss contingencies hinge on situations that may cost the company money in the future. However, keep in mind that these events haven't yet happened and, indeed, may never happen.

Let's get crackin' on these contingencies. First up, discussing legal woes.

Is this thing on? Recording contingent liabilities

You typically record contingent liabilities in the footnotes to the financial statement (see Chapter 21) instead of as an actual part of the financial statements. However, if a loss due to a contingent liability meets two criteria, it needs to be accrued as part of the company's financial statement.

These two criteria must be met for this accrual to take place:

The possibility of the loss event happening must be *probable*, which means that the future event will likely occur. Taking the guarantee of obligation example from earlier, if the debtor business has gone out of business and the owners have disappeared into the night, it is indeed probable that the lender will come after the back-up guarantor to pay off the remaining amount of the loan.

The amount of the loss can be *reasonably estimated*, which means you can come up with a highly accurate loss dollar amount. In the previous example, the loss is reasonably estimated because it should be the remaining balance on the loan plus any additional charges the lender tacked on in accordance with the obligatory note.

If the loss contingency meets these two standards for accrual, the journal entry involves a debit to a relevant loss account and a credit to a liability account. For example, the company could take the debit to loss on guaranteed debt and a credit to some sort of noncurrent liability account, such as amount due on guaranteed obligations.

Litigation

Litigation occurs when the company either is actively involved in a lawsuit that it hasn't yet settled or knows that a filing of legal action against the company is imminent, a common type of contingent liability. Most publicly traded companies have at least a few litigation disclosures in their footnotes to the financial statements (see Chapter 21).

You'll almost never see a legal contingent liability show up on the balance sheet. Until the jury returns with a judgment and award, companies can seldom predict the outcome of litigation with enough certainty to meet the criteria for booking the accrual.

Here's a typical disclosure of pending litigation:

"On October 31, 2012, shareholders filed a class action complaint against the Company in the U.S. District Court. At this time, it's not possible to predict the potential financial impact on the Company of an adverse action."

Guarantees

This situation occurs if a company guarantees the obligation of another. For example, you might have someone with more established credit co-sign on your first auto loan.

If you don't make the payments, the lender expects the cosigner to step up to the plate — ruining her credit if she doesn't (this is the stuff of Judge Judy!).

This topic is more of an advanced financial accounting topic. For your intermediate accounting class, just remember that, in some instances, the fair value (see Chapter 3) of the guarantee is recorded as a current liability.

Warranties

As a consumer, you're probably very familiar with product *warranties.* They cover repairs or replacement if a product fails to work within a certain period of time. Based on what you bought, the warranty may be either an assumed part of the purchase price or something you elect to buy, usually at the time of purchase.

To bring this point home, I discuss a common business warranty situation and show you how to account for it under the *expense warranty approach,* which estimates warranty cost using prior experience.

My second example talks about the sales warranty approach, which covers extended warranties, an add-on cost to the purchase.

Expense warranty approach

A great example for the expense warranty approach is the guarantee of performance relating to the purchase of tractors from the manufacturer.

Farmer John's Tractors issues a six-month warranty covering numerous performance and repair issues. Assume that if the tractor breaks down within the six-month warranty period, the purchaser can send it back to be fixed, free of charge. In addition to disclosures the company has to make in footnotes to the financial statements (see Chapter 21), Farmer John's has to figure and book an estimate of how much it costs to fulfill the terms of the warranty.

A popular way to estimate warranty expense is to use a percentage of sales. This percentage is normally figured historically. If in the past the company incurred an actual warranty expense of 3 percent, until the facts change, 3 percent is the estimate.

In January, Farmer John's sells $500,000 of tractors. Historical warranty expense is 3 percent of sales. So the estimated warranty liability is $15,000 ($500,000 × 3%). Also during January, Farmer John's has actual expenses of

$5,000 for labor and $2,500 for materials to fulfill warranty claims (total of $7,500). Keep in mind that the $7,500 doesn't include only warranty costs for September purchases, but includes purchases going back six months as well.

Ready to see how to journalize the warranty transactions? Figure 14-3 gives you the lowdown on the entry to book the estimate and record actual warranty expenses.

Warranty Expense	15,000.00	
Estimated Warranty Liability		15,000.00

Figure 14-3:
Recording
accrued
and actual
warranty
expenses.

To record estimated warranty expense for January

Estimated Warranty Liability	7,500.00	
Labor Expense		5,000.00
Materials Expense		2,500.00

To record estimated warranty expense for January

Sales warranty approach

Every time you buy a computer, flat-screen television, or some other type of appliance, you know it's coming — the dreaded extended warranty pitch!

Any additional warranty a customer purchases is recorded in the books by crediting cash and debiting unearned warranty revenue. Then the warranty is written off using the straight-line method.

For example, let's say that Farmer John's also sells heavy-duty trucks to haul the tractors around on a flatbed. The trucks come with a four-year or 48,000-mile (whichever comes first) standard warranty. Farmer John's also offers customers an extended warranty that protects the buyer for an additional three years or 24,000 miles for $1,800.

Assume that a customer buys the extended warranty on January 2, 2012, and, as of December 31, 2016, Farmer John hasn't had to perform on the extended warranty. Figure 14-4 shows how to account for this transaction.

Figure 14-4:
Recording
sales
warranty
transac-
tions.

2012: year of purchase:

Cash	1,800	
Unearned warranty reserve		1,800

December 31, 2016

Unearned warranty revenue	600	
Warranty revenue		600

2016 warranty revenue at $1,800/3 years

Environmental issues and asset retirements

In certain instances, companies have to report a liability when they have a future cost (obligation) associated with its retirement. Most intermediate accounting textbooks mention the following four types of assets that are environment issues: closing landfills, decommissioning nuclear plants, closing down oil and gas wells, and closing down mines.

Each type of "dirty" asset has different costs associated with its retirement. This topic isn't one for an intermediate accounting class. You just need to know how to handle the related costs (which are given to you as part of any homework assignment or test question on this subject).

Normally, this equation has two components: interest expense and the discounted fair value of the obligation. I discuss fair value in Chapter 3 and present value tables in Chapter 8, so take a walk over to those chapters if you want to brush up on these topics.

You just need to know how to handle the related costs (which are given to you as part of any homework assignment or test question on this subject).

Suppose that Expert Drilling erects an oil platform on January 1, 2013, with an estimated useful life of ten years. The cost to dismantle the platform is estimated at $650,000, the present value of the asset retirement obligation (ARO) is $450,000, and interest expense for 2013 is $12,500.

Figure 14-5 shows you how to account for the platform and the obligation in 2013.

January 1, 2013

Oil platform	450,000	
Asset retirement obligation		450,000

December 31, 2013

Depreciation expense	45,000	
Accumulated depreciation		45,000

Figure 14-5: $450,000 ARO divided by 10 years estimated useful life = $45,000
Recording
oil platform
and ARO.

Interest expense	12,500	
Asset retirement obligation		12,500

Finally, at the end of its useful life, it actually costs $675,000 to dismantle the platform. This figure goes on the books as a debit to asset retirement obligation for $650,000 and a debit to loss on ARO for $25,000 ($675,000 – $650,000). The credit goes to cash for the cost of $675,000.

Chapter 15

Planning for Long-Term Obligations

. . . .

In This Chapter

▶ Discovering how a company raises cash

▶ Identifying long-term liabilities

▶ Accounting for notes payable

▶ Reporting gain or loss on debt extinguishment

▶ Accounting for bonds

. . . .

*I*f you own a car you financed, you're probably all too familiar with *long-term debt:* loans that won't be paid off by the end of the next 12-month period. Well, companies have long-term debt, too. A company usually uses current debt as a vehicle to meet short-term obligations like payroll and incurs long-term debt to finance company assets.

In this chapter, I give you the lowdown on two types of long-term debt: notes and bonds payable. *Notes payable* are debt a company takes on mostly through lending institutions such as banks to finance asset purchases – like a car or building. *Bonds payable* are typically issued by hospitals and munici-palities to fund expansion (although corporations can issue them too).

This chapter walks you through the facets of this complicated topic, to pre-pare you to tackle your intermediate accounting homework assignments and tests.

Managing Long-Term Debt

It's an immutable fact of running a business that at one point or another the company will have to take on long-term debt to keep their business a going concern. After all, unless the business owner is just running the business for fun — they will want to increase operations in the hopes of making more money.

Just like when you financed a vehicle or home purchase, how you structure the long-term debt affects the expense of borrowing the money. After all, didn't you shop around for interest rates and evaluate the wisdom of financing the loan for a certain number of years over another?

Well, businesses are the same way, only ramped up, as they can carry millions of dollars of debt on their balance sheet. So, managing the debt service is crucially important as minute differences in terms can have a large effect interest-wise on the bottom line.

If the company needs to raise cash to purchase assets, expand existing operations, or maybe even buy another company and decides to do so by accumulating long-term debt, they evaluate the relative merits of available forms of long-term debt. The most common types of long-term debt are mortgages, notes payable, and bonds payable. The next few sections discuss mortgages and notes payable. I get into bonds payable in the "Accounting for Bonds, James Bonds" section, later in this chapter.

The many faces of notes payable

Notes payable are formal written documents that spell out how money is being borrowed. This type of agreement between a lender and a borrower specifies *principal* (amount borrowed), *rate* (how much interest the company pays to borrow the money), and *time* (length of the note).

Notes payable are issued in four different ways: face; no-face; no-interest; and no-face, interest. These terms may make lending and borrowing seem like a silly game of peek-a-boo, so take a look at their definitions.

Face

Face is the easiest type of note to account for. With this type of note, the present value of the note payable is the same as its *face,* which is the amount stated on the note. This sameness results because the *effective* interest rate, which is the market interest rate, and the *stated* interest rate (what's printed on the face of the note receivable) are the same.

Market is the interest rate for a note of similar risk. For example, if one company loans another company $5,000 at an effective and stated rate of 10 percent due in three years, the journal entry for the creditor to record issuance of the note is to debit cash and credit notes payable for $5,000. Pretty straightforward, right?

Then each year, the creditor records interest expense at $500 ($5,000 × .10). When the company pays off the debt at the end of the three years, the creditor records a credit to cash and a debit to notes payable for $5,000. Another item of debt bites the dust!

No-face, zero-interest

This type of note payable issues for the present value of the cash the creditor receives from the lender. Chapter 8 talks about the present value of 1 and an annuity of 1, so head there for more on that topic. For now, just keep in mind that the future value of 1 is assumed to be worth more than the present value of 1.

With that caveat in mind, let's say Green Corporation borrows $20,000 from Blue, Inc., with payment due in five years. Green figures that the present value of the $20,000 is $13,612 using an implicit and effective interest rate of 8 percent. The difference between $20,000 and $13,612, or $6,388, is the discount on notes payable. Figure 15-1 shows how to journalize this transaction.

Find the present value of $13,612 by using the present value of 1 table (see Chapter 8). The factor at the intersection of 8 percent and five periods is .6806. And $20,000 × .6806 = $13,612.

Figure 15-1:
Journalizing a zero-rate-interest-bearing note payable.

Cash	13,612	
Discount on notes payable	6,388	
Notes payable		20,000

The discount on notes payable account is a contra liability account. It follows the note payable, amortized over the five-year life. It moves from the balance sheet to the income statement via interest expense using the effective interest method. Figure 15-2 gives you a bird's-eye view on how this works, assuming that the effective interest rate is 8 percent.

Schedule of Discount on Notes Payable Amortization
Effective Interest Method
0% Note Discounted at 8%

	Interest Expense	Discount Amortized	Carrying Amount
Date of Issue			$13,612
End of year 1	$1,089**	$1,089	14,701
End of year 2	1,176	1,176	15,877
End of year 3	1,270	1,270	17,147
End of year 4	1,372	1,372	18,519
End of year 5	1,481	1,481	20,000
	$6,388	$6,388	

Figure 15-2: Discount amortization schedule: zero-rate-interest-bearing note.

** $13,612 × .08 = $1,089. $13,612 + $1,089 = $14,701.

Journalize the first year by debiting interest expense for $1,089 and crediting discounts on notes payable for the same amount. For the second year, debit interest expense for $1,176 and credit discounts on notes payable for the same amount — and so on for the remaining three years.

No-face, interest bearing

Now that you've tackled zero-interest-bearing notes payables, you can dig into interest-bearing ones. Going back to the $20,000 example from the "No-face, zero-interest" section, the note payable has a stated (face) interest rate of 6 percent. At that stated rate, interest is $1,200 per year ($20,000 × .06). Green pays interest to Blue at the end of each year.

You know that the present value of the principal is $13,612. However, you also need to figure out the present value of the interest portion of the note. Use the present value of an annuity of 1 table for the interest because it is a series of payments.

The factor at the intersection of 8 percent and 5 years in the present value of an annuity of 1 table is 3.9927. The present value of the interest is $4,791 ($1,200 × 3.9927). Add the two present value figures to get the carrying value of the note, which is $18,403 ($13,612 + $4,791). Subtract $18,403 from the face value of the note receivable to get the discount of $1,597 ($20,000 – $18,403).

Figure 15-3 shows how to journalize this transaction and Figure 15-4 gives you the lowdown on the amortization table used to prepare the journal entry.

To record the creditor's interest payment at the end of each year, journalize the first year by crediting discounts on notes payable for $272 and debiting interest expense for $1,472. The credit goes to cash for $1,200. For the second year, you credit discounts on notes payable for $294, debit interest expenses for $1,494, and credit cash for $1,200 — and so on for the remaining three years.

Figure 15-3:
Recording discounted note payable.

Cash	18,403	
Discount on notes payable	1,597	
Note payable		20,000

Note Payable Discount Amortization
Effective-Interest Method
6% Note Discounted at 8%

	Cash	Interest Revenue	Discount Amortized	Carrying Amount
Date of Issue				$18,403
End of year 1	$1,200	$1,472**	$272	18,675
End of year 2	1,200	1,494	294	18,969
End of year 3	1,200	1,518	318	19,287
End of year 4	1,200	1,543	343	19,630
End of year 5	1,200	1,570	370	20,000
	$6,000	$7,597	$1,597	

Figure 15-4:
Discount amortization schedule: interest bearing note payable.

** $18,403 × .08 = $1,472. $1,472 − $1,200 = 272. $18,403 + $272 = $18,675.

Walking through non-cash notes

Sometimes companies exchange notes for value other than cash. In that case, use the stated interest rate unless one of these three circumstances exists: 1) there is no stated interest rate; 2) the stated interest rate is unreasonable — for example, not in line with what's fair for the marketplace; or 3) the face amount of the note differs materially from the cash price of the property/good/service.

If one of these is present, use the fair market value of the property, goods, or service subject to the note transaction to approximate the present value of the note receivable.

Discussing mortgages payable

The most common type of note payable is a *mortgage*, which is used to finance the purchase of real property assets such as land and building. The property *collateralizes* the mortgage, which means the property is held as security on the mortgage. If the company defaults on the mortgage, the lending institution seizes the property and sells it in an attempt to pay off the loan.

Mortgages require a formal closing procedure that's typically done at the offices of a *title company,* an independent middleman that coordinates the rights and obligations during the sale for the buyer, seller, and mortgage company. As in the purchase of a personal residence, reams of paperwork (such as the mortgage document and the transfer of the property's title) are passed back and forth among the buyer, seller, and closing agent for approval and signature.

Another type of long-term debt involves capitalized leases. A company doesn't always buy its fixed assets — sometimes it leases them (more on fixed assets in Chapter 11). In this scenario, the lessee, the person leasing the property, records the capital lease as both a leased asset and a leased liability. Read more about accounting for leases in Chapter 18.

Treasury bonds defined

I find that students always need a quick refresher at this point in their intermediate accounting class to tie in Treasury bonds to regular bonds. Sometimes they get confused and think that Treasury bonds are debt that somehow relate to treasury stock. Not true. (However, if you're hankering for some treasury stock information, hop on over to Chapter 16.)

Treasury bonds are debt the government of the United States issues to pay for government projects. As with any bond, repayment of principal is accompanied by a fixed (or variable in some new, inflation-proof U.S. bonds) interest rate.

Treasury bonds have nothing to do with *treasury stock,* which is corporate stock the issuing corporation buys back. Make sense? See the "Accounting for Bonds, James Bonds" section later in this chapter to understand how to account for corporate bond debt.

The dark side of debt-free

Finally, that wonderful day comes when the debt is paid off. You may not think of it as a thorny accounting situation — and it isn't, as long as the debt is held to maturity. In other words, there's no problem as long as the debtor doesn't pay it off early.

However, if an event occurs that leads a company to pay off debt (whether a note or a bond) early, the company may have to figure gain or loss on the transaction. The regular amortization journal entries did not zero out any discount or premium on the debt payable.

If the acquisition price is greater than the carrying value of the debt, there's a loss on extinguishment. A gain occurs if the acquisition price is less than the carrying value.

A good example of how gain may occur is the accounting for callable debt, which means the issuer can pay off the debt before the maturity date. In the business world, this scenario happens if the interest rate falls and it's possible to reissue the debt at 6 percent. This situation is often referred to as the debt being callable.

Need an example on the accounting for the early extinguishment of debt? You ask, I deliver!

Imagine that a company repurchases a note payable for $104,000 whose face value was $100,000. It was issued at a discount, of which $3,000 isn't yet amortized at the date of repurchase. Gain or loss on the transaction?

For your answer, see Figure 15-5.

Figure 15-5: Reacquisition price		$ 104,000
Figuring Net carrying amount:		
gain or loss on the early		
extinguish- Face value	$ 100,000	
ment of Unamortized discount	(3,000)	97,000
debt. Loss on debt repurchase		$ 7,000

Remember that a business can remove the debt from its balance sheet only if one of the following occurs:

✔ The debtor pays the creditor and is totally relieved of the obligation. For example, the debt was for $10,000 and the debtor paid the creditor the full $10,000 plus all required interest.

✔ The creditor legally releases the debtor from any further obligation. For example, the creditor agrees to cancel a portion of the debt.

This chapter doesn't discuss troubled debt restructuring, which is an advanced financial accounting topic. This takes place when there are market or legal reasons why terms of the debt are modified. A good example of this when the financial institution lowers the interest rate they are charging the business for the debt. On the personal side, you may have had friends participating in a residential short sale, which means a house is sold for less than the mortgage debt still owed on it with the lender taking a loss on the sale.

Accounting for Bonds, James Bonds

Bonds are long-term lending agreements between a borrower and a lender. For example, when a municipality (such as a city, county, town, or village) needs to build new roads or a hospital, it issues bonds to finance the project. Corporations generally issue bonds to raise money for capital expenditures, operations, and acquisitions.

The selling price of bonds, like publicly traded stock, is normally set by what the market will bear. The issuer of the bond sets the interest rate, which is known as the stated, coupon, face, contract, or nominal rate. All five terms mean the same thing — the interest rate given in the bond indenture.

You can compare a bond indenture to any type of legal financing document that you may have signed to finance a house or car. It describes the key terms of the bond issuance, such as maturity date and interest rate.

The people who purchase a bond receive interest payments during the bond's term (or for as long as they hold the bond) at the bond's stated interest rate. When the bond *matures* (the term of the bond expires), the company pays back the bondholder the bond's face value.

A bond is either a source of financing or an investment, depending on which side of the transaction you're looking at. Because this is a chapter on long-term liabilities, it looks at this transaction from the source of financing viewpoint.

Valuing bonds payable

A company can issue bonds either at *face value* (also known as *par value*), which is the principal amount printed on the bond; at a *discount,* which is less than face value; or at a *premium,* which means the bond sells for more than its face value. Usually face value is set in denominations of $1,000.

You need the present value tables I discuss in Chapter 8 to help in valuing bonds in the real world. Luckily for your intermediate accounting class, the chapter on bonds references the correct table but gives you the factor so you don't have to do the heavy lifting yourself. I follow the same practice for my discussion.

GAAP prefers the effective interest method when accounting for bonds issued at a discount or a premium. When using the *effective interest* method, you amortize using the carrying value of the bonds, which is face plus unamortized premium or minus unamortized discount.

Figuring out the present value of a bond

Quick and dirty, here's your introduction to valuing bonds. A company issues a $100,000 bond due in four years paying 7 percent interest annually at year end. So that's $7,000 interest expense per year ($100,000 × .07).

Market rate for similar bonds is 11 percent. You have to use two tables to figure this one out.

Use the present value of 1 table for the bond face value factor (.65873) and the present value of an annuity for the interest payment factor (3.10245).

The present value of the bond is $65,873 ($100,000 × .65873). The present value of the interest payments is $21,717 ($7,000 × 3.10245).

GAAP allows the straight-line method if the result is materially the same: straight line versus effective. In fact, your financial accounting class may use only the straight-line method in its chapter on bonds. Keep in mind that International Financial Accounting Standards (IFRS) requires use of the effective interest method.

Issuing at par value

This one is the easiest type of bond transaction to account for. The journal entry to record bonds that a company issues at face value is to debit cash and credit bonds payable. So if the corporation issues bonds for $100,000 with a five-year term, at 10 percent, the journal entry to record the bonds is to debit cash for $100,000 and to credit bonds payable for $100,000.

A bond with a face value and market value of $1,000 has a bond price of 100 (no percent sign or dollar sign — just 100). Bonds issued at premium have a bond price of more than 100. Issued at a discount, the bond price is less than 100.

The rate of interest investors actually earn is known as the effective yield or market rate. If the bond sells for a premium (see the section "Recording bonds issued at a premium" later in this chapter), its market rate is lower than the rate stated on the bond. For example, if the face rate of the bond is 10% and the market rate is 9%, the bond sells at a premium.

On the flip side, if a bond sells at a discount (see the section "Accounting for discounted bonds"), its market rate is higher than the rate stated on the bond. For example, if the face rate of the bond is 10 percent and the market rate is 11 percent, the bond sells at a discount.

Payback time!

You may be wondering how to address interest payments. Suppose the terms of the bond call for interest to be paid *semiannually*, which is every six months. Further suppose that the bonds in the example I give in the section "Issuing at par value" are issued on July 1 and the first interest payment isn't due until December 31. The interest expense is principal ($100,000) multiplied by face rate (10%) multiplied by time (½ year). So your journal entry (see Chapter 4 for more information about preparing journal entries) on December 31 is to debit bond interest expense for $5,000 and credit cash for $5,000.

Accounting for discounted bonds

A *bond discount* is relevant when a bond issues at less than face value. Going back to the example earlier in this chapter in the "Figuring out the present value of a bond" sidebar, how do you account for this transaction?

To recap, the bond's face is $100,000, the present value of the bond is $65,873, and the present value of the interest payments is $21,717 (rounded). Figure 15-6 shows how to calculate the discount on bonds payable.

Figure 15-6: Calculating discount on bonds payable.

Maturity value of the bond		$ 100,000
Present value of the $100,000 bond	$ 65,873	
Present value of interest payable	21,717	(87,590)
Discount on bonds payable		$ 12,410

The journal entry to record this transaction is to debit cash for $87,590 and debit discount on bonds payable for $12,410. The credit is to bonds payable for $100,000 ($87,590 + $12,410).

Now, what about the interest expense and amortization of the bond discount? Going back to the facts in the sidebar, this bond pays $7,000 ($100,000 × .07) interest annually at year end. So that's $7,000 interest expense per year. And remember, the effective interest rate is 11 percent.

Figure 15-7 shows the schedule of bond discount amortization for this issuance.

	Cash Paid	Interest Expense	Discount Amortized	Carrying Amount
				$87,590
Year 1	$7,000	$9,635	$2,635	$90,225
Year 2	7,000	9,925	2,925	93,150
Year 3	7,000	10,247	3,247	96,397
Year 4	7,000	10,603	3,603	100,000

Figure 15-7: Bond discount amortization schedule. Figure the interest expense by multiplying the carrying amount of the bond by the effective interest rate of 11% ($87,590 × .11 = $9,635). The discount amortized is the difference between cash paid and interest expense ($9,635 − $7,000 = $2,635).

The journal entry to record Year 1 is to debit interest expense for $9,635. The credits go to discount on bonds payable for $2,635 and cash for $7,000.

Recording bonds issued at a premium

When a bond is issued at a *premium,* its market value is more than its face value. To make the concept come alive for you, consider a common example you will see in your intermediate accounting textbook.

Using the same facts and circumstances from the section "Accounting for discounted bonds," earlier in this chapter, imagine that, for the same $100,000, the investor is willing to accept an effective interest rate of 6 percent. Using the present value tables, the present value of the $100,000 bond is $79,209 ($100,000 × .79209). The present value of the interest payable is $24,256 ($7,000 × 3.46511). Figure 15-8 shows how to calculate the premium on this issuance.

Figure 15-8:
Calculating premium on bonds payable.

Maturity value of the bond		$ 100,000
Present value of the $100,000 bond	$ 79,209	
Present value of interest payable	24,256	(103,465)
Premium on bonds payable		$ 3,465

The journal entry to record this transaction is to debit cash for $103,465. You have two accounts to credit: bonds payable for the face amount of $100,000 and premium on bonds payable for $3,465, which is the difference between face and cash received at issuance.

Similar to the example in Figure 15-7, the premium of $3,465 has to be amortized for the time the bonds are outstanding. Quick and dirty, for Year 1, cash paid is $7,000, interest expense is $6,208 ($103,465 × .06), and the premium amortized is $792 ($7,000 – $6,208). For Year 2, cash paid remains $7,000, interest expense is $6,160 [(103,465 – 792) × .06], and the premium amortized is $840 ($7,000 – $6,160). And so on for Years 3 and 4.

Corporations raise money to purchase assets in one of two ways: debt or equity. This chapter talks about debt. Chapter 16 gives you the lowdown on equity, which means the company sells shares of its own stock to investors.

Convertible bonds

Before you exit this chapter, I want to give you one more tie-in between debt in this chapter and equity in Chapter 16. Convertible bonds (debt) can be converted into common shares of stock (equity) at the option of the owner of the bonds.

The conversion feature makes convertible bonds more attractive to potential investors because it's possible to reap the benefits of the following circumstances: cash-in increases if the amount of dividends regularly being paid to shareholders is higher than the interest earned on the bonds; and the value of the company's common stock increases over the value of the bonds.

Oddly enough, debt can end up making a company money. This is called financial leverage, and it takes place when the borrowed money is expected to earn a higher return than the cost of interest payable on the debt. Additionally, interest expense on debt is a tax deduction, whereas dividends payable to investors are not. Based on many factors that combine advanced financial accounting and finance, the company may also end up in a better position due to the decrease in taxes payable.

Chapter 16

Letting Owners Know Where They Stand: The Equity Section

In This Chapter

▶ Walking through how corporations raise capital

▶ Gaining a view of the incorporation process

▶ Thinking about the different parts of paid-in capital

▶ Understanding how corporations pay their investors

▶ Calculating earnings per share (EPS)

▶ Discussing convertible stock and warrants

*P*art IV of this book is all about debt and equity, which are two ways a company can raise funds for business. Read Chapter 14 for a discussion on current debt, such as accounts payable, and Chapter 15 for the scoop on two types of long-term liabilities: notes and bonds. This chapter talks about equity.

Here we cover the nitty-gritty of how stockholders' interest in a corporation shows up on the balance sheet. This interest reflects in the equity section and in a few different types of accounts. These include additional paid-in capital, retained earnings, and capital stock.

This chapter helps you understand the difference among common, preferred, and treasury stock. It also talks about dividends and how companies account for them, and it includes a discussion on noncash dividend transactions, such as property and stock dividends.

But that's not all — you also get a tutorial on retained earnings, which is the total profit the business has brought in that it hasn't paid out as dividends. To wrap it all up, you walk through the equity section of a balance sheet for a corporation and see how income statement events affect the statement of changes in stockholders' equity. Plus, you get a tutorial on earnings per share.

Recording Stockholder Interest

This chapter is all about equity, which shows the combined total of each and every owner's investment in the business. A company can organize itself as one of three types of entities: sole proprietorship, corporation, or flow-through entity such as a partnership. Your intermediate accounting textbook homes in on the corporation equity accounts. I follow the same treatment in this chapter.

Stockholders' equity represents the claim shareholders of the corporation have to the company's net assets. Stockholders' equity has three common components: paid-in capital, treasury stock, and retained earnings. Paid-in capital and treasury stock involve transactions dealing with the corporate stock issuances. Retained earnings shows income and dividend transactions.

The sole proprietorship has two unique equity accounts: owner's capital and owner withdrawals. The owner's capital accounts show cash and other contributions, such as equipment the owner makes to the business. Owner withdrawals shows money and other assets the owner takes from the business to convert to personal use.

Partnerships mimic sole proprietorships, in that the equity section has capital and withdrawal accounts. Instead of owner capital and owner withdrawals, though, it's partner capital and withdrawals.

Business, incorporated

If a business wants to operate as a corporation, it has to prepare and file articles of incorporation, which is also known as a corporate charter, with the Secretary of State in whatever state it wants to operate. The *articles of incorporation* cover the basics about the company, such as its name and address, the stock it issues (what type and how many shares), and the *registered agent*, who is the person the Secretary of State contacts with any questions about the corporation.

The type of information a state needs for the incorporation is a matter of state statute and can be found online by doing a search for the specific state's name and the word *statute*. For example, I did a Google search on the phrase "Illinois state statutes," and the correct website was number one in my search results.

In general, if you scroll through the various statute titles, you should find one called *business organizations* or something similar. The statutes for the state of Illinois list this at the bottom in Chapter 805: Business Organizations.

Another term for equity is *net assets*, which is the difference between assets, or the resources a company owns, and liabilities, which are claims against the company.

Distinguishing Between Different Types of Ownership

In the prior section, I list the three common components to stockholders' equity as paid-in capital, treasury stock, and retained earnings. I didn't mention capital stock, which perhaps you thought was an oversight. Well, there's a method to my madness, because corporate stock is a component of paid-in capital. You can read all about paid-in capital in the upcoming section aptly titled "Paid-in capital." For now, I want to explain the difference between the two types of corporate stock ownership: common and preferred.

Common stock

Common stock represents residual ownership in the corporation. *Residual ownership* consists of any remaining net assets after preferred stockholders' claims are paid.

To be a real business, at least one share of common stock has to be issued. After all, somebody has to own the corporation!

Common stockholders elect the *board of directors,* who oversee the business. The board of directors elects, appoints, or hires the corporate officers (president, vice president, secretary, and treasurer), who handle the day-to-day operations of the business.

Net assets are total assets minus total liabilities.

Preferred stock

Preferred stock also shows ownership in the corporation. However, preferred stock contains traits of both debt and equity. If a corporation sells its assets and closes its doors, preferred shareholders get back the money they invested in the corporation plus any *dividends* owed to them, which is money paid the shareholders based on their proportionate stock ownership (for more info, see the section in this chapter "Spotting Reductions to Stockholders' Equity"), before the common stockholders get their piece of the pie.

GAAP dictates that you properly describe stock transactions on the balance sheet. Figure 16-1 shows the proper balance sheet descriptions for the following common and preferred stock:

- **Common stock, $5 par value, 500,000 shares authorized, 250,000 shares issued December 31, 2013:** The value of the stock in the corporate articles of incorporation is $5 (remember, this is usually an arbitrary number); the total number of shares the corporation can sell at any one time is 500,000; and as of December 31, 2013, 250,000 shares have been sold to investors.

- **Preferred stock, 5 percent, $200 par value, cumulative, 30,000 shares authorized, issued, and outstanding:** Since preferred stock has a debt-like characteristic, the amount of return the corporation has to pay is printed on each share. In this description, it is 5 percent. The face value per the corporate charter is $200. The limit for the number of shares the corporation can issue at any one time is 30,000. All 30,000 have been sold to investors.

Following the rules for issuing stock

A company's articles of incorporation always have a section (or article) that sets the limit for the number of shares that can be authorized, issued, and outstanding by the corporation at any one time. The custodian of the stock, who may be an employee of the company or an unrelated registrar, keeps track of the number of shares outstanding to make sure the company doesn't issue more than is allowed.

Wondering what authorized, issued, or outstanding means? *Authorized* is the upper limit on the number of shares the company can issue. Issued means the company sold stock to an investor and received cash or some other benefit in return. After stock is issued, it is classified as outstanding for as long as it's in the hands of investors. The company can buy back outstanding shares of stock, called treasury stock. I fully explain treasury stock in the section "Buying treasury stock," later in this chapter (issued minus treasury stock equals outstanding).

Figure 16-1:
Capital stock balance sheet descriptions.

Stockholders' Equity

Capital Stock:

Preferred stock, 5%, $200 par value, cumulative, 30,000 shares authorized, issued and outstanding.	6,000,000.00
Common stock, $5 par value, 500,000 shares authorized, 250,000 shares issued at December 31, 2013	1,250,000.00

Paid-in capital

Now that you have the 411 on capital stock, let's look at the larger equity box that capital stock sits in, which is paid-in capital. Paid-in capital represents money the shareholders in the corporation invest in the business (contributed capital). It consists of purchases of common stock, preferred stock, and additional paid-in capital.

Don't worry, you're not seeing double! Additional paid-in capital is a subset of paid-in capital and is the excess over par value that shareholders paid to buy the stock.

Par value is what's printed on the face of the stock certificate, reflecting the cost of the stock. Wondering how par value is determined? Whoever was in charge of originally forming the corporation decided on the amount of par value. Most of the time, it's an insignificant amount selected arbitrarily.

For example, the par value for Green, Inc.'s common stock is $20 per share. An investor buys 100 shares for $25 a share. The addition to Green's common stock account is $2,000 (100 shares at $20 par value). Additional paid-in capital is $500, which is calculated by multiplying those 100 shares by the excess the investor pays for the stock over its par value (100 shares × $5).

Some states allow no-par capital stock. One good reason for doing this is the fact that there's usually no relationship between par and market price of stock.

Retained earnings

Retained earnings shows the company's total net income or loss from the first day it's in business to the date on its balance sheet. See Chapter 5 for information on how to figure net income (loss). In comparison to paid-in capital, which is contributed, retained earnings is earned capital minus dividends.

Keep in mind, though, that dividends, a topic I discuss later in the section of this chapter "Spotting Reductions to Stockholders' Equity," reduce retained earnings. *Dividends* are earnings paid to shareholders based upon the number of shares they own.

For example, Green, Inc., opens its doors on January 2, 2013. On January 2, retained earnings is 0 because the company didn't previously exist. From January 2 to December 31, 2013, Green has a net income of $150,000 and pays out $50,000 in dividends.

On January 1, 2014, retained earnings is $100,000 ($150,000 – $50,000). Then, to figure retained earnings as of January 1, 2015, you add or subtract the amount of income the company made or lost during 2014 (and subtract any dividends paid) to the $100,000 prior balance in retained earnings.

Now that you understand the two components for stockholders' equity, paid-in capital and retained earnings, Figure 16-2 shows you an abbreviated balance sheet as of the first day of the financial period, homing in on the equity section of a balance sheet.

Paid-in capital includes purchases for common stock, preferred stock, and additional paid-in capital. Figure 16-2 is abbreviated, so it doesn't break out the three components for the paid-in capital amount of $90,000.

Briefly review Figure 16-2 it and keep it in the back of your mind. I give you a blown-out example of financial statement relationships and their effect on stockholders' equity in the "Spotting Reductions to Stockholders' Equity" section of this chapter.

Don't worry — you get to the third component, treasury stock, later in this chapter.

Figure 16-2:
Stockholders' equity on the balance sheet.

Total assets		$200,000
Total liabilities		$ 50,000
Stockholders' equity:		
Paid-in capital	$90,000	
Retained earnings	60,000	
Total stockholders' equity		$150,000
Total liabilities and stockholders' equity		$200,000

Spotting Reductions to Stockholders' Equity

Very few transactions directly affect stockholders' equity. The two biggies are dividends and treasury stock. Another type of transaction, *prior-period adjustments,* or corrections of errors, comes up in Chapter 19.

Both dividends and treasury stock usually reduce equity, but they're completely different types of transactions. Not all dividends reduce equity. Wondering why? I explain all in the next section.

Dividends isn't an account. You'll never find it in the chart of accounts, which is a listing of all accounts set up to handle a company's transactions.

Paying dividends

Dividends are distributions of company earnings to the shareholders. They can be in the form of cash, stock, or property. Most *unrelated investors* (not directly involved with the day-to-day operations of the business) probably prefer to receive cash dividends. After all, who doesn't like cash? However, stock dividends can be quite profitable in the long run when investors finally get around to selling the shares they receive as stock dividends.

Dividends are not an expense of doing business. They're a balance sheet transaction only, serving to reduce both cash (in the case of cash dividends) and retained earnings.

The following sections provide examples and definitions of all four types of dividends.

Cash dividends

Shareholders of record receive payment in the form of cash or electronic transfer based on how many shares of stock they own. However, to pay cash dividends, a company must meet two conditions: It can't pay cash dividends unless there are positive retained earnings, and it must have enough ready cash to pay the dividends.

For example, imagine that you own 2,000 shares of common stock in ABC Corporation. ABC has both a surplus of cash and positive retained earnings, so the board of directors decides to pay a cash dividend of $10 per share. Your dividend is $20,000 (2,000 shares × $10).

Property dividends

In this case, the corporation issues a dividend for one of the assets of the corporation. It could be any asset: inventory, equipment, vehicle, whatever.

When a company issues a property dividend, it has to restate the value of the distributed asset at fair value; see Chapter 3 and record gain or loss on the transaction.

The life of a cash dividend

The company's board of directors is in charge of deciding when and how much of a dividend to issue. However, unless it's a closely held corporation, the board can't just wake up one morning and decide that today's the day to distribute some cash! The dividend cycle consists of three events:

Declaring the dividend: This is the date the board of directors authorizes the dividend. When a dividend is declared, the company has a legal responsibility to pay it.

The company records this legal responsibility by reducing retained earnings and increasing a short-term liability: dividends payable. The dollar amount reducing retained earnings and increasing the liability is the dividend per share multiplied by all shares outstanding. So if the

company has 5,000 shares outstanding and declares a dividend of $2 per share, the amount is $10,000 ($2 × 5,000 shares).

Recording the dividend: The recording date determines who receives the dividend. All shareholders of record on that date get the payment. If you sell your shares of stock after the declaration date but before the recording date, you aren't entitled to receive the dividend. No entry is made in the financial records.

Paying the dividend: Last but certainly not least, the cash dividends are paid out. Stock dividends are issued. Paying cash dividends reduces both cash and dividends payable. For example, if the total dividends paid were $10,000, you debit dividends payable and credit cash for $10,000 each.

Journal entries for a property distribution

Suppose that, instead of issuing a cash dividend, ABC Corporation decides to distribute inventory on the books for $100,000. It declares this intent on December 26, 2013, for distribution of shareholders of record as of December 15, 2013. The inventory will change hands on January 10, 2014. Gain on distribution at fair value is $10,000 on both December 26 and January 10.

The following are the two journal entries ABC needs to make:

On December 26, 2013, the date of declaration, the company has to debit inventory for the difference between cost and fair value ($10,000). Inventory is debited, and an account such as unrealized holding gain is credited for $10,000. ABC also has to debit retained earnings and credit property distributions payable for $110,000 ($100,000 cost + $10,000)

and

On January 10, 2014, the date of distribution, the company needs to reduce the liability account to zero and also show the reduction to inventory. Accomplish this by debiting property distributions payable and crediting inventory for $110,000.

Stock dividends

Corporations normally issue stock dividends when they're low in operating cash but still want to throw the investors a bone to keep them happy. Although no money immediately changes hands, issuing stock dividends operates the same as cash dividends: Each shareholder of record gets a certain number of extra shares of stock based on how many shares that shareholder already owns.

This type of dividend is expressed as a percentage rather than a dollar amount. For example, if a company issues a stock dividend of 5 percent, and the investor owns 1,500 shares, that investor receives an additional 75 shares of stock (1,500 × .05).

Your intermediate accounting textbook also briefly mentions liquidating distributions. These distributions aren't dividends because making the distribution isn't contingent on having retained earnings. Instead, the funds come from paid-in capital. As a reminder, paid-in capital consists of purchases for common stock, preferred stock, and additional paid-in capital.

Calculating the reduction to retained earnings for stock dividends

Per GAAP (see Chapter 1), if the stock dividend is less than 20 to 25 percent of the common stock outstanding, the company uses the fair market value (FMV) of the stock for the transaction instead of the par value.

For example, a company issues a 5 percent stock dividend at a time when it has 50,000 shares of $20 par value common stock outstanding. At the date of declaration of the stock dividend, the FMV of the stock was $25. *Fair market value* is what an unpressured person would pay for the stock in an open marketplace.

The stock dividend totals 2,500 shares (5% × 50,000). The net effect is to decrease retained earnings by $62,500 (2,500 × FMV of $25 per share) and increase common stock dividends distributable by $50,000 (par value of $20 × 2,500 shares). Additional paid-in capital increases by the difference between the two figures: $12,500 ($62,500 − $50,000).

At the date of distribution, common stock increases by $50,000 and the common stock dividends distributable reduces to zero.

One other type of stock transaction that doesn't reduce retained earnings is a stock split. A stock split increases the number of shares outstanding by issuing more shares to current stockholders proportionately by the amount they already own. Stock splits are typically done when a company feels the trading price of its stock is too high because this artificially reduces the price per share.

Time for an example of a stock split. Imagine that ABC Corporation stock is trading for $100, and the company feels this high price affects the average investor's desire to purchase the stock. To get the price of the stock down to $25 per share, the company issues a four-for-one split. Every outstanding share now is equal to four shares.

Building on the beginning-of-the-year information in Figure 16-2, I want to show you how various accounting events reduce and increase stockholders' equity. Figure 16-3 shows changes in stockholders' equity (the fourth financial statement) at year end, assuming that total assets increase by $30,000, total liabilities decrease by $15,000, and cash dividends in the amount of $50,000 were paid to stockholders.

Income Statement

For the Year Ending December 31, 2013

Revenue	$ 1,500,000
Expenses	1,405,000
Net Income	$ 95,000

Statement of Changes in Stockholders' Equity

For the Year Ending December 31, 2013

Paid-in capital	$ 90,000
Retained earnings:	
Beginning balance	$ 60,000
Plus net income	95,000
Less cash dividends	(50,000)
Ending balance	$ 105,000
Total changes in stockholders' equity	$ 195,000

Balance Sheet

For the Year Ending December 31, 2013

Total assets	$ 230,000
Total liabilities	$ 35,000
Stockholders' equity:	
Paid-in capital	$ 90,000
Retained earnings	105,000
Total stockholders' equity	$ 195,000
Total liabilities and stockholders' equity	$ 230,000

Figure 16-3: Showing changes in stockholders' equity.

Buying treasury stock

Treasury stock is shares of corporate stock that a company previously sold to investors and has since bought back. It may seem strange for a company to do this. After all, isn't the point in selling stock to raise capital?

A corporation may opt to remove shares from the open marketplace for many reasons. For example, a corporation may buy back shares of its own stock to prevent a hostile takeover. Fewer shares trading in the open market reduces the chance of another company purchasing a controlling interest in the corporation.

You record treasury stock on the balance sheet as a contra stockholders' equity account. *Contra accounts* carry a balance opposite to the normal account balance. Equity accounts normally have a credit balance, so a contra equity account weighs in with a debit balance.

Your intermediate accounting textbook covers three different treasury stock transactions: purchasing, selling, and retiring. All three are pretty easy to journalize after you get the hang of it. Time to get going hanging this treasury stock wallpaper!

- ✔ **Purchase:** The journal entry is to debit treasury stock and credit cash for the purchase price. For example, if a company buys back 10,000 shares at $5 per share, the amount debited and credited is $50,000 ($10,000 \times \$5$).

- ✔ **Sale at more than cost:** If the company reissues all 10,000 shares of treasury stock at a price higher than what it paid to purchase it (say it sold the purchased stock at $6 per share), the journal entry is to debit cash for $60,000 ($10,000 \times \$6$) and credit treasury stock for $50,000 and paid-in capital from treasury stock for $10,000 ($60,000 – $50,000).

- ✔ **Sale at less than cost:** If the company reissues all 10,000 shares of treasury stock for $4 per share, the journal entry is to debit cash for $40,000 ($10,000 \times \$4$), debit paid-in capital from treasury stock for $10,000, and credit treasury stock for $50,000.

- ✔ **Retiring:** If the company retires treasury stock, the journal entry is to debit the paid-in capital account that relates to the retired treasury stock and credit treasury stock.

Figure 16-4 builds upon Figure 16-3, showing what a statement of stockholders' equity (the fourth type of statement) looks like if the company has 10,000 shares of treasury stock purchased for $5 per share.

Figure 16-4: Stockholders' equity with treasury stock.

Stockholders' equity:	
Paid-in capital	$ 90,000
Retained earnings	105,000
Total paid-in capital and retained earnings	195,000
Less cost of treasury stock	50,000
Total stockholders' equity	$ 145,000

You're gonna need a warrant for that: Reviewing stock warrants

It's not a topic covered in expansive detail for intermediate accounting, but I want to make sure you at least have basic knowledge of this topic. So here goes! Stock warrants grant the right to their holder to buy or sell the stock that's the subject of the warrant, at a fixed price up to the date the warrant expires. The warrant's multiplier determines the amount of stock that's bought or sold. For example, a stock warrant with a multiplier of 1 entitles the holder to one share for each warrant.

Per generally accepted accounting principles, recording any sort of gain or loss on treasury stock transactions isn't appropriate.

Computing Earnings per Share

Earnings per share (EPS) shows the spread of net income when you divvy it up between shares of stock *outstanding,* which means the stock has been issued and is in the hands of the investor. Potential investors in a corporation like to see this type of information so they can make educated investment decisions. Let's face it, if your motivation for buying stock in a corporation is to bring in some dividend income, you want to be able to compare the dividends your top picks are paying their current investors.

Rounding out this chapter, I show you how to calculate EPS for a simple capital structure and give you very basic information on EPS in a complex capital structure.

Simple capital structure

If a company issues only common stock or common stock and nonconvertible preferred stock outstanding, with no convertible securities, stock options, warrants, or other rights outstanding, it has a simple capital structure. Examples of *convertible securities* are bonds and preferred stock that the investor can change into common stock.

Calculate EPS by dividing income available to common shareholders by the weighted-average number of common shares outstanding for the period. Weighted-average is figured by weighting the shares by the fraction of the period in which they're outstanding. For example, if the company has 10,000 shares of stock outstanding in January, February, and March, its weighted average is 2,500 (10,000 × $\frac{3}{12}$).

Suppose that ABC Manufacturing Corporation has net income of $473,400. During the year, the corporation has 38,000 outstanding shares of $4.50, $70 par value preferred stock, and weighted-average number of common shares outstanding totals 205,000. The owners of the 38,000 shares of preferred stock get a dividend of $4.50 per share first, which equals $171,000 (38,000 shares × $4.50 per share).

This figure has to be subtracted from net income before figuring the EPS of common stock ($473,400 − $171,000 = $302,400). Dividing $302,400 by the shares of common stock outstanding (205,000) equals $1.48 EPS of common stock.

If net income includes items such as extraordinary gains or losses, a separate EPS is required for each major component of income, as well as for net income. See Chapter 5 for more information on gains and losses.

Complex capital structure

If items that could cause a potential dilution to EPS exist, the company's capital structure is complex. Potential sources of dilution are convertible securities, stock options, and warrants. In such a case, you have to show both basic and diluted EPS.

Figure diluted EPS similarly to basic EPS, adjusting the number of common shares outstanding that would be issued if the potentially dilutive shares had been issued.

Presenting both basic and diluted EPS gives the user of the financial statements the "worst case" scenario for EPS, relating to any exercise of existing options or the conversion of existing securities.

Check out Figure 16-5 for an abbreviated income statement showing how basic EPS looks, including extraordinary items, too (see Chapter 5 for more information). Plus, I throw in a line item reflecting diluted EPS.

Net income	$100,000
Basic EPS calculation:	
Income from continuing operations	$ 3.50
Extraordinary items	(.62)
Net income available for common stockholders	$ 2.88
Diluted EPS:	
Income available to common stockholders adjusted For the effects of assumed exercise of options and conversion of bonds	$ 1.45

Figure 16-5: Showing EPS on the income statement.

Part V

Accounting for Advanced Intermediate Issues

"Annuities? Equity income? Tax–free municipals? I say we stick the money in the ground like always, and then feed this guy to the sharks."

In this part . . .

1 cover more advanced accounting topics, building upon information your intermediate accounting course touches on in prior chapters. These chapters help you better understand related topics in your textbook and provide an introduction to the more complex discussions you'll encounter if you decide to continue with advanced financial accounting courses.

For example, Chapter 17 talks about everyone's favorite topic, income taxes. Since generally accepted accounting principles (GAAP) often differs from Internal Revenue Code (IRC), revenue and expense differences may arise between the two. You find out about both types of differences: temporary and permanent. You also get info on how to account for tax deferrals, which directly relate to temporary differences, and get the skinny on interperiod and intraperiod tax allocations.

Chapter 19 explains the two different types of leases, capital and operating, and tells you how to account for both. I approach this topic from the standpoint of both the lessee (the party doing the leasing) and the lessor (the party who owns the property the lessee is using). Specifically, I discuss operating, direct financing, and the more advanced topic of sale-type leases. Plus, you find out how to account for *residual value,* which is what the asset is worth when the lessor decides to retire it.

In Chapter 20, you find out how to fix inadvertent mistakes in the financial statements. Also covered is how to account for a change from one accounting method to another and what to do when you find out that an accounting estimate is incorrect.

Finally, I bring it all home by reviewing revenue recognition guidelines. This chapter discusses point-of-sale revenue and how to account for revenue using different contracting methods. You also learn about the installment method, which occurs whenever purchases are made but not fully paid for at point of sale or delivery. Finally, to wrap up revenue into a tidy package, this chapter discusses franchise sales.

Chapter 17

Accounting for Income Taxes

. . . .

In This Chapter

▶ Looking at the difference between financial and taxable income

▶ Walking through temporary and permanent differences

▶ Talking about deferrals

▶ Understanding the difference between income tax payable and expense

▶ Considering the net operating loss effect on income taxes

▶ Calculating interperiod and intraperiod tax allocations

. . . .

*A*lthough preparing income tax returns isn't part of your job description as a financial accountant, knowing how to account for income taxes is. Financial statements prepared according to generally accepted accounting principles (GAAP) differ from financial information you figure for income tax returns, so you may find revenue and expense differences between the two. In this chapter, you read about both types of differences: temporary and permanent.

In addition, you look at how to account for tax deferrals, which directly relate to temporary differences, and operating losses, which reduce taxable income in previous or subsequent years.

In this chapter, I also give you the scoop on the difference between interperiod tax allocations and intraperiod tax allocations, and I walk you through a two-year interperiod tax allocation.

You guessed it: Financial statement preparation and disclosure issues have finally raised their ugly heads. Let the fun begin.

Reviewing Income Tax Reporting

Intermediate accounting is all about reporting using financial accounting standards, including generally accepted accounting principles (GAAP); see Chapters 1 and 2. In this chapter, you switch gears somewhat, as reporting for income taxes doesn't use GAAP — it uses the Internal Revenue Code (IRC).

Before you start blustering about the Internal Revenue Service (IRS) and the unfair amount of taxes you have to pay as an individual, keep in mind that the IRS is only the enforcement agency. Congress (your elected representatives) enacted the Internal Revenue Code in Title 26 of the United States Code (26 U.S.C.).

Like your intermediate accounting textbook, this chapter only touches on accounting for income taxes for a corporation. Any further discussion about taxation of different types of business entities (see Chapter 6 for more about different types of business entities) is really a topic for your taxation classes.

You may be thinking that it's not logical that financial accountants have to worry about income taxes. After all, that's part of the job description for a tax accountant, right? Well, although it is the main bailiwick of tax accountants, under GAAP, financial accountants have tax-related work to do as well. Never fear, we touch on all these tax-related responsibilities in this chapter!

Identifying financial income versus taxable income

In addition to using different standards for financial income (also known as *book income*) versus taxable income, the entities and individuals interested in financial accounting and taxable income are different.

The users of taxable income are usually governmental, whereas the users of financial income are typically individuals or businesses.

- ✔ **Governmental:** Any local, state, or federal taxing agency. Most of the time, though, whenever you think about taxes, the image of good old Uncle Sam and the IRS immediately jumps into your head.

- ✔ **Individuals/businesses:** This class of user includes stock exchanges if the business is *publicly traded,* which means anyone with the money and desire can purchase shares of company stock in an open marketplace. This category includes investors like you and me interested in finding a safe bet to invest our leftover cash, as well as creditors who closely scrutinize the financial statements to make sure the company likely will be able to pay back any loans eventually made.

In the next couple sections, I walk you through both types of income: financial and tax. So get out your calculator and checkbook — it's time to talk taxes!

Financial income

You show financial income on the income statement; see Chapter 5 for more on that. All earned and recognizable revenue minus all allowable expenses per GAAP gives you *income before taxes.* Income before taxes gives users of the financial statements a clear picture on how well the company performs during the financial period. After all, taxes are a somewhat involuntary disbursement of income instead of an accounting event that causes income.

Figure 17-1 shows a simple example of income before taxes.

Income before taxes is also known as *pretax financial income* or income for financial reporting purposes.

Figure 17-1:
Income
before
taxes.

Penway, Inc
Financial Income Under GAAP
For the Twelve Month Period Ending December 31, 2013

Revenue	$150,000
Expenses	65,000
Income before taxes	$ 85,000

Now, you may be thinking, "Okay, but what about income tax expense and the bottom-line net income?" Well, don't start rustling around in your intermediate accounting textbook to find the magic GAAP income tax formula. You figure income tax for financial reporting using the same tables as you do for tax reporting.

Because the goal of this chapter is *not* to test your ability to accurately figure income tax expense using the IRC income tax tables, I use a constant tax rate of 40 percent in all examples (your intermediate accounting textbook uses a constant tax rate, too).

Using a constant tax rate of 40 percent, income tax expense for the income before taxes in Figure 17-1 is $34,000 ($85,000 × .40). Figure 17-2 shows this financial accounting provision for income taxes.

Figure 17-2:
Financial
income
provision
for income
taxes.

Income before taxes	$ 85,000
Income tax expense	34,000
Net Income	$ 51,000

Taxable income

Using IRC as your guide, you figure how much total income to include and which expenses are allowable to reduce the total income. Taxable income is that bottom-line number you report on the appropriate tax return.

Most companies report different financial and taxable income, for this reason: Accounting management prepares the financial books using a full accrual method but, for the tax return, uses a *modified cash method,* which uses some elements of GAAP and some elements of the cash method. For example, the company may accelerate asset depreciation (see Chapter 12 for more on this).

Time to don that cap and gown: Graduated income tax rate

Like individuals, corporations in the U.S. have a *graduated income tax rate,* which means the tax rate goes up based on taxable income. The following figure shows the amount of tax based on taxable income. For example, if the corporation has taxable income of $68,000, federal income tax is $12,000 ($7,500 + [68,000 − $50,000] × .25).

Over–	But not over–	Tax is:	Of the amount over–
$0	$50,000	15%	$0
50,000	75,000	$7,500 + 25%	50,000
75,000	100,000	13,750 + 34%	75,000
100,000	335,000	22,250 + 39%	100,000
335,000	10,000,000	113,900 + 34%	335,000
10,000,000	15,000,000	3,400,000 + 35%	10,000,000
15,000,000	18,333,333	5,150,000 + 38%	15,000,000
18,333,333	- - - - -	35%	0

Using the cash method of accounting, total income is recorded when it's received. In other words, money changes hands and the company doesn't have an accounts receivable; see Chapter 9. Ditto for expenses: The company records expenses only when the expenses paid — the company doesn't have an accounts payable; see Chapter 14.

The gap between book and tax income generally results from three categories of differences: temporary, permanent, and loss carryforwards/carrybacks. Yikes, not sure how the three differ? Let's take a look.

Understanding temporary differences

Temporary differences occur because financial accounting and tax accounting rules are somewhat inconsistent when determining when to record some items of revenue and expense.

Because of these inconsistencies, a company may have revenue and expense transactions in book income for 2013 but in taxable income for 2012, or vice versa.

Two types of temporary differences exist. One results in a *future taxable amount,* such as revenue earned for financial accounting purposes but deferred for tax accounting purposes. This may happen if a company uses the cash method (see Chapter 1) for tax preparation.

The second type of temporary difference is a future deductible amount. The company is reporting an expense on the current tax return but reports it for financial statement purposes in the future. Depreciation is a great example of this (see Figure 17-3).

Now, it's important to keep in mind that temporary differences smooth out, given enough time. Excess financial income over taxable income in one year eventually reverses as an excess of taxable income over financial income in another year (or vice versa). Because of this, accounting geeks also refer to temporary differences as timing differences.

Quite a few accounting events lead to a temporary difference for book versus tax. In this section, I briefly go over three that commonly occur: accrued liabilities, depreciation, and estimates. Your intermediate accounting book may discuss others. If you understand the concept behind these, you'll breeze through any others your textbook mentions.

✔ **Accrued liabilities.** Liabilities are claims against a business, such as *contingent liabilities*, which is money the company may have to pay out in the future based on events that haven't yet come to fruition. Under financial accounting, a business has to record liabilities when they're most probably incurred and the dollar amount can be reasonably estimated.

This rule ensures that the users of the financial statements have relevant information for evaluating the merits of one company against another. Not properly booking accrued liabilities usually understates expenses, which overstates net income. It's also a pretty big deal when doing ratio analysis; see Chapter 22.

For tax purposes, liabilities aren't included until all events establishing and substantiating the liability take place and the liability is reasonably estimated. An example is accruing wages payable to officers of the corporation, which IRC specifically disallows. The company can't expense those outlandish bonuses until it cuts the checks!

✔ **Depreciation.** Most accounting books emphasize this example of a temporary difference: For book purposes, the company may use straight-line depreciation (see Chapter 12), whereas for tax purposes, it may use a more accelerated method, such as *IRC Section 179.* Under certain circumstances, IRC Section 179 allows a business to write off 100 percent of the cost of the asset in the first year of use. Financial depreciation methods, on the other hand, call for the asset to be expensed over both the contemporaneous and future years.

To make this concept a little easier to understand, Figure 17-3 shows the timing difference when using financial versus tax depreciation methods. In this example, for book purposes, the company uses straight-line depreciation for an asset costing $12,000 with no salvage value and a useful life of three years.

As you can see, the same $12,000 ends up on the income statement as a depreciation expense. However, for tax purposes, it all gets expensed in year 1; for book purposes, it's spread over three years.

Figure 17-3:
The timing difference between book and tax depreciation.

	Year 1	Year 2	Year 3
Book	$ 4,000	$4,000	$4,000
Tax	$12,000	0	0

✔ **Estimates.** Estimates are any expenses for which the company figures a reasonable amount, such as *warranty costs,* which is the cost to repair items sold to customers, or *allowance for bad debts,* which is how much in accounts receivable the company reckons it won't collect from customers. For more on accounts receivable, see Chapter 9. For more on collecting from customers, flip back to Chapter 5.

A company can't deduct estimates as an expense on its tax return until it actually incurs the cost. The IRC has strict criteria for deducting bad debts. For example, a bona fide creditor–debtor relationship must exist, and the debt must be positively *uncollectible* (for example, the debtor files for bankruptcy and the company is not a secured creditor).

Tax credits are another, more advanced cause behind a difference in book versus taxable income. This is really a subject for a federal taxation class, but for now, know that a business can receive a tax credit, or a dollar-for-dollar reduction in taxes, for many different reasons. For example, a business qualifies for a tax credit if it hires a certain class of disadvantaged employee.

Reviewing permanent differences

A temporary difference eventually smoothes itself out over time, but permanent differences won't ever be the same in terms of book versus tax. A *permanent difference* is an accounting transaction that the company reports for book purposes but that it can't (and never will be able to) report for tax purposes.

Permanent differences arise because GAAP allows reporting for a particular transaction but the IRC does not. As with temporary differences, quite a few accounting events lead to a permanent difference.

In this section, I discuss five common ones: penalties and fines, meals and entertainment, life insurance proceeds, interest on municipal bonds, and the special dividends received deduction.

✔ **Penalties and fines.** These expenses occur when a business breaks civil, criminal, or statutory law (and gets caught!). Say that a company breaks a local zoning ordinance or an employee gets a speeding ticket while driving the company car to conduct company business.

The company deducts any fines assessed against book income, but IRC 162(f) disallows a penalty/fine expense for tax purposes. The company never gets to reduce taxable income for the expense — thus a permanent difference between net and taxable income.

The M-1 is not just a U.K. motorway

Tax accountants report taxable income on the relevant tax return. For a corporation, the federal form is Form 1120, "U.S. Corporation Income Tax Return." You can check out Form 1120 at the IRS website, www.irs.gov/pub/irs-pdf/f1120.pdf. Tax accountants reconcile temporary and permanent differences between book and tax on page 5 of this form using Schedule M-1.

✔ **Meals and entertainment.** Companies can expense 100 percent of the cost to provide business-related meals and entertainment that they incur in the normal course of business for book purposes. However, under IRC 274(n), for tax purposes, the business can expense, at most, only 50 percent of that same cost, unless certain exceptions apply. In taxes, as in life, there's no free lunch.

✔ **Life insurance proceeds.** If a corporation receives life insurance upon the death of an employee, it's income for financial accounting but never for taxable income. As for the premiums paid for the life insurance on key employees, the company can expense them for book but not tax purposes.

✔ **Interest on municipal bonds.** Municipal bonds are debt instruments (see Chapter 15) a local government issues to fund a project, such as a new highway. Under GAAP, you add this income to net income. For federal tax, it's generally never taxed (although this may not be true in some states). Likewise, any expenses incurred in obtaining tax-exempt income are deductible for book but not tax purposes.

✔ **Special dividend received deduction.** Dividends a company receives from other businesses in which they have ownership are taxable at less than 100 percent, depending on the amount of ownership. For financial accounting purposes, you include all dividends a company receives as income.

For the dividend received deduction, if the company has less than 20 percent ownership in the other business, the company deducts 70 percent. For example, if the dividend is $100, the company reports only $30 as taxable income.

For 20 to 80 percent ownership, the business deducts 80 percent of the dividend. For more than 80 percent ownership, the company doesn't report any of the dividend as taxable income.

Explaining tax deferrals

If a company has any sort of temporary difference, it has to report on its financial statements any deferred tax effect due to the temporary differences. So the company has to figure out the tax effect when book and taxable income catch up with each other and recognize the amount of tax that will be payable or refunded.

Two types of tax deferrals exist:

✔ **Deferred tax liability.** Temporary differences that increase the amount of tax to be paid in future periods create a deferred tax liability. For example, let's say depreciation causes a temporary difference in book versus tax that results in book income tax expense of $25,000 and, under tax reporting, assesses the business income tax payable of $15,000.

The difference between the two, $10,000 ($25,000 – $15,000), is the deferred tax dollar amount. Because income tax expense is more than income tax payable, the $10,000 is a deferred tax liability. It's a liability because the $10,000 represents income taxes that will be payable in the future after the temporary depreciation difference evens out. The amount represents money the business will eventually owe to the government, so it is a liability.

✔ **Deferred tax asset.** A deferred tax asset occurs when taxes payable in the future are less (or anticipated refunds are more) because of deductible temporary differences. Reversing the figures from the deferred tax liability example (income tax expense is $15,000 and income tax payable is $25,000), the $10,000 difference between the two figures is a deferred tax asset. It's an asset because income tax payable will be less in the future after all temporary differences are reduced to zero, and the $10,000 will reduce the amount of tax payable to Uncle Sam.

Taking Advantage of Net Operating Losses

It's a fact of life in the business fast lane that companies don't always have more revenue than expenses every year. It's not necessarily a bad thing, and it can happen for many reasons, including moving the company facilities or expanding the company into new markets.

Operating losses are a tough pill to swallow. Pharmaceutical companies can show enormous losses for years while developing new drug products that become enormously profitable.

Broadly speaking, a *net operating loss* (NOL) occurs when the company has more deductions than revenue on the tax return. Of course, as with most tax-related subjects, there's a bit more to it than that. But this isn't a tax accounting class, and I want to go only as far down that road as I need for you to understand this part of your intermediate accounting class.

Note that I mentioned the tax return in the previous paragraph. For financial accounting, an NOL is an occurrence that investors and lenders note through review of the financial statements — but there's no special form for NOLs as there is for tax accounting.

However, a company has to disclose the facts and circumstances surrounding an NOL so the users of the financial statements understand what is going on. See Chapter 21 for more info about disclosure notes for the financial statements.

Depending on the facts and circumstances surrounding the NOL, both sets of users may not be dismayed at all. For example, many drug companies post net operating losses while doing research to develop new drugs that will eventually be extraordinarily profitable.

However, I know you're sitting on the edge of your seat wondering how an event such as an NOL can be advantage for a company. Here's the skinny on that: An NOL reduces the amount of tax the company paid on earnings in the past or has to pay going forward into the future.

Under the IRC, a business usually has the option of carrying the NOL back to past years, to get a refund against taxes already paid in past years. If a company chooses to, it can forgo the carryback period and apply the NOL to tax returns not yet filed.

The IRC rules that govern carrying the NOL forward or backward are extensive and aren't covered in your financial accounting class. The next two sections provide the basics, in case you decide to take taxation or more accounting classes.

Identifying loss carrybacks

If a business decides to carry back the net operating loss to prior years, it files the relevant tax form showing a reduction in taxable income for the NOL; it results in a refund of previously paid income tax.

For example, Penway, Inc., has a net operating loss (NOL) of $40,000 in 2014 and opts to carry back the loss to 2012, a year in which the company had a taxable income of $30,000. The remaining $10,000 NOL goes to 2013, another year with taxable income, exhausting the NOL in full.

After the applicable IRS service center accepts and processes the returns — the returns also may be subject to exam, which slows the process — the company gets a refund using the tax rate in effect for the $30,000 taken back to 2012 and the remaining $10,000 taken back to 2013. For this example, assume that the income tax effect is a refund for 2012 of $450 and, for 2013, of $1,500.

The 2012 refund cannot be $15,000 (a 50 percent tax bracket). If using the NOL to wipe out the full $30,000, the company would be in the 15 percent tax bracket.

Before you tax junkies start to get into a dither about me not using the IRC Section 1211 five-year carryback for 2008 and 2009 small business returns, I want to keep this old school and use the two-year carryback period.

GAAP states that you have to record the expected refund on the current books. Your journal entry (see Chapter 4) debits an asset account such as income tax refund receivable and credits an income statement account such as benefit due to loss carryback for the tax effect of $5,500 ($4,500 + $1,500).

Understanding loss carryforwards

Suppose Penway, Inc., decides to forgo the carryback period and instead uses the NOL as a *carryforward*. In other words, the company elects to forgo carrying back the NOL and instead carries it forward to offset expected taxable income in subsequent years.

You can carry NOLs forward 20 years. So this isn't as much of a gamble as you may think, as long as the business expects to continue in business (and eventually have net income).

Forgoing the carryback period can be a business choice or can happen when the company has no taxable income in prior years and has nothing to carry the NOL back to.

Using the same facts and figures as in the "Identifying loss carrybacks" section of this chapter, Penway, Inc., decides it doesn't make sense to go through all the hassle and expense of amending prior years to get a refund of $5,500.

The value of valuation accounts

Sometimes future events don't play out the way we want them to. There's no crystal ball to help us know what will happen. Well, anytime a company books a deferred tax asset and over time realizes that chances are good (higher than 50 percent chance) that it won't be able to utilize the deferred tax asset, it may need to use a valuation account.

For example, suppose that a company has a loss carryforward, and halfway into the 20

years, it reckons that it won't be able to use the entire amount of the loss carryforward.

Using its best judgment, the company estimates that $100,000 of the deferred tax asset associated with the loss carryforward won't be used.

This estimate is booked via a journal entry debiting income tax expense and crediting the valuation account: *allowance to reduce deferred tax asset to expected realizable value* for $100,000.

It has a new product hitting the market in 2015 that it feels will be a winner. Upper management is relatively confident that the company will be able to absorb the $5,500 by year-end 2015. And, happy days, management was right. The company has contemporaneous taxable income for 2015 of $100,000. The actual taxable income after carrying the NOL forward is $60,000 ($100,000 – $40,000).

No Form 1139 or amended return is needed: The company reports the NOL as a deduction on its tax return for the year in which it takes the NOL.

To get this on the books, debit the account deferred tax asset and credit the account benefit due to loss carryforward for the tax effect in 2015 for the appropriate dollar amount using 2015 tax rates. In this case, assuming that the 2015 tax rate is 40 percent, the dollar amount for the journal entry is $16,000 ($40,000 – .40).

Checking Out Interperiod Tax Allocation

Interperiod tax allocation means you recognize the tax effect of accounting events in the years in which the events are recognized for financial reporting purposes. By doing this, you're matching income tax expense with the related revenues.

I discuss the importance of matching revenue and expenses, which accountants call the *matching concept,* in Chapter 2.

In the next section, we go over the four principles of the method you use to make this interperiod tax allocation, the *asset-liability method.* This method does the best job of matching revenue with income tax expense.

The asset-liability method

Although there are several different allocation methods, GAAP currently requires that companies use the asset-liability method for interperiod tax allocation. If the Financial Accounting Standards Board (FASB) and GAAP prefer one method over another, you can bet the farm that the preferred method comes the closest to giving users of the financial statements consistent and comparable results.

Your GAAP guide may truncate this to just the liability method. Don't let that confuse you: Both terms mean the same thing.

The asset-liability method provides these desired results through the use of the following four principles:

1. Recognize a current tax liability or asset, with the associated estimated tax payable or refund on the current tax return.

2. Recognize the same for the estimated future tax effect of all temporary differences.

    You ignore permanent differences, because they won't ever be the same book versus tax.

3. Use enacted tax laws and rates to measure the effect of the deferred tax liabilities and assets; don't look into the crystal ball to guess what the IRC and tax rates may change to in the future.

4. Establish a valuation account to reduce any deferred tax assets that the company likely won't be able to utilize (with a higher than 50 percent chance of this).

Looking at interperiod tax allocation using the asset-liability method

To bring this concept to life, in this section, you walk through a typical inter-period tax allocation computation. Consider the facts behind the allocation:

Penway, Inc., has two temporary differences. The first is the depreciation expense for assets the company purchased in the current year. Penway purchased $250,000 in fixed assets (see Chapters 11 and 12) in 2013. Of the $250,000 purchase price, Penway elects to take the special IRC 179 expensing depreciation for $100,000.

Without getting into all the oohs and aahs of depreciating assets (you can do enough of that in Chapter 12), assume that, using an appropriate tax method for the remaining adjusted depreciable base of $150,000 ($250,000 – $100,000), tax depreciation for 2013 is $30,000 and, for 2014, is $48,000. Under GAAP, assuming the use of an allowed method, depreciation is $25,000 for both 2013 and 2014. Figure 17-4 shows the future taxable temporary differences.

2013	Tax	GAAP	Future taxable amount
Purchase Price	$250,000	$250,000	
Depreciation	30,000	25,000	
IRC 179	100,000	0	
2013 depreciation	130,000	25,000	
Basis at 12/31/2013	$120,000	$225,000	($105,000)
2014	Tax	GAAP	
Depreciation	$48,000	$ 25,000	
2014 depreciation	48,000	25,000	
Basis at 12/31/2014	$72,000	$200,000	($128,000)

Figure 17-4: Penway, Inc., calculating future taxable amounts.

The second temporary difference is for *prepaid insurance,* which reflects insurance that Penway, Inc., paid for in advance of the benefit period. Penway has prepaid insurance of $50,000 in 2013 and $25,000 in 2014.

Using the earlier facts and circumstances, Figure 17-5 shows the computation of deferred income tax for this interperiod tax allocation.

	12/31/2013	12/31/2014
Future deductible temporary difference		
Prepaid insurance	$ 50,000	$ 25,000
Future taxable temporary difference		
Asset purchase	(105,000)	(128,000)
Net taxable temporary difference	(55,000)	(103,000)
Effective tax rate	40%	40%
Ending deferred income tax liability	(22,000)	(41,200)
Beginning deferred income tax liability	0	(22,000)
Deferred income tax expense	($22,000)	($63,200)

Figure 17-5: Penway, Inc., deferred income tax computation.

Warming Up for Financial Statement Preparation

To provide useful information to the users of the financial statements, GAAP tells you exactly how to prepare the financial statements when you have income tax expense or benefit. In this section, I give you an overview of income statement and balance sheet preparation.

Other chapters discuss these financial statements and events in much more detail. As I mention them, I reference the associated chapters so you can flip back and forth between this chapter and others, if you want to read more on a particular topic.

Reporting on the income statement

If you liked interperiod tax allocation, you'll love this section's topic: intraperiod tax allocation. For the income statement, you use *intraperiod tax allocation,* which means you allocate income tax expense or benefit to continuing operations (normal day-to-day operations), discontinued operations (company segments no longer functional), extraordinary items (unusual accounting stuff), and prior-period adjustments (corrections of errors taken directly to retained earnings).

I discuss continuing and discontinued operations and extraordinary items in Chapter 5. Find out about prior-period adjustments in Chapter 19.

Using intraperiod tax allocation, the income tax effect of each of these items reports with the individual item.

The point to remember is that extraordinary items, discontinued operations, and prior-period adjustments are shown *net of tax,* which means the accounting event and the related tax show up as one line item on the financial statement.

Look back to Figure 17-2. It shows income before taxes, income tax expense, and net income as three different line items. Figure 17-2 doesn't show income from continuing operations — that designation isn't necessary, as there were no other types of income or loss.

Now check out Figure 17-6, showing the netting effect of taxes and extraordinary items, discontinued operations, and prior-period adjustments.

	Income from continuing operations before income taxes	$85,300
	Income taxes	16,325
Figure 17-6:	Income from continuing operations	$68,975
Intraperiod	Gain on disposal of business segment (net of income taxes of $4,380)	10,824
tax	Extraordinary loss on litigation (net of tax benefit of $3,910)	(11,500)
allocation.	Prior period adjustments (net of income taxes of $3,200)	5,321
	Net income	$73,620

Showing the effect on the balance sheet

You know from earlier in this chapter that temporary differences create two balance sheet accounts: deferred tax liability and deferred tax asset.

Take a moment to review the "Explaining tax deferrals" section of the chapter if you want a refresher.

To show the effect of tax deferrals on the balance sheet you have to consider three different questions: Are they current or noncurrent? Can deferral accounts be netted? How do you figure the correct netted amount? Well, that last one gives you a sneak peek at the answer for the second!

Classifying the deferrals as current or noncurrent

You classify a tax deferral as current or long term depending on the specific asset or liability to which it relates. For example, the estimate for allowance for bad debt ties to accounts receivable, which is a current asset. So this portion of the tax deferral is current.

If the tax deferral doesn't specifically relate to any asset or liability, you classify it as current or long term based on when you expect it to reverse. For example, the portion of the temporary difference for excess donations that you anticipate carrying forward for more than 12 months is long term. Chapter 7 shows a complete balance sheet with these accounts.

Netting tax-deferred accounts

You might be wondering whether you can net out deferred tax asset and liability accounts. For example, imagine that your current deferred tax asset is $7,800 and your current deferred tax liability is $5,400. Can you just show the difference of $2,400 ($7,800 – $5,400) as a deferred tax asset? Not unless the deferred tax assets and liabilities are for the same taxing jurisdiction. So you can net all that relate to the Internal Revenue Service (IRS). But you can't net those related to the IRS and a specific state's department of revenue.

Calculating deferred current and noncurrent netting

If your deferrals are all to the same tax jurisdiction, you figure the netting effect by summing the various current deferred tax assets and liabilities. If the net effect is an asset, you report it on the balance sheet as a current asset. And vice versa if the net is a liability.

For example, if current deferred tax assets total $54,000 and current deferred tax liabilities are $45,000, you have a current deferred tax asset of $9,000 ($54,000 – $45,000).

Then do the same for your noncurrent deferred tax assets and liabilities. So if you have a noncurrent deferred tax asset of $10,000 and a noncurrent deferred tax liability of $35,000, you have a noncurrent deferred tax liability of $25,000.

Wow, those last couple sections show a lot of figures and calculations! If your head is spinning, take heart: You're heading into the last section of this chapter, which discusses income tax disclosure. I promise, you don't need a calculator.

The Big Reveal: Income Tax Disclosure

In the *notes to the financial statements,* which are additional information at the end of the financial statements (see Chapter 21), companies spell out in greater detail how they handle accounting events related to income tax.

In most cases, the external users of the financial statements need the underlying facts behind the numbers on the financial statements to weigh the relative merits of a company before investing in it or loaning it money.

Consider a typical disclosure note for income taxes:

Deferred tax assets and liabilities are recognized for tax consequences of temporary differences between financial reporting and tax reporting. The tax rate used to determine the deferred tax assets and liabilities is the enacted tax rate for the year and manner in which we expect the differences to reverse.

Valuation allowances are recorded to reduce deferred tax assets to the amount that will more likely than not be realized. The company records taxes collected from customers and remitted to the appropriate governmental authority on a net basis.

The company also discloses any income tax examinations in progress by governmental agencies and their expected outcome.

Chapter 18

Accounting for Leases

Most businesses need *tangible fixed assets,* such as property, plant, and equipment (PP&E) for their day-to-day operations. Instead of laying out the money to purchase fixed assets, many companies opt to lease equipment. Both the lessee and the lessor have advantages when leasing. For example, a major advantage to leasing fixed assets is that a company can get 100 percent financing, greatly increasing its cash flow (more on this in Chapter 7).

In this chapter, you look at leasing from the point of view of both the *lessor* (the party that owns the leased asset) and the *lessee* (the party that's acquiring the right to use the asset). You need to get familiar with the operating and capitalization methods of recording leases by the lessee. You also walk through the journal entries a lessee makes to record a lease under both these methods.

In addition, you read about how to classify and account for leases for the lessor. Specifically, I discuss operating, direct-financing, and the more advanced topic of sale-type leases. Plus, you look at how to account for *residual value,* which is what the asset is worth when the lessor decides to retire it.

Reviewing Lease Basics

Businesses don't always buy their *fixed assets,* which include property, plant, and equipment. (See Chapter 11 for more on that area.) Sometimes they lease those assets. You've probably been a party to a lease yourself at some time: Even if you own your own home now, you probably rented either a house or an apartment in the past.

Signing a lease on an apartment is rarely more complicated than coughing up the cash and signing on the bottom line, but business leases are trickier. So you can't automatically equate a business lease to a personal rental. When renting an apartment, you have no claim to it after your lease expires. Depending on how a business lease is set up, however, a company may be the eventual owner of the leased equipment. The terms of the lease also have an effect on how financial accountants book the lease payments.

Leasing instead of flat-out purchasing business assets has grown in popularity over the past couple decades. The reason is that although businesses need tangible assets, they don't want to tie up money in acquiring these assets. Enter the lease, which is a way to get property, plant, and equipment while eliminating the up-front costs inherent in purchasing.

Normally, a lease involves two parties. The *lessor* owns the property and grants the *lessee* the right to use it. In today's marketplace, lessors fall into three classes: banks, captive leasing companies, and independents.

Even after all these years working in accounting, sometimes my brain freezes when trying to remember which party is which. I use a weird mnemonic device: own-or (owner) goes with less-or (lessor).

✔ **Banks:** Many banks conducting what you consider "normal" bank activities (such as accepting money on deposit and lending the funds back out) also have leasing subsidiaries. These subsidiaries acquire all manner of fixed assets and then lease them to businesses.

✔ **Captive leasing companies:** These leasing companies are subsidiaries of parent companies and handle the leasing of the parent company's tangible assets. For example, Ford Motor Credit is the captive leasing company for Ford Motor Company. Ever leased a car you hated? You probably ended up feeling like a captive!

When a business owns more than 50 percent of another business, the investor business is called a parent and the investee is the subsidiary, or sub, for short.

✔ **Independents:** Any leasing company that's not a bank or a captive falls into this category. It's hard for independents to make a buck in this economy. They lack the financing power and availability of ready cash of a bank. Independents also don't have the built-in customer base available to leasing companies with parents such as Ford and other large manufacturers.

An interesting fact about leases is that the lessor doesn't necessarily own the fixed asset just prior to entering into a lease agreement. Sometimes purchasing the fixed asset is contingent upon finalizing the lease agreement. In other words, as part of the agreement, the lessor commits to purchasing the leased asset. This situation may happen if the piece of equipment is expensive or isn't an asset in high demand.

Identifying leasing advantages

Leasing brings six major advantages, and all directly involve the company's cash flow. Essentially, the advantage to leasing over buying is that there's usually no large outlay of cash at the beginning of the lease as there is with an outright purchase.

This topic ties in closely with the time value of money, which is the subject of Chapter 8. Depending on how the parties structure the lease, leasing may end up costing the business less money than buying.

Of course, as with many intermediate accounting extravaganzas, it's not quite that simple. Without further ado, let's get to a full explanation of those advantages!

- ✔ **100 percent financing:** Many business leases come with 100 percent financing terms, which means no money changes hands at the inception of the lease. Can you imagine what a boon to cash flow this can be? Well, it's not totally cash-free, because the lessee has to make the lease payments each month. But many times the assumption is that the company will be making the payments from future cash flows — in other words, from enhanced revenues that the company earns because of the lease.

- ✔ **Obsolescence:** Another advantage to leasing is working around *obsolescence,* which means the company anticipates frequently replacing the fixed asset. For example, many of my larger clients lease rather than purchase their computer equipment so they can stay current with new and faster computer processing technology.

- ✔ **Flexibility:** Asset flexibility is another leasing advantage. Based on the relationship between the lessor and the lessee, the lease may be for either just a few months or the entire expected life of the asset. Or let's say an employee for whom the company leases a vehicle leaves the company. Predicated on the terms of the lease, the company doesn't have to worry about advertising the car for sale and trying to find a buyer, as it would with an owned vehicle — the company just turns the car back in to the leasing company.

✔ **Lower-cost financing:** Based on many different variables, a company may be able to utilize tax benefits associated with leasing. I mention this consideration only briefly here because your intermediate accounting textbook discusses it in greater detail. This topic is a more complicated tax issue that is more appropriate for your taxation classes.

✔ **Tax advantages:** Separate from any tax benefit a company may gain, lease payments can reduce taxable income (see Chapter 17) in a more appropriate manner than depreciation expense (see Chapter 12). I discuss this topic later in this chapter in the section "Reviewing operating leases." For now, remember that you treat operating leases like rentals by expensing the entire lease payment when the business makes it.

Before you get all excited about paying fewer taxes, there's usually only a *timing* difference in taxes paid with leased versus purchased assets. I discuss timing issues in Chapter 17. Basically, taxes saved today will eventually have to be paid tomorrow.

✔ **Off-balance-sheet financing:** Finally, operating leases provide off-the-books (or balance sheet) financing. In other words, the company's obligation to pay the lease, which is a liability, doesn't reflect on the balance sheet (see Chapters 14 and 15 for more on liabilities). This can affect a financial statement user's evaluation of how solvent the company is because he will be unaware of the debt—hence the importance of footnotes to financial statements. See Chapters 2 and 21 for more about required disclosures to the financial statements.

Working jointly, the Financial Accounting Standards Board (FASB) and the International Accounting Standards Board (IASB) have initiated a joint project to develop a new approach to lease accounting, to ensure that assets and liabilities that arise under leases extending 12 months past the balance sheet date are recognized in the statement of financial position.

Round-table discussions started in 2010. Most currently, on July 21, 2011, the two boards reexposed their revised proposals for leasing standards, allowing interested parties to comment on revisions since August 2010. I discuss both FASB and IASB in Chapter 1.

Understanding the nature of leases

To understand the nature of a lease, you must have a handle on the circumstances surrounding a transaction that make it a lease versus a sale. You also need to get familiar with the contractual goodies you may see on leases.

Leasing versus purchasing

The first job is to make sure the arrangement between the parties is indeed a lease. Basically, a lease gives the lessee the exclusive right to use an asset that the lessor owns for a specific period of time in exchange for an agreed-upon payment. Obviously, the big clue here that it's a lease is the fact that the arrangement isn't permanent: It's for a specific period of time.

Capitalizing versus expensing

Your intermediate accounting textbook homes in on the subject of capitalization of leases when discussing the nature of leases. Going back to Accounting 101, *capitalization* means that you record the cost of the purchase on the balance sheet as an asset rather than on the income statement as an expense.

Chapter 12, which discusses depreciation, also provides info about capitalization for purchased assets.

Accountants have to follow certain rules when deciding to capitalize a lease. I briefly mention them here — don't worry, though, I go over each later in the chapter.

A lease is capitalized if it meets any of the following criteria:

- ✔ Ownership of the property transfers to the lessee at the end of the lease term.

- ✔ The lease contract includes a bargain purchase option.

- ✔ The lease term is at least 75 percent of the leased property's economic life.

- ✔ The present value of the minimum lease payments is at least 90 percent of the fair value of the leaser property.

If you're not meeting the criteria, you expense the lease payments.

While on the subject of capitalization, you need to know that direct costs of acquiring a lease, such as real estate commissions and legal fees, must be combined with the lease and expensed over the lease term.

Paying contingently

Some leases provide for payments from the lessor that hinge on future events that aren't known at the time of signing. For example, I once had a retail client whose lease called for extra payments if overall tenancy fell below a certain percentage. Yikes! Not good if there's a mass exodus of tenants from the mall.

It's the nature of the beast that some leases have service aspects, such as routine maintenance. Although the cost of any service element of a lease isn't that big of a deal under GAAP, it must be allocated under the new rules the FASB and the IASB are currently hatching.

Accounting for the Lessee

How companies book leased assets differs depending on whether the lease is capital or operating and whether they're the lessor or the lessee. This section discusses the lessee. But don't worry, I get to the lessor in the next section!

Look to the FASB Accounting Standards Codification Section 840 for more info on lease accounting.

The lessee records the lease agreement and lease payments differently, depending on whether the lease is written as a capital or operating transaction. A major difference between the two types of leases is that operating leases have no aspects of ownership with immediate versus delayed expensing.

Reviewing operating leases

The easiest type of lease to account for, an *operating lease,* has no aspects of ownership. And guess what? Because of this lack of ownership, this type of lease doesn't affect the balance sheet as either an asset or a liability. The cost of the lease payments goes on the income statement as rental expense.

Figure 18-1 shows how to journalize an operating lease if the lease agreement calls for a monthly lease payment of $2,500 relating to equipment rental.

Figure 18-1:
Journalizing
the lessee
operating
lease
payment.

Equipment rental expense	2,500	
Cash		2,500

One more pesky operating lease issue

If the company leasing the equipment pays a broker a finding fee for the lease, any payment made to the broker must be capitalized and amortized equally over the lease period. Let's say the arrangement results in a ten-year lease with a finder's fee of $20,000. The fee expense of $2,000 ($20,000 ÷ 10) must be reported every 12 months.

The finder's fee originally books as an increase to an asset account and a decrease to cash for $20,000. When the cost moves to the income statement, an expense account such as professional fees is increased and the original asset account is decreased by $20,000 ($2,000 annually over ten years, or $20,000 ÷ 10). And at the end of the ten-year period, the asset account reduces to zero.

It just doesn't get any easier than this. There's no pesky fixed-asset accounting to deal with. This simple transaction reduces revenue by the total amount of the lease payment. The cash account is reduced by the same amount. No muss, no fuss — that's the extent of accounting for operating leases on the lessee side.

You usually treat subleasing, in which the lessee further rents the asset to another party, as an operating lease.

Walking through capital leases

Now on to those devilish capital leases! They're more complicated to account for than operating leases because they have characteristics of ownership. The lessee assumes all the responsibilities, benefits, and risks of owning the leased asset. Therefore, the cost of the leased asset goes on the balance sheet in a manner similar to a purchase (see Chapter 11), as both an asset (the classification of which depends on the type of the leased asset) and a lease payable, which is a liability. Flip over to Parts III, IV, and V for more on assets and liabilities.

Now, remember when I briefly mentioned the criteria for capitalizing leases in the "Understanding the nature of leases" section of this chapter? Well, now you get into the nitty-gritty of the four characteristics of capital leases — and only one of them needs to be met for the lease to be capital.

Many companies are under the misguided impression that as long as the lease agreement states it's an operating lease, it's okay to treat it as such. Not true. If the lease agreement contains certain characteristics, it's deemed a capital lease.

- ✔ **Transferring ownership:** If the lease transfers ownership of the asset from the lessor to the lessee, it's a done deal. Additionally, because the lessee now owns the leased asset, the lessee also has to depreciate it; see Chapter 12 to brush up on how to depreciate assets.

- ✔ **Buying at a bargain:** The lessee has the option to purchase the leased asset for a nominal amount at the end of the lease. This option is also known as a bargain purchase. Both terms mean the same: The lease has a clause allowing the lessee to purchase the leased asset for an amount sufficiently lower than its expected fair market value, or what an unpressured party would pay for the same asset in an open marketplace at the date this purchase option comes into play.

GAAP gives little guidance on what constitutes "significantly lower." Financial accountants take into consideration many factors, such as the age and condition of the asset, when setting a figure for the sufficiently lower criteria.

- ✔ **Testing economic life:** The total lease period is at least 75 percent of the estimated economic life of the asset. Economic life is merely an estimate of how long the lessor reckons it will use the asset. So if the estimated economic life of the leased asset is 5 years, you treat any lease whose term is more than 3.75 years as capital ($5 \times .75 = 3.75$). And as an additional monkey wrench thrown into the whole extravaganza, if the lease starts in the last 25 percent of the life of the asset, companies can't use the economic life test to classify a lease as capital.

- ✔ **Recovering investment test:** The present value of the lease payments is at least 90 percent of the fair value of the asset. Present value represents current worth (at the signing of the lease) of the total number of lease payments for the assets.

No textbook handy? Use the suggestion I give in Chapter 8, to use an Excel or similar spreadsheet program to figure present value. You can also find the present value of an annuity of $1 table at www.accountingformanagement.com.

Testing, testing . . . (at 75 percent)

Well, let's hope you get a better grade than that on your intermediate accounting final exam! However, this testing at 75 percent has nothing to do with grades and everything to do with whether a lease is capital or operating. The following figure shows an example of the 75 percent rule at work.

Estimated remaining economic life per independent appraisal	10 years
Total economic life per industry valuation guide	20 years
Lease term	8.5 years

Does the lease term pass the 75 percent test?

Yes! 8.5 years in the lease term divided by 10 years remaining economic life = 85 percent.

Does the lease term start in the last 25 percent of total economic life?

No! You figure this answer by subtracting estimated remaining from total economic life (20 −10 =10). Dividing that figure by total economic life of 20 years gives you 50 percent (10 divided by 20). So the lease is starting in the last half of the asset's life.

Is this a capital lease?

Yes!

Understanding financial statement presentation

After taking a gander at the "Reviewing operating leases" section of this chapter, you can see that financial statement presentation for operating leases is a snap. Unless you have an event such as a finder's fee, no part of the transaction is capitalized. You treat the entire extravaganza as a straight-out expense.

Capital leases are a bit more complicated. But don't worry — by the time you get to the end of this section, you'll be working through the lessee capital lease accounting like a pro! In this section, I show you how to journalize a capital lease transaction and how to reflect a capital lease on the balance sheet and income statement.

For the lessee, capital leases affect both the asset and liability sections of the balance sheet. The lessee also has to allocate the liability between current and long-term liabilities.

This situation is a lot easier to work through if you have a fleshed-out example to follow, so here's one now:

Recovery in fewer than 12 steps

No you're not getting ready for a trip to rehab! It's time to calculate the 90 percent test. To figure out the present value of the lease payments, you have to find the minimum lease payment, deduct any executory costs included in that minimum lease payment, and factor in the discount rate.

Whoosh! You've got a lot of work to do. Time to get crankin'. Here are the facts and figures for your exciting walk down recovery lane:

The fair value of the asset is $130,000;

The lease term is for five years;

The lease payments are $35,000 per year;

Executory costs are $2,000 per year for property taxes; and

The borrowing rate on the lease is 10 percent. The *borrowing rate* is the interest rate the

company incurs if it finances and purchases instead of leasing the asset.

To solve this 90 percent puzzle, you need the assistance of a present value table of an annuity of 1 table (see Chapter 8 for more info on the tables and *annuities,* which are a series of payments made or received). Flip open your intermediate accounting textbook to the correct page showing this table. Find the 10 percent column and trace down that column until you get to Period 5. The number at the intersection is 3.7908.

Next, multiply $33,000 ($35,000 lease payment − $2,000 executory cost) times 3.7908. You get $125,096, which is your present value of the lease payments. Is $125,096 at least 90 percent of the fair value of the asset? Yup, it sure is, because 90 percent of the fair value of $130,000 is $117,000.

On October 1, 2012, Michael, Inc., leases a machine from a captive leasing company for a monthly rental of $50,000. The term of the lease is 12 years, and the company reckons that the useful life of the machine is five years. There's no salvage value and no maintenance payments. Michael plans to use the straight-line method of depreciation, which you can read more about in Chapter 12.

Borrowing money to pay for this type of transaction would cost Michael 12 percent per year. Michael makes the lease payments at the beginning rather than the end of each month.

Keep in mind the following facts:

- ✔ To figure the asset and liability, you need to check out the present value of an annuity of 1 table to get the factor. The factor of 76.899 is at the intersection of 144 periods (12 years × 12 months in each year) and 1 percent (12 percent ÷ 12 months in a year). Remember, the lease payment is monthly, not yearly. The asset and liability amounts are 3,844,950 (the monthly lease payment of $50,000 × 76.899).

- ✔ The depreciation amount per month is $26,701 ($3,844,950 lease liability ÷ 144 periods).

✔ Interest expense per month is figured on the unpaid balance at the end of the month multiplied by 1 percent. Book this at the end of the month. For the first month, the interest expense is $37,950 ($3,794,950 [$3,844,950 lease liability – $50,000, the payment made on October 1] × .01)

First, let's tackle the journal entries, which I show in Figure 18-2. The journal entry is a three-part process that involves booking the acquisition of the leased asset, divvying up the lease payment between principal and interest, and recording depreciation for the leased asset.

To record the inception of the lease on January 1, 2012:

Lease Receivable	160,000	
Equipment		160,000

To record payment on December 31, 2012:

Cash	92,192	
Lease Receivable		76,192
Interest Revenue		16,000

To record payment on December 31, 2013

Cash	92,192	
Lease Receivable		83,808
Interest Revenue		8,384

Figure 18-2: Recording capital lease transactions.

Well, that example wasn't too horrifying was it? Remember also that these are the journal entries for the lessee, not the lessor (you get to the lessor next!). Looking at the accounts you affect in the journal entries, some are balance sheet accounts and some are income statement accounts. Now do an account/financial statement round-up — see Table 18-1.

Table 18-1   Account/Financial Statement Round-Up

Balance Sheet	Income Statement
Lease Equipment — Fixed Asset	Interest Expense
Lease Liability — Liability (current and long-term)	Depreciation Expense
Cash — Current Asset	
Interest Payable — Current Liability	
Accumulated Depreciation — Contra-asset Account	

Now that you have your journal entry accounts classified by financial statement, it's time to figure out the current versus long-term amounts for the lease liability presentation on the October 31, 2012, balance sheet.

This fairly simple intermediate accounting textbook procedure is easy to understand when checking out the lease amortization schedule. The lease amortization schedule shows how the amount of the lease payment is divvied up between interest and reduction of lease liability.

Figure 18-3 shows a partial lease amortization schedule for Michael, Inc. This schedule reflects three payments Michael made at the beginning of October, November, and December and the accrual of three months' worth of interest from October 1, 2012, through December 31, 2012.

Figure 18-4 shows a partial balance sheet reflecting the lease transaction. Pull the numbers for the liabilities from the lease amortization schedule. Figure accumulated depreciation by multiplying the monthly amount of $26,701 by three months (October, November, and December). The income statement, which isn't shown, is affected by reducing net income by both the interest and depreciation expense.

Michael, Inc.
Balance Sheet
December 31, 2012

	Assets			Liabilities	
Figure 18-3:	Property, Plant, Equipment		Current:		
Partial lease	Leased property	3,844,950		Interest payable	110,349
amortization	Less: Accumulated			Lease liability	39,651
schedule.	depreciation	80,103	Noncurrent:		
		3,764,847		Lease liability	3,805,299

Michael, Inc.
Balance Sheet
December 31, 2012

	Assets			Liabilities	
Figure 18-4:	Property, Plant, Equipment		Current:		
Partial	Leased property	3,844,950		Interest payable	110,349
balance	Less: Accumulated			Lease liability	39,651
sheet.	depreciation	80,103	Noncurrent:		
		3,764,847		Lease liability	3,805,299

Accounting for the Lessor

Now that you have the skinny on accounting for the lessee, it's time to address the lessor. As a refresher, the lessor is the party to the lease that owns the leased asset. In this section, you look at the three classes of leases by the lessor and how to account for each one.

Plus, just as I did with the lessee, I want to get this party started with a discussion of the lessor benefits of leasing. Three major ones stand out: residual value, interest income, and tax incentives. I discuss each in turn:

- ✔ **Residual value:** Residual value is what the leased asset is worth when it finishes its last contract and is sold to another party. Think of rental cars. A company like Avis retires its rentals after a certain number of miles and sells them to individuals or rent-a-wreck-type car-rental agencies.

- ✔ **Interest income:** This category is the revenue the lessor receives from the lessee for the financing aspect of the lease. In the prior section "Understanding financial statement presentation," interest expense for the lessee is $37,950. Well, interest expense for the lessee is interest income for the lessor. Ching-ching!

- ✔ **Tax incentives:** Asset ownership can reduce the taxable income of the lessor, including assets not actively put in use by the lessor. In other words, these assets are ones that the lessor rents out to the lessee.

Identifying classification of leases

The lessor looks at many different types of criteria when deciding how to structure its leases. Obviously, the most important standard for the lessor is profit driven: how much this lease will increase its bottom-line income. The lessor also looks at the credit standing of the lessee and how long of a lease term the lessee requires. Based on those facts, plus many other specifics to the company and industry, lessors may choose to classify lease agreements as operating, direct-financing, or sales-type.

Understanding operating leases

Thinking back to the discussion of operating leases in the "Accounting for the Lessee" section of this chapter, it was a pretty simple matter for the lessee to account for an operating lease. Well, good news! Accounting for an operating lease is just as easy for the lessor.

The sticky-wicket part of this for the lessor is that the lessor has to make sure it's okay to record the lease as operating. To qualify as an operating lease, the lease must meet the capitalization criteria on the lessee's side *and* meet both of the following conditions:

- ✔ Collectability of the minimum lease payments from the lessee is reasonably predictable. The bare-bones definition of the *minimum lease payments* is the minimum rental payments called for by the lease over the term. *Reasonably predictable* means what a sensible person can expect to happen under normal circumstances.

- ✔ No important uncertainties surround the leasing event; for example, any future costs associated with the lease are reasonably predictable and the responsibilities of the lessor are substantially complete.

So even if the lessee treats the lease as a capital lease, if collectability on the part of the lessor is uncertain, the lessor has to record the transaction as an operating lease. The lessor leaves the asset on its balance sheet (depreciating it normally) and merely records lease payment from the lessee as a debit to cash and a credit to rental revenue.

Figure 18-5 shows how the facts from Figure 18-1 record on the lessor's financial statements.

To record the inception of the lease on January 1, 2012:

Lease Receivable	160,000	
Equipment		160,000

To record payment on December 31, 2012:

Cash	92,192	
Lease Receivable		76,192
Interest Revenue		16,000

Figure 18-5: Journalizing lessor operating lease revenue.

To record payment on December 31, 2013

Cash	92,192	
Lease Receivable		83,808
Interest Revenue		8,384

Talking about direct-financing leases

A direct-financing lease exists when it (a) does not meet the criteria to be classified as an operating lease and (b) the lessor realizes interest income (but not profit or loss) on the transaction. The lessor's cost for the asset is the same as the fair market value of the asset, so the lessor's profit on the transaction is limited to the interest income they earn to service the lease.

Booking a direct-financing lease

Just for fun, you can journalize a typical direct-financing lease arrangement between Robson Leasing Company and Green Manufacturing, which starts on January 1, 2012. Here's the info relating to this transaction:

1. Robson's cost and fair value for the equipment is $160,000, with a useful life of two years and no salvage value (read more about fair value in Chapter 3).

2. Robson wants a return of 10 percent on this arrangement. Going to the present value of an annuity of 1 table in your intermediate accounting textbook, the factor at the intersection of 10 percent and 2 periods is 1.7355.

3. Each lease payment totals $92,192 ($160,000 ÷ 1.7355).

4. Interest revenue for the first year is $16,000 and for the second year is $8,384.

And check out the following journal entries, showing you how to get this transaction on the books.

To record the inception of lease on January 1, 2012:

Lease Receivable	160,000	
Equipment		160,000

To record payment on December 31, 2012:

Cash	92,192	
Lease Receivable		76,192
Interest Revenue		16,000

To record payment on December 31, 2013:

Cash	92,192	
Lease Receivable		83,808
Interest Revenue		8,384

Suppose a company needs a certain type of equipment to make its products but doesn't have the money to purchase the equipment itself. The company contracts with a leasing company that agrees to purchase the asset, entering into a lease agreement with the lessee.

 Functionally, this is the equivalent of a straight-out loan. The lessor uses an amortization schedule, which shows how much of the lease payment goes to principal versus interest, booking the interest portion as revenue and reducing the amount of lease receivable carried on their books by the principal portion. House owners — sound familiar? It's the same theory as your mortgage payment allocation.

Reviewing sales-type leases

This topic is a more advanced leasing topic, so in this section, I give you only a brief explanation of sales-types leases. More information about this type of lease is in the upcoming section of this chapter titled "Working Through Advanced Leasing Topics."

In a nutshell, in a sales-type lease, the lease doesn't qualify as operating and the lessor realizes a profit or (loss) on the transaction in addition to the normal interest revenue. Baldly put, the accounting for sales-type leases seems pretty straightforward. This type of lease is more complicated, but don't worry — in the next section, I give you the info you need to be a sales-type lease star in your intermediate accounting class!

Understanding financial statement presentation

Financial statement presentation for the lessor is somewhat an opposite situation from lessee presentation. Your intermediate accounting textbook doesn't cover this in detail because the chapter primarily concerns itself with the presentation for the lessee.

However, I still want to throw out some basic presentation facts for operating and direct-financing leases. I discuss sales-type leases in the next section of this chapter, and in Chapter 21, I go over disclosure issues for both the lessee and the lessor.

- ✔ If the lessor treats the lease as operating, the fixed asset stays on the lessor's balance sheet and is depreciated. Lease payments go on the income statement as revenue.

- ✔ If the lessor treats the lease as direct-financing, the fixed-asset account is removed and a new asset account, lease receivable, takes its place. The interest portion of the lease payment goes on the income statement as revenue; the principal portion reduces lease receivable.

Working Through Advanced Leasing Topics

In this section, I elaborate on sales-type leases and residual value. Up to this point, I've not factored in residual value because accounting for it is complex. However, I do want to give you an overview of the subject and add it to the mix in accounting for sales-type leases. Ready to get started? I kick off this thrilling section (please, contain your excitement!) with residual values.

Figuring out residual value

Looking back to the lessor leasing advantages, residual value is what the leased asset is worth when it finishes up its last contract and is sold to another party. If residual value exists (the lessor may simply junk the asset instead of selling it), you must factor in its present value at the inception of the lease. I show you how to do this in the next section, "Accounting for sales-type leases."

Residual value can be guaranteed, which means that the lessee affirms that the leased asset will be worth a certain amount at the end of the lease contract. If the asset's value is less than this guaranteed residual value, the lessee has to make additional payments to the lessor to make up the difference.

Accounting for sales-type leases

Finally! You get to the much ballyhooed discussion of accounting for sales-type leases. I'll try to make sure it lives up to the hype!

Okay, just to recap, a sales-type lease exists when (a) the lease does not meet the criteria to be classified as operating and (b) the lessor realizes both interest income and a profit or (loss) on the transaction. Therefore, the fair market value of the leased asset is more than the lessor's cost to purchase the asset.

Consider an example of how to account for this type of lease: Green Manufacturing walks over to the other side of the table and leases a computer system to ABC Corp.

Green pays $120,000 to buy the computer system and leases it to ABC for $150,000 on January 1, 2012. Green reckons that the computer equipment will have a residual value of $10,000. The lessee doesn't guarantee this residual value.

The term of the lease is six years. Rounding out the picture, Green wants a rate of return of 11 percent, and the first lease payment is due on January 1, 2012.

Here are your initial calculations to get this bad boy on the books:

- ✔ Find the present value of the residual value, which is $5,346 ($10,000 × .5346). Go to the present value of 1 table at 11 percent for six periods — the factor is .5346.

- ✔ Calculate annual rent, which is $30,804. Because ABC makes the payment at the beginning of each period, use the present value of an annuity of 1 due table. At the intersection of 11 percent and six periods, you see that the factor is 4.6959.

  To get the annual rent, you have to subtract the present value of the residual value from the total lease amount ($150,000 – $5,346 = $144,654). Then divide $144,654 by the annuity factor of 4.6959.

- ✔ Figure the $114,654 cost of goods sold amount by subtracting the present residual value from the price Green pays for the equipment ($120,000 – $5,346 = $114,654).

- ✔ Interest receivable at December 31, 2012, is $13,112 ([$150,000 – the January 1, 2012, payment of $30,804 = 119,196] × .11).

Figure 18-6 shows you how the journal entries play out for the first year of this sales-type lease.

To record the inception of lease on January 1, 2012:

```
Lease Receivable      150,000
Cost of Goods Sold    114,654
    Sales                          144,654
    Inventory                      120,000
```

Figure 18-6: Booking year one journal entries for a sales-type lease.

To book the lease payment on January 1, 2012:

```
Cash                   30,804
    Lease Receivable                30,804
```

To book accrued interest income on December 31, 2012:

```
Interest Receivable    13,112
    Interest Income                 13,112
```

Chapter 19

Fessing Up: Correcting Errors and Reporting Changes in Methods

----

In This Chapter

▶ Understanding and recognizing accounting changes

▶ Reporting accounting changes

▶ Accounting for estimates

▶ Fixing mistakes

----

*L*ife is full of changes, and some can be pretty inconvenient. This chapter takes a look at how to best handle changes in an accounting method, such as switching one way of valuing inventory to another. For example, your company may switch to using last-in, first-out (LIFO) instead of its previous first-in, first-out (FIFO) method.

Human error is as inevitable as change, and this chapter also talks about how to gracefully (and correctly) handle those hair-raising moments when an accountant discovers he made an inadvertent error in reporting accounting transactions in the current or previous accounting period. Don't worry — this chapter helps you figure out how to properly fix and forgive such errors.

The chapter also takes a look at changes in accounting estimates. An accounting estimate is merely your best guess on how a future account-ing transaction will play out. These future events are out of your control, so when they actually come to fruition, many times you'll have to reflect a change between your best guess and the actual.

Change Is Good (Even for Accounting Methods)

The whole purpose of preparing financial statements is to give the interested external users of the financial statements relevant, comparable information to use in making their investment decisions. When a company decides that the old way of booking certain accounting events no longer gives a fair, full, and complete financial picture, it's time to consider a change in accounting methods.

I introduce you to the various users of the financial statements in Chapter 1. But to save you from having to flip over there now, here it is in a nutshell: External users run the gamut, from shareholders evaluating the relative merits of buying stock in a company, to banks deciding whether to extend credit to a company.

Three types of accounting changes crop up: change in *accounting principle,* or a change from one generally accepted accounting principle (GAAP) to another; change in *accounting estimate*, or a company's "best guess" on how to handle an accounting event that hasn't yet come to its final conclusion; and change in *reporting entity,* which means the current financial statements show a different mix of companies than the ones reflected on prior years' statements.

As with just about everything you hear in your intermediate accounting class, the Financial Accounting Standards Board (FASB) determines the specific categories in which to classify these accounting changes; see Chapter 1 for more on that. Each of the three categories uses a different method to show the effect of the change on the financial statements.

Corrections of errors, which are inadvertent mistakes, don't qualify as an accounting change, although this chapter addresses that topic, too. You find out how to handle these errors, also known as restatements, in the upcoming section "Mea Culpa: Analyzing Errors."

This chapter introduces all three accounting changes, plus how to correct errors. First up, you find out about changes in accounting principle.

Reporting Changes in Accounting Principles

At this point in your accounting studies, no one has to tell you that financial accountants use GAAP to record a company's accounting events, such as recording revenue, paying bills, or purchasing an asset. But in some instances, GAAP doesn't dictate only one way to handle accounting transactions. Depending on what's going on, you may have more than one acceptable way to handle the same event. Therefore, a change in accounting principle moves from one generally accepted accounting principle to an alternate that the business prefers.

The overriding determining factor in which GAAP method is preferable is that the method provides a fair, full, and complete accounting for transactions you report on the income statement. Change generally happens for three legitimate reasons:

✔ Management prefers the new accounting method over the old.

✔ Management wants to adopt a recently released, brand new accounting principle.

✔ Management received more reliable data for an estimate. (See the upcoming section "Changes in Estimates" for more info.)

When the company opts for a change in accounting principle, you guessed it: There's a GAAP for that! Your intermediate accounting textbook discusses three possible alternatives for reporting the change on the financial statements: *currently* (right now), *retrospectively* (recasting previous statements, and addressing the change on the present set of financial statements) and *prospectively* (in the future). While there are three possible alternatives, GAAP allows only one of the three.

Very small closely held companies with no outside reporting requirements tend to use the easiest method possible: currently.

Because your intermediate accounting textbook discusses all three, more info follows about the allowed and alternative methods:

Reporting changes currently

The easiest method to use is for the business to show the cumulative effect of the change in the current-year income statement as an irregular item that's reported after net income from continuing operations. For more on that, hop over to Chapter 5. Do nothing to adjust any prior-period financial statements.

Understanding retrospective-effect accounting changes

You report accounting changes using retrospective application when you show the difference between the retained earnings balance at the beginning of the year in which a change is reported and what the retained earnings should have been after applying the accounting change retrospectively in all affected prior periods.

Gone retro: The retrospective application

The FASB requires the use of the retrospective application, and the IFRS generally requires it as well, so here are the steps for retrospective application:

1. Calculate the effect of the accounting change and adjust the carrying balances of any affected assets or liabilities to show the effect. For example, if the company changes accounting methods to use one depreciation method instead of the originally used one, the asset and accumulated depreciation balances on the balance sheet will most likely change.

2. Take your offsetting entry to retained earnings. If your calculation for number 1 changes both assets and liabilities, record the difference to *net assets* (which is assets minus liabilities) for your offsetting entry.

3. Adjust prior-year financial statements shown for comparison purposes so that the prior-year financial statements are on the same basis as the contemporaneous (current) statement. For example, if the current year is 2012, the 2008, 2009, 2010, and 2011 (and possibly further back) financial statements may be included with the current one, you also have to reflect the change in accounting method for all prior-year financial statements. See Figure 19-3 for an example of a comparative income statement.

Changing inventory valuation methods to LIFO

One change of accounting principle may be from using FIFO to using LIFO to account for inventory. Chapter 10 is all about inventory, so if you want to know more than basic inventory concepts, check out that chapter before you continue to read this sidebar. Here's a thumbnail sketch of both methods:

LIFO: The company assumes that its newest items (the ones it most recently purchased) are the first ones sold.

FIFO: The company assumes that the oldest items in its inventory are the ones first sold.

That being said, to account for a change in valuing inventory from any other method to LIFO, the company uses the opening inventory balance for figuring all subsequent LIFO calculations. So there's no going back. If the company is making the change in 2012, it uses the inventory figure on the balance sheet as of 1/1/2012 as the starting point in figuring cost of goods sold.

You aren't required to do some blown-out disclosure in the notes to the financial statements (see Chapter 21). You simply need to show in the notes to the financial statements how much of a change is taking place, in both net income and earnings per share (EPS), by using LIFO instead of the previously used method; take a look at Chapter 16 for more. You also have to note that current and prior-year financial statements are not comparable because the change isn't retrospectively applied.

Using prospective effect for accounting changes

With this method, companies don't recast opening balances to show the effect of the change in accounting principle. Depending on the circumstances, prospectively is okay when there's an impracticability exception to adjusting prior periods under GAAP. This situation may arise when the business can't determine the effect as a whole or can't determine the effect to a specific financial period. In this case, the business spreads the accounting change over current and future financial statements, as needed.

To recap your GAAP guidelines for changes in accounting principle:

Use the retrospective approach:

1. Adjust all prior-period comparative financial statements (see Figure 19-3 for an example of a comparative income statement).

2. Disclose in the year of change the effect on net income and *earnings per share* (*EPS* — basic EPS is net income divided by the weighted-average number of shares of common stock; see Chapter 16 for an expanded version of this) for all prior periods you show on the comparative financials.

   I discuss disclosure issues in Chapter 21.

3. Take the adjustment to beginning retained earnings for the earliest year you present in comparable statements.

   See Figure 19-5 for a comparable statement of retained earnings.

4. If figuring out the prior-period effect is impractical, follow GAAP's impracticality exception:

   a. Do not adjust prior-year income.

   b. If the change in accounting principle is a change to LIFO, use the opening inventory in the year LIFO adopts as the base-year inventory amount (see the sidebar "Changing inventory valuation methods to LIFO" for more info).

   c. Disclose the effect of the change on your current year and explain why you didn't employ the retrospective approach.

Changes in Estimates

Thinking about estimates you make in your personal life, how often do you think your best guesses end up being correct? If you're like me, it depends on many factors, such as the level of certainty you have while making the estimate and how far into the future you're speculating.

Certainly, guessing how long it's going to take me to drive into the office if I leave before rush-hour traffic swings into high gear results in a better guess than figuring out the current direction of the economy!

Well, businesses have to give many accounting events their best guess to satisfy the matching principle espoused by GAAP (see Chapter 2). Estimates arise because sometimes, until the whole transaction comes to fruition, the company isn't 100 percent sure how much revenue or expense to book.

Several chapters in this book that discuss income statement and balance sheet events cover estimates you make for financial statement purposes. For example, many facets of depreciating (see Chapter 12) assets are estimates. In this chapter, I discuss this and other common accounting transactions that require you to calculate an estimate for financial statement purposes.

When a company comes up with a method for calculating various estimates, it doesn't mean that the estimate or estimation method is set in stone. Future events affecting the validity of the estimate can be just as much of a guess as the estimate itself. So changes in estimates are frequently made as new and better evidence is gathered. The factor may be as simple as getting closer to the date when the transaction upon which the estimate was made nears completion.

Reviewing estimates

Your intermediate accounting book probably goes over at least five big estimates: customers who don't pay their bills, inventory that takes a dump, tangible asset issues, deferred costs, and warranty servicing. I fully discuss each of these in other chapters of this book, but here's a thumbnail sketch of each so you don't have to jump back and forth between this chapter and others.

✔ **Uncollectible accounts receivables:** Sometimes those wily customers either decide not to pay your invoices or go out of business before they pay. Unfortunately, part of running a business is the realization that customers occasionally will fail to pony up the cash.

GAAP requires that businesses extending credit to their customers estimate how much of accounts receivable — I discuss this more in Chapter 9 — will eventually prove to be uncollectible. This estimate involves both reducing net income, by increasing bad debt expense, and reducing the book value of accounts receivable for the amount of the estimate, by increasing the contra-asset account allowance for uncollectible accounts.

Contra accounts carry a balance opposite to the normal account balance. Because accounts receivable normally has a debit balance, the contra asset account allowance for uncollectible accounts has a credit balance.

✔ **Obsolete inventory:** This category involves inventory that has gone out of style, that has been damaged, or that, in some other way, is no longer sellable. Under GAAP, the company estimates disposition value for the obsolete items, subtracts the estimate from the book value of the `obsolete inventory`, and sets aside the difference as a reserve. When the company disposes of the obsolete inventory or makes a change in the estimated amount, the company adjusts the reserve to reflect these changes.

Clear as mud? Let me clean it off for you with an example. Robson Corporation has 100 widgets in its inventory, with a cost of $50,000 that it deems obsolete for its purposes. Initially, Robson reckons it will be able to sell the widgets for $10,000, a reduction in value of $40,000 ($50,000 – $10,000). As negotiations continue, the estimate changes to $12,000, so the company must book an adjustment to the reserve estimate for $2,000 ($12,000 – $10,000). Figure 19-1 shows the journal entries for these transactions.

To record the estimate for the reserve:

Cost of goods sold	40,000	
Reserve for obsolete inventory		40,000

Figure 19-1:
Journalizing
obsolete
inventory.

Adjust the estimate ($10,000 - $8,000):

Reserve for obsolete inventory	2,000	
Cost of goods sold		2,000

- ✔ **Tangible asset issues:** Tangible assets, also called fixed assets, include property, plant, and equipment (PP&E), such as computers, desks, and manufacturing equipment. When a company purchases long-term (with an expected useful life of more than one year), tangible assets, it has to depreciate them, which spreads the cost of a long-term asset over its expected useful life. Take a look at Chapter 12 for more on tangible assets.

  When depreciating assets, a company has to make two important estimates: how long it will be able to use an asset and the salvage value of the asset. Salvage value is how much a company assumes it will be able to get for a long-lived asset when it comes time to dispose of it.

  Regarding salvage value, the company can't be 100 percent sure how much it will get upon disposing of the asset until the transaction actually occurs.

  Wondering how a company makes tangible asset estimates? Experience can be useful. For example, a company usually trades company vehicles when they hit the five-year mark. The useful life for depreciation purposes, then, is five years.

- ✔ **Deferred costs:** Deferrals are costs taking place in the current period that you expense in a future period. So the costs show up on the balance sheet as an asset until it's time to move them to the income statement as an expense. A good example is an insurance premium paid to a company covering a 12-month period. See Chapter 17 for information about tax deferrals, which show the tax effect when book and taxable income differs.

- ✔ **Servicing warranties:** When a company sells a product with a warranty or performance guarantee, it recognizes the estimated cost of servicing the warranty in the same financial period in which the revenue from the sale is booked. You usually figure the cost of the warranty by using an estimate you base on recent experience.

  For an example of how to figure warranty costs, let's say that, for ABC, Inc., in the last two years, the actual cost of performing on product warranties was 2 percent of net sales. If gross sales are $100,000 and sales discounts (which are discounts the company gives to its best customers) are $2,000, net sales are $98,000 ($100,000 – $2,000). Taking 2 percent of $98,000 is $1,960, which is the company's estimate for warranty expense.

Read Chapter 14 for the full story about warranties. Calculating the estimate for warranties is a frequent midterm or final exam question, so in Chapter 14, I also walk you through a typical warranty estimate transaction, complete with the appropriate journal entries.

Handling changes prospectively

Now that you can identify which accounting events lead to estimates, it's time to find out what to do if the estimate is inaccurate. Remember, until the accounting event plays out to its logical conclusion, you won't know if your best guess is correct! And as you saw in the obsolete inventory example in the previous section of this chapter, estimates can change midstream, too.

Changes in accounting estimates have to be recognized currently and also prospectively, if appropriate. So if the change in accounting estimate affects both the current and future years, the effect is shown in the current financial period and all other applicable ones.

The current and future financial statements show the effect of the change in estimate, but no change is made to prior-period financial statements.

To bring this home for you, consider that the Robson Corporation purchases equipment on January 1, 2012, for $500,000. The company estimates this equipment to have a ten-year useful life with a salvage value of $20,000. The depreciable base is $480,000 ($500,000 – $20,000). Straight-line depreciation per year is $48,000 ($480,000 ÷ 10 years of useful life).

The company decides at the beginning of year 8 (2020) to revise the estimated useful life to 15 years, with a new estimate of $5,000 for salvage value. Accumulated depreciation is $336,000 ($48,000 × 7 years). Book value at 1/1/2020 is $164,000 ($500,000 – $336,000).

So how do you account for this bad boy? First, what's the entry to correct prior years' depreciation? Think about it. There's no entry, since you handle changes in estimates prospectively.

But what do you have to do? Figure 19-2 shows the journal entry and its analysis.

Book at 1/1/2020	$164,000
Less estimated salvage value	(5,000)
Remaining depreciable base	$159,000
Divided by remaining useful life (15 years – 7 years)	8 years
Depreciation expenses 2020 ($159,000 divided by 8 years)	$19,875

Figure 19-2: Reporting a change in estimate for depreciation.

December 31, 2020 journal entry to record depreciation expense:

Depreciation expense	19,875	
Accumulated depreciation		19,875

| Book at 12/31/2020 ($164,000 – $19,875) | $144,125 |

Yikes! What do you do if a change in accounting principle causes an estimate change (see the section earlier in this chapter called "Reporting Changes in Accounting Principles")? When in doubt, treat the difference as a change in estimate. Your intermediate accounting textbook calls this a "change in estimate effected by a change in accounting principle."

In the classroom, I find that many students assume that a change in estimate always affects more than one year. To clear up this misconception, suppose that a business originally estimates the useful life of a piece of manufacturing equipment to be 15 years. When year 12 rolls around, the machine is obviously on its last legs and will be junked at year-end. Well, changing the useful life of the machine to 12 years in year 12 of its expected useful life doesn't affect any future periods — only the current one.

To recap your GAAP guidelines for changes in accounting estimates:

Use the current and prospective approach:

1. Use the new estimate for all current and future financial statements.

2. Don't restate any prior years that you show on comparative financial statements (see Figure 19-3 for an example of a comparative income statement); likewise, leave the beginning balance of retained earnings alone.

Understanding Changes in Reporting Entities

Reporting entities are combinations of businesses a parent company shows collectively on its financial statements, also known as *consolidated financial statements.* Your intermediate accounting textbook probably briefly goes over three different ways that changes in reporting entities can occur.

Imagine that a parent company (investor) owns more than 50 percent of another business, and the investee business is the subsidiary.

I mimic the brief treatment here. Any further expansion on the three is more of an advanced financial accounting issue:

- ✔ The parent shows consolidated financial statements instead of a past practice of showing individual financial statements for each subsidiary.

- ✔ The parent changes the mix of subsidiaries it shows on the consolidated financial statements.

- ✔ A change in companies included in the combined financial statements occurs. A combined financial statement mingles assets, liabilities, and equity results from operations for two or more affiliated companies.

  An *affiliated company* either 1) has ownership of less than 50 percent of the voting stock in another company or 2) when combining with another company, is a subsidiary (along with its combining company) of a third company.

Don't consider business combinations reported using the pooling method. Treat them as a change in reporting entity.

The important aspect to remember for your intermediate accounting class is how to handle these changes on the financial statements. Use retrospective treatment to show changes to reporting entities. *Retrospective treatment* means you have to restate all prior-period financial statements included with the current financial period, for comparison purposes.

For example, if the current period is 2014 and the company shows 2012 and 2013, too, both those years have to be restated, but not 2011 or prior years. Figure 19-3 gives an example of an income statement showing more than one financial period.

	2012	2013	2014
Sales - net	$ 225, 365	$ 259,170	$ 285,087
Cost of goods sold	101,414	116,626	128,289
Gross profit	123,951	142,544	156,798
General & administrative expenses	47,000	47,350	48,520
Income before taxes	76,951	95,194	108,278
Income taxes at 40%	30,780	38,078	43,311
Net income	$ 46,171	$ 57,117	$ 64,967

Figure 19-3: Income statement for years ended December 31.

To recap your GAAP guidelines for changes in reporting entities:

If you use the retrospective approach:

1. Restate the financial statements of all prior periods you show on comparative financial statements.

    See Figure 19-3 for an example of a comparative income statement.

2. Disclose in the year of change the effect on net income and *earnings per share (EPS)* for all prior periods you show on the comparative financials.

    Basic EPS is net income divided by the weighted-average number of shares of common stock — see Chapter 16 for an expanded version of this. I discuss disclosure issues in Chapter 21.

Mea Culpa: Analyzing Errors

Let's face it, nobody's perfect. In the sometimes-harum-scarum world of GAAP interpretation and booking accounting events, mistakes do happen. And just as you do with changes in estimates, the important point is to make sure that you correct any inadvertent mistakes in reporting accounting transactions on the financial statements in complete accordance with the way generally accepted accounting principles (GAAP) — and that you do so as soon as you discover those mistakes.

Wondering what the difference is between an inadvertent error and fraud? Errors aren't deliberate. Fraud takes place when there's a deliberate intent to mislead the users of the financial statements.

Reviewing types of errors

For your intermediate accounting class, you need to understand several types of inadvertent errors. I discuss the most prevalent here:

- ✔ **Change in accounting principle from non-GAAP to GAAP:** This is considered an error only because you're going from non-GAAP to GAAP. For example, the company may switch from using the cash method of accounting to using the accrual method. See the section at the beginning of this chapter titled "Reporting Changes in Accounting Principles" for how to handle changes from one GAAP accounting principle to another GAAP accounting principle.

- ✔ **Math mistakes:** These mistakes occur when the financial accountant, or the accounting software, just flat-out fails to record something correctly. As a good example, maybe you're totaling a column of figures and you make a mistake adding them up; the mistake then affects some aspect of data entry into the accounting software system and flows through to the financial statements.

- ✔ **Bad-faith estimates:** The company adopts an estimate, such as useful life, for an asset that, at the inception, is clearly unrealistic.

- ✔ **Incorrect recognition:** The company doesn't accrue or defer expenses and/or revenues appropriately. *Improper presentation* is another concern: In this case, you fail to show the transaction in the right way on the financial statement. For example, maybe you take an expense to the balance sheet instead of to the income statement.

- ✔ **Interpretation of facts:** The accountant misuses or misinterprets currently available information. Figuring salvage value on an asset is an easy-to-understand example. Let's say that the best information available at the time for salvage value for a particular asset is that its worth at disposal will be $5,000. The financial accountant unilaterally decides not to use this figure, but uses $10,000 instead.

Inadvertent errors fall into three broad categories: math mistakes, improperly applied GAAP, and incorrect interpretation of facts available at the time the financial statements are issued.

Letting sleeping dogs lie with counterbalancing errors

When any of the types of errors I explained earlier occur and they're *counterbalancing*, which means the error naturally corrects itself over two financial periods, accounting management of a company (with the concurrence of their financial statement auditors and following Security and Exchange Commission [SEC] rules — see Chapter 1 for guidance) may decide to not take any action.

For example, let's say that the financial accountant messed up in recording depreciation in one year. Even though the depreciation entry in the second year was incorrect, the two errors resulted in a zero net effect for the two years combined. If the books for both financial periods have already been closed, no further action may be necessary — especially if the error is immaterial. The financial accountant just moves on, making sure year 3 and forward is done correctly.

Righting the wrong

As soon as an error is found, it must be corrected. How you correct the error under GAAP depends on the type of error, the number of financial periods the error affects, how the error affects financial statement presentation, and whether the error is counterbalancing.

To straighten out the messy mistakes and give the users of the financial statements accurate data for ratio analysis (discussed Chapter 22), you have to ask yourself these three questions:

- ✔ **What is the type of error?** We just discussed this. If you need a quick refresher, see the prior section in this chapter, "Reviewing types of errors."

- ✔ **What do I need to do to fix it?** Sometimes a simple journal entry is enough. Other times, a direct correction to retained earnings for a prior-period adjustment is on the accounting menu.

- ✔ **Do the financial statements have to be restated?** *Restatement* means previously issued financial statements are revised, to correct the error. If the error is material or prior-period financial statements are shown with the current year (see Figure 19-3 for an example), restatement of the financial statements is a must.

Take two: Statement restatement

When restating the financial statements, follow these three steps:

1. Adjust the balances of any assets or liabilities at the beginning of the newest financial period shown in the comparative statements for the cumulative effect of the error.

2. The other side of the correction goes to retained earnings.

3. Lastly, you have to correct the error on each of the comparative-year financial statements. Your intermediate accounting textbook may refer to this as *period-specific effects*.

The notes to the financial statements detail the restatement, giving all necessary info surrounding the event, such as the nature of the error and the effect on net income (both gross and net of income tax). Read all about it in Chapter 21.

Walking through correction of errors

Before I wrap up this chapter, I want to show you an example of how to journalize error corrections both when the books haven't been closed and when they have. I also show you how to prepare the associated restated retained earnings statement.

For this example, Robson Corporation discovers the following errors in January 2013 relating to 2012 accounting transactions. The books for the 12 months ending December 31, 2012, are still open. All years prior to January 1, 2012, are closed:

- ✔ A math mistake was made, and depreciation expense is understated by $35,000.

- ✔ Robson failed to recognize and accrue salaries payable of $3,000.

- ✔ The company switches from using the cash method to using the accrual method to book revenue, resulting in understated net sales of $20,000.

- ✔ Robson further notices that depreciation expense for years prior to January 1, 2012, is understated by an additional $50,000.

Figure 19-4 shows the adjusting journal entries Robson needs to make at December 31, 2012.

Figure 19-4: Adjusting journal entries to correct errors.

	Debit	Credit
1 Depreciation expense	35,000	
Accumulated depreciation		35,000
2 Salary expense	3,000	
Salaries payable		3,000
3 Accounts receivable	20,000	
Sales		20,000
4 Retained earnings	50,000	
Accumulated depreciation		50,000

Figure 19-4: Adjusting journal entries to correct errors.

Robson Corporation shows two comparative years, 2011 and 2012, on its statement of retained earnings. Figure 19-5 shows how to reflect the adjusting journal entries from Figure 19-4.

Robson Corporation
Retained Earnings Statement
For the Year Ending

	2012	2011
Retained earnings, January 1, unadjusted	$125,000	
Less prior period adjustment	(50,000)	
Retained earnings, January 1, adjusted	75,000	83,000
Add: Net income*	37,000	42,000
Retained earnings, December 31	$112,000	$125,000

*Net income prior to the discovery of the errors is	$ 55,000
Depreciation expense	(35,000)
Salary expense	(3,000)
Sales	20,000
2012 Net income	$ 37,000

Figure 19-5: Restating retained earnings.

To recap your GAAP guidelines for changes because of errors:

If you to use the restatement approach:

1. Correct all prior-period financial statements shown on comparative financial statements. See Figure 19-3 for an example of a comparative income statement.

2. Restate the beginning balance of retained earnings for the first period shown on a comparative statement of retained earnings if the error is prior to the first comparative period. See Figure 19-5 for an example on how to do this.

Chapter 20

Is That You, Revenue? Revenue Recognition Concepts

*T*ime to go over some basic concepts of revenue recognition. What is revenue? How do companies record it? Revenue is recognized only when it is *earned* and *realizable.* This chapter looks at what those two terms mean and also explores revenue that is recognized at point-of-sale, both before and after delivery.

I also explain the two methods to account for long-term contracts under Accounting Standards Codification (ASC) 605-35. In addition, I help you determine what to do accounting-wise when customers return (or have the right to return) their purchases. Finally, to wrap up revenue into a tidy package, I introduce franchise sales and revenue disclosure notes to the financial statements.

Reviewing Guidelines for Recognition

Financial accounting and generally accepted accounting principles (GAAP) (see Chapter 1) guidelines state that you record revenue when it's earned and realizable and you record expenses when they're incurred. Wondering what the criteria are for earned and realizable? The *earned* criteria are satisfied when the seller satisfactorily performs on his contract with the customer. *Realizable* means that the seller has an actual expectation of collecting the money for the job from the customer.

The accrual method takes cash out of the equation, as money changing hands doesn't determine whether you recognize a transaction. Because of this, a company has accounts receivable, which shows money customers owe to the business, and accounts payable, which shows all money a company owes to its vendors.

Your intermediate accounting textbook also refers to this as the *sales basis,* which means that the company records revenue from the sale of a product or service on the date of the sale or delivery. However, based on the unique facts and circumstances of the revenue transaction, a company also records certain items of income before the entire transaction comes to fruition. For example, they use the percentage-of-completion method for long-term contracts and after the revenue transaction is complete. An example of revenue recognition after completion of the job is the installment-sale method.

If you can't quite call to mind the particulars of the percentage-of-completion or installment-sale methods, don't worry. You'll get familiar with both of these methods later in this chapter. I discuss the percentage-of-completion in the "Contracting Methods" section of this chapter and installment sales in the "Delaying Revenue Recognition" section. Before you get into the nitty-gritty of revenue recognition, here's a brief rundown on the four types of revenue transactions:

- ✔ **Inventory sale:** This type applies when a merchandising or manufacturing company sells inventory to a customer. A *manufacturer* makes the product the merchandiser sells. For example, Amana sells washing machines that it manufactures to Sears for sale to consumers like you and me.

- ✔ **Providing a service:** Services aren't *tangible* — you can't touch or feel them. Examples of service providers are accountants and physicians.

- ✔ **Allowing use of an asset:** In this case, the company allows another business to use something that the company owns. For example, Penway, Inc., owns an office building that it leases to Michael Manufacturing.

- ✔ **Sale of a noninventory asset:** Gain or loss takes place upon disposing of an asset (see Chapter 5 for more info about gains and losses). Imagine that Penway, Inc., decides it no longer wants to be a landlord. Penway asks Michael Manufacturing if it wants to buy the office building it's presently leasing, and the business agrees. Based on numerous factors, Penway will either lose or make money on the sale of the office building.

The Financial Accounting Standards Board (FASB) and the International Accounting Standards Board (IASB) are currently in the process of replacing guidance for revenue recognition with a new global accounting standard that will apply a single set of principles to all revenue transactions. See Chapter 1 for more information.

Point-of-Sale/Delivery Revenue

Point-of-sale/delivery is just another way of saying that the company records revenue when it's earned and realizable. I give you two examples of this: one involving a retail store and the other taking place in a service provider type of business:

- ✔ **Retail store:** You desperately need a new microwave, so you hustle on down to your favorite discount department store. After selecting the best in your price range, you take it to the checkout, where the clerk scans the barcode, adds sales tax, and tells you the grand total you owe on the sale. After the clerk swipes your credit card and gets approval from the issuer of your credit card, you're the proud owner of a new microwave and the store has a completed point-of-sale transaction.

- ✔ **Service provider:** The service provider for this example is a printing company. Penway, Inc., orders business cards with its new business telephone numbers from Curry's Printing. When Curry's runner drops off the completed order and Penway accepts it, the revenue transaction is considered to be delivered and complete.

Now, just to shake up the fairly simple concept of point-of-sale/delivery, some events reduce the amount of gross revenue per the customer contract for revenue transactions. The two biggies are sales discounts and returns. We look at these now.

Reporting sales discounts

Sales discounts are reductions in price that a business gives to a good customer who pays early or buys in volume. For example, a customer's invoice may be due in 30 days, but if the customer pays the invoice within 10 days, the terms of the contract allow him to automatically take a 2 percent discount. So if the original invoice amount is $2,000, the customer can reduce the actual amount he pays by $40 ($2,000 × .02).

Discounting a volume purchase occurs anytime a seller gives the buyer a break when placing a larger order. It's similar to deals you occasionally see in the grocery store when you buy two and get the third item free.

You book revenue transactions involving sales discounts for the entire (gross) amount of the invoices. However, transactions involving volume discounts are booked at the discounted amount. See Chapter 5 for more information on booking these types of transactions.

Returning sales

It's a sad day indeed when a customer returns a purchase for a refund —
but it's a basic fact of doing business for many companies. Your job as an
accountant is to recognize the difference between these types of transactions
and understand how to account for them.

I talk about the garden variety of occasional sales returns and allowances in
Chapter 5. In this chapter, you look at how to handle returns for companies
that have such a high rate of returns that, in some cases, the business has to
put off recognizing revenue.

A good example of this concept is doing business with a mega-chain store
such as Wal-Mart or Target, which affords its own customers a very liberal
return policy. Any wholesaler marketing products through such a store usually has a contractual agreement allowing the retailer to send returns to the
wholesaler. This policy can also include products that didn't sell.

Entering into a contract that allows for liberal refunds is a cost of doing business when selling to a large retailer: The wholesaler usually moves a tremen-
dous amount of product through the retailer and wouldn't be able to achieve
that volume with smaller chain stores.

What to do? Well, looking to the Financial Accounting Standards Board
(FASB) for guidance (see Chapter 1), you record revenue from sales in which
the buyer has the right to return the merchandise only if specific conditions
are met. Drum roll please — here they are!

- The contractual terms regarding the price are substantially fixed or
  determinable at the date of sale, which is the good ol' point of sale.

- The buyer has paid or is obligated to pony up the bucks for the sales
  transaction. In addition, this obligation is not contingent on the buyer
  being able to sell said merchandise.

- The buyer's obligation to make good on the contract with the seller will
  not change if the buyer loses possession of the merchandise through
  events such as theft, fire, or natural disaster.

- The buyer has *economic substance,* which means it's in business to make
  a profit and isn't tied to its relationship with the seller.

- The seller doesn't have to take significant actions in the future to make
  the product sellable by the buyer; the buyer is ready to put the product
  to use.

- The seller can reasonably estimate future returns.

What happens if these six conditions aren't met? Well, the seller has to delay recognizing part of the sale or the entire sale until the contractual return period has expired or the six conditions come to fruition, whichever comes first.

You need to take away two major points from this section about returning sales:

- ✔ If the customer has the right to return the product for a full refund and the seller is uncertain about the probability that the customer will take advantage of this aspect of the contract, the seller must delay recording any portion of the sale until the refund period elapses.

- ✔ If the seller has an insignificant risk of returns and can reasonably estimate them, two different *contra-accounts,* which are accounts carrying a balance opposite to their normal balance (more on that in Chapter 4), get the transaction on the books. The sales returns and allowances account (the contra revenue account) is debited, and the allowance for sales returns and allowances account (the contra asset account) is credited for the amount of the estimate.

Understanding buyback agreements

Consider this sticky wicket: What happens accounting-wise if a seller has a *buyback agreement* with the buyer, meaning that the seller agrees to buy back the merchandise sometime in the future? Can and should the seller record this transaction as revenue?

The defining aspect of the transaction is whether it qualifies as a sale or *financing transaction,* which occurs when the seller is providing 100 percent financing (the buyer doesn't have to pony up any cash) and the seller agrees to repurchase the merchandise at the end of the financing agreement.

Financing transactions are basically rental agreements — kind of like if you lease a car from a dealership for three years and then have to return it. Explore these types of transactions more in Chapter 18.

The following conditions must be met for the transaction to qualify under GAAP as a sale:

- ✔ Ownership of the goods transfers from the seller to the purchaser at point of sale/delivery.

- ✔ The purchaser has no restrictions on the use of the goods.

Accounting for a sale with buyback

Penway, Inc., sells merchandise to Michael Manufacturing for $200,000, which carries a cost to Penway of $110,000. Penway agrees to buy back the merchandise from Michael at the end of three years for *fair value,* or what an unpressured purchaser in an open marketplace would pay. See Chapter 3 for more information about fair value. Penway receives payment in full and places no restrictions on the use of the merchandise.

This illustration shows how Penway records this sale with buyback.

Cash	200,000	
Sales Revenue		200,000
Cost of Goods Sold	110,000	
Inventory		100,000

Loading and channel stuffing

Last but not least in this discussion of point-of-sale revenue is the irritating topic of loading and channel stuffing. Both terms mean essentially the same thing: transactions taking place when a company entices its customers to buy more product than they could possibly need or sell.

This type of behavior probably doesn't seem too logical. Why would a company do this, and why would the vendor agree? Channel stuffing normally occurs at year-end. Plain and simple, it's just a way for the company to artificially inflate revenue. Could this help bonuses?

When this occurs, there's always the unspoken agreement that the vendor can return the unneeded product after the first of the year for a full refund. Vendors agree for many different reasons, maybe because they participate in channel stuffing themselves or they receive favorable purchasing terms from the company in exchange for the consideration.

GAAP doesn't allow these types of transactions to be booked without an appropriate allowance for sales returns. And if the company abides by GAAP, it has little reason to book this *window dressing* (artificially distorting results to make the company look better) type of revenue transaction.

Another insidious practice is a side agreement, which is a verbal agreement that changes the terms of the sale. For example, a vendor may place an order buying 5,000 items at $100 per item, with the expectation that before the invoice is due to be paid, the seller will reduce the price per item to $50. Side agreements are another way to artificially inflate gross receipts.

Contracting Methods

Two methods account for long-term contracts: the percentage-of-completion method and the completed-contract method. *Long-term contracts* span more than an accounting year. In other words, the company starts the contract in May 2012 and doesn't finish it until January 2014. The really interesting aspect of accounting for long-term contracts is the fact that the percentage-of-completion method allows for revenue recognition before delivery, and the completed-contract method employs point-of-sale revenue recognition.

Although recognizing revenue before delivery seems to fly in the face of GAAP, Accounting Standards Codification (ASC) 605-35 specifically allows for it.

In this section, I home in on *long-term construction contracts.* The construction industry has three main groups: building, nonbuilding, and specialty trade construction.

Yes, I know this is hard to believe, but the *building category* includes office buildings, warehouses, single, and multifamily dwellings. *Nonbuilding construction* includes items such as highway and street construction, large bridges, and refineries. The major *specialty trades* include electrical, plumbing, roofing, and heating and air-conditioning.

Those types of contracts qualify as long-term construction contracts. Now it's time to explore the two different methods of accounting for them. First up: percentage-of-completion.

The new model of revenue recognition the FASB and the IASB has devised may cause differences in the way companies apply contracting methods, such as in what costs are capitalized or which measurements for completion apply.

Percentage-of-completion method

Use the percentage-of-completion method when you record revenue from long-term contracts in stages. With this method, you recognize revenue, costs, and gross profits throughout the life of each contract, based on a periodic measurement of progress. Accountants use two specific accounts in the chart of accounts (see Chapter 4) for the percentage-of-completion method (PCM):

- ✔ **Construction in process:** This inventory asset account shows accumulated construction costs and gross profit earned as of the date of the balance sheet.

- ✔ **Billings on construction in process:** Use this contra inventory account to accumulate progress billings.

GAAP dictates that businesses with long-term contracts use the PCM when both the estimates regarding progress made toward completion of the contract and the revenue and costs associated with the contract are reasonably dependable — *and* when all the following additional conditions are met:

- ✔ **Terms of the contract:** The contract must clearly spell out enforceable rights regarding the goods or services, the consideration exchanged, and the terms of settlement.

- ✔ **Buyer obligations:** There's a reasonable expectation that the buyer will live up to his end of the contract.

- ✔ **Contractor obligations:** There's a reasonable expectation that the contractor will live up to his end of the contract.

Accounting for the PCM method can be quite subjective and open to error.

Reporting PCM on the balance sheet

For each contract in progress at year-end, reduce the total cost incurred to date plus the estimated earnings by the total amount of billings rendered, to arrive at a net balance.

For each contract, the net balance is a debit if the total costs and estimated earnings exceed the billings; it's a credit if the billings exceed the costs and estimated earnings. PCM asset and liability accounts can't be netted or offset against each other.

All contracts that have a debit balance are added together with the total shown as an asset on the balance sheet; all contracts that have a credit balance are added together with the total shown as a liability on the balance sheet.

International Accounting Standard (IAS) 11 (see Chapter 1 for more information) includes instructions to use the percentage-of-completion method when the outcome of a construction contract can be reasonably estimated. If the outcome cannot be reasonably estimated, no profit should be recognized. Contract revenue should be recognized only to the extent that contract costs are incurred.

Completed-contract method

The completed-contract method (CCM) is easier to account for than the PCM. Using the CCM, a contracting company doesn't recognize either revenue or expense transactions relating to the contract until the contract is completely finished. Companies that use the CCM must have some sort of accounts to hold these transactions until recognition.

But, hey, here's some good news: Companies don't have new account names to memorize! Businesses use the same two accounts to hold the value of these transactions for CCM as they use for the PCM.

- **Construction in process:** This inventory asset account shows accumulated construction costs as of the date of the balance sheet.
- **Billings on construction in process:** Use this contra inventory account to accumulate progress billings.

The CCM generally results in the greatest tax deferral, compared to other long-term contract accounting methods, because the general rule is that all contract income and contract-related expenses (both direct and indirect) are deferred until the taxable year in which the contract is completed.

Generally, a company should use the CCM when one of the following conditions exists:

- The company deals mostly with *short-term contracts,* which are those that don't span a year-end.
- The company doesn't meet the criteria to use PCM, which I discuss in the earlier section "Percentage-of-completion method."
- Inherent risks exist beyond the scope of normal business risks, such as a potential scarcity of a natural resource needed for the project (for example, because of extreme weather conditions)

Long-term construction accounting methods

ABC Construction Company has an $800,000 contract for a major office building. ABC's cost to construct is reasonably estimated at $500,000. During the first month of the job, ABC has the following transactions relating to the contract:

1. Pays $30,000 for permits

2. Receives an invoice for $15,000 from a subcontractor

3. Prepares the first progress billing for $100,000

For the PCM, you base both revenue and gross profit on how much of the job is complete. First, divide costs to date $45,000 ($30,000 + $15,000) by total estimated costs of $500,000, giving you a job completion percentage of 9 percent. Then use this percentage to figure the reportable revenue of $72,000 ($800,000 × .09) and gross profit of $27,000 ([800,000 − 500,000] × .09). Which method best shows the economic reality of the transaction? Most accountants agree that, for long-term contracts, the PCM is best: Revenue is recognized as it's earned.

The following illustration shows how to record the three accounting events using the accrual, PCM, and CCM methods.

	Accrual	Completed Contract	Percentage-of Completion
Revenue	$100,000	$ 0	$72,000
Costs	45,000	0	45,000
Gross profit	$ 55,000	$ 0	$27,000

CCM can be used only for two types of long-term contracts: home construction contracts and any other contract that's expected to be completed within two years, provided that the company's average annual gross receipts for the prior three years do not exceed $10 million.

Delaying Revenue Recognition

Now that you've walked through the PCM, which recognizes revenue before delivery, it's time to look at three methods that recognize revenue after delivery: the installment method, cost-recovery method, and deposit method. Ready? Here we go.

Handling the installment method

Installment sales take place whenever purchases are made but not fully paid for at point of sale or delivery. For example, Penway, Inc., wants to totally revamp the office with swanky new furniture and fixtures, but it prefers not to lay out the cash for the purchase all at once upon receipt of the furniture.

Penway finds an office furniture supplier that's willing to take payments over the next five years. Using the *installment method,* the office furniture supplier recognizes the revenue for this sale in the periods it receives the payments from Penway instead of at point of sale/delivery.

The theory behind delaying recognition for financial statement purposes is that the risk of not collecting on the installment sale receivable is greater than an accounts receivable. To refresh your memory, accounts receivable reflects all money customers owe to a business for completed sales transactions and due within a shorter time, such as 30 days (see Chapter 9).

To cover the realizable aspect of revenue recognition, the revenue is booked as it is received; you also book the related gross profit at the same time. Consider the following example:

ABC, Inc., sells inventory to XYZ, Inc., for $750,000. XYZ signs an installment sales contract requiring that it pay $100,000 down and $130,000 per year for the next five years, with the first payment also due at signing. Thus, the initial payment is $230,000 ($100,000 + $130,000).

ABC's cost of inventory sold is $400,000. ABC's gross profit on the whole she-bang is $350,000 ($750,000 – $400,000). ABC also has to figure out the gross profit percentage, which is 46.667 percent (otherwise rounding doesn't make journal entries work) ($350,000 ÷ $750,000).

All your facts and figures line up, so let's journalize this transaction! Figure 20-1 shows the journal entries to record the sale and the five years of installment sale entries.

To record the installment sale:

Installment Accounts Receivable (A/R)	750,000	
Installment Sales		750,000
Cost of Goods Sold	400,000	
Inventory		400,000
Cash	230,000	
Installment A/R		230,000

To record year one gross profit:

Installment Sales	750,000	
Cost of Goods Sold		400,000
Deferred Gross Profit		350,000
Deferred Gross Profit	108,100 ($230,000 x .47)	
Realized Gross Profit on Installment Sale		108,100

Figure 20-1: Journaling an installment sale.

To record realized gross profit for each year, 2 through 5:

Deferred Gross Profit	61,100 ($130,000 x .47)	
Realized gross profit on Installment Sales		61,100

Recording the cost-recovery method

The installment-sale method isn't exactly an optimal way of recording sales transactions, and the cost-recovery method takes it down another notch. If a company isn't reasonably assured of recovering the cost of the goods sold if the buyer defaults on the financing arrangement, the sales transaction records it using the cost-recovery method. Under the *cost-recovery method,* the seller can't record profit on the sales transaction until the customer's payments cover at least the cost of the goods sold.

If you're planning to take an advanced financial accounting class, file in the back of your mind that the cost-recovery method differs slightly if the debt is nonrecourse: Then the borrower isn't liable for any unrecovered portion of the debt. In other words, the customer owes nothing if the goods are repossessed for nonpayment and the value of the repossessed goods is less than the balance on the debt.

So how do you figure gross profit for a simple cost-recovery transaction? Suppose Baldwin Park Manufacturing sells a machine costing them $50,000 to Grand Central Freight, which has a dubious credit history, for $72,000. The terms of the contract call for payments of $36,000, $24,000, and $12,000 over a three-year period.

Figure 20-2 shows how to figure gross profit if the Baldwin Park and Grand Central transactions play out according to the contract.

	Year 1	Year 2	Year 3
Cash collected	$36,000	$24,000	$12,000
Revenue	72,000		
Cost of goods sold	50,000		
Deferred gross profit	22,000	22,000	12,000
Less recognized gross profit	0	10,000 **	12,000
End of period deferred gross profit	$22,000	$12,000	$0

Figure 20-2: Figuring gross profit using the cost-recovery method.

** The unrecovered cost at the end of the year 1 is $14,000 ($50,000 − $36,000). $24,000 − $14,000 = $10,000.

One additional method that your intermediate accounting textbook quickly discusses is the deposit method. This method comes into play when the buyer gives the seller a deposit on the eventual transaction. The seller records this as a liability, like customer advances.

Reviewing Franchise Sales Transactions

If you've ever yelled your lunch order into a drive-through clown's mouth or rented a car from those guys who "try harder," you're probably familiar with the concept of franchises. A *franchise* is a business that perhaps started as a one-location shop but grew to be so popular that the original owners allowed other individuals to open shops using the same concept or name in other geographic locations.

The parties to a franchise are the *franchisor,* the party granting the business rights, and the *franchisee,* the individual purchasing the right to use the franchisor's business model and name.

The franchisor faces special issues. First, the franchisor doesn't recognize revenue until after substantially performing all material services per the franchise agreement. For example, the franchise agreement may call for the franchisor to provide a certain amount of training to the franchisee.

Also, if the initial franchise fee required at the time of signing the franchise agreement is large compared to the *continuing fees* (usually a percentage of sales), the franchisor defers a portion of the initial fee, recording it as earned through future services rendered to the franchisee. In addition, two other considerations apply when accounting for franchises:

- ✔ **Bargain purchases:** If the franchise agreement gives the franchisee the right to make bargain purchases from the franchisor after paying the initial franchise fee, the franchisor must defer recognizing as revenue a portion of the initial franchise fee if the following conditions exist:

  - The item's bargain price is less than its normal selling price.

  - The bargain price doesn't allow the franchisor a reasonable profit on the transaction.

- ✔ **Purchase option:** If the franchise agreement contains a clause allowing the franchisor to purchase the franchisee's location and this likely will eventually occur, the franchisor records the initial franchise fee as a liability instead of revenue. That's because the initial franchise fee is, in essence, a future payable to the franchisee.

The Full Monty: Revenue Disclosure

In the *notes to the financial statements,* which are additional information at the end of the financial statements (see Chapter 2), companies spell out in greater detail how they recognize various revenue transactions.

In most cases, the external users of the financial statements need the underlying facts behind the numbers on the financial statements to weigh the relative merits of a company before investing in it or loaning it money.

Consider this typical disclosure note for revenue recognition:

> The company recognizes revenue when persuasive evidence of an arrangement exists, delivery of goods has occurred, the sales price is fixed and determinable, and collectability is reasonably assured. This means we generally recognize revenue when legal control of our goods transfers to our customers. Title usually transfers upon shipment to or receipt at our customer's locations, which is determined by contract. Our sales terms do not allow for a right of return except for matters related to any manufacturing defects on our part.

Part VI
The Part of Tens

The 5th Wave   By Rich Tennant

"Hello—forget the company's financials, look at the CEO's Facebook page under '25 Things the SEC Doesn't Know About Me.'"

In this part . . .

This last part of the book — featured in every *For Dummies* book — offers some top-ten lists for your consideration. I provide a quick look at ten common disclosure notes to the financial statements and explain ten ratios helpful for evaluating the relative merits of investing in a company.

Chapter 21

Ten Common Notes to the Financial Statements

*T*his chapter walks you through the explanatory notes to the financial statements. *Explanatory notes* are discussions of items that accompany the financial statements, which are the income statement (covered in Chapter 5), the balance sheet (see Chapter 6), and the statement of cash flows (discussed in Chapter 7). These notes are important disclosures that further explain numbers on the financial statements. The reason for these notes harkens back to fulfilling the needs of the external users of the financial statements.

"External users of the financial statements" is just a fancy way of saying people like you or me who may be interested in investing in the business. Users may also be banks thinking about loaning the company money or governmental agencies making sure the company has complied with reporting or taxation issues.

So information that can't easily be gleaned from reviewing the financial statements has to be spelled out in notes and disclosures, to explain how or why a company handles a transaction. External users then can understand what is going on and have a level playing field to compare the financial statements of two companies.

The notes are part of the *corporate annual report,* which provides shareholders with financial and *nonfinancial* (for example, public relations goals) information about the company's operations in the past year. These notes come after the financial statements in the corporate annual report, in the same order as presentation of the financial statements (notes for income statement accounts come first, then the balance sheet, and finally items reflecting on the statement of cash flows).

Instead of discussing every type of note you'll ever encounter in a financial statement, this chapter covers ten common ones. Let's get started.

Showing the Basis for Presentation

The first order of business when preparing explanatory notes is explaining, in general, the business and significant accounting policies. Some businesses tackle these two topics in different notes. The first can be called "Basis for Presentation," and the second, "Accounting Policies." I discuss both in this chapter.

For such a note, the company gives a thumbnail sketch of the business. Common topics for discussion include what the company is in the business of doing and how it does that work. For example, does the company manufacture the product itself or contract it out?

For now, at least (see Chapter 1 for more information about convergence), a U.S. company states in this section that its financial statements are prepared in accordance with accounting principles generally accepted in the United States (good ol' GAAP!). If applicable, the company also explains the use of estimates, as with the allowance for doubtful accounts, which is money it reckons customers will fail to pay (see Chapter 9), and impairments, which is how the company accounts for assets that are no longer useful (see Chapter 12).

Alternatively, the company may have just one note, called "Summary of Business and Accounting Policies," which combines the information in this section of the chapter and the next.

Advising on Significant Accounting Policies

Information about accounting policies assists financial readers in better interpreting a company's financial statements, thus resulting in a more fair presentation of the financial statements. A note is needed for each significant accounting choice by the company.

Financial accountants use the terms *footnote*, *note*, and *explanatory note* pretty much interchangeably as all three terms represent the same explanatory information.

At the very least, the explanatory notes should include what depreciation methods are in use (see Chapter 12), how a company values its ending inventory (see Chapter 10), the basis of consolidation (see the "Consolidating Financial Statements" section in this chapter), accounting for income taxes (see Chapter 17), information about employee benefits (see the "Spelling out Employee Benefits" section of this chapter), and accounting for intangibles (see Chapter 13).

Here's an example of a note — we'll call it Note 15, for income taxes:

NOTE 15: TAXES:

Income before taxes was $7.68M, and the provision for federal taxes was $2.39M, an effective tax rate of 31.1 percent. Deferred income taxes reflect the net tax effects of temporary differences between the carrying amounts of assets and liabilities for financial reporting versus tax reporting purposes.

Depreciating Assets

I discuss *depreciation,* which is spreading the cost of a long-term asset (see Part III) over its useful life (which may be years after the purchase) in Chapter 12. Inventory valuation methods, which is how a businesses values its ending inventory, is the topic of Chapter 10. The methods a company opts to use for both depreciation expense and inventory valuation can cause wild fluctuations in the amount of assets shown on the balance sheet and the amount of net income (loss) shown on the income statement.

The user needs to know which methods the company uses when comparing financial statement figures with another company's figures. Differences in net income could merely be a function of depreciation or valuation methodology, and the user would be unaware of that fact without the footnote.

Valuing Inventory

Companies have two inventory issues that must be disclosed in the notes: the basis upon which the company states inventory (lower of cost or market) and the method in use to determine cost. GAAP allows three different cost flow assumptions: specific identification; weighted average; and first in, first out (FIFO). For the full accounting scoop on inventory, see Chapter 10.

Accounting for depreciation and inventory is usually addressed in whichever note gives a summary of accounting policies.

Assuming that Note 1 addresses depreciation and inventory, here's a truncated example of how one looks:

NOTE 1: SUMMARY OF BUSINESS AND ACCOUNTING POLICIES:

We compute inventory on a first-in, first-out basis. The valuation of inventory requires that we estimate the value of obsolete or damaged inventory.

We compute depreciation for financial reporting purposes using the straight-line method, generally using a useful life of two to five years for all machinery and equipment.

Disclosing Subsequent Events

The company also has to address any subsequent events that happen after the close of the accounting period. How the company handles this type of event hinges on whether the event is a Type I or Type II event.

Type I events affect the company's accounting estimates booking on the financial statements. *Type II events* aren't on the books at all before the balance sheet date and have no direct effect on the financial statements under audit. The purchase or sale of a division of the company is a classic example of a Type II event.

Type II events are also called nonrecognized events. Here's why: If they're material, they must be disclosed in footnotes to the financial statements, but the financial statements don't have to be adjusted.

Assuming that Note 21 addresses the event subsequent to the balance sheet date, and the balance sheet date is 12/31/2012, here's a truncated example of how one looks:

NOTE 21: SUBSEQUENT EVENT

On April 1, 2013, we entered into an agreement to sell our ownership interests in our Green division to Blue Manufacturing for approximately $10 million in cash. The transaction is subject to certain regulatory approvals. We expect the transaction to close in the fourth quarter of 2013.

Explaining Intangibles

Intangible assets aren't physical in nature, like a desk or computer. Two common examples of intangibles are *patents,* which are licensing for inventions or other unique processes and designs, and *trademarks,* which are unique signs, symbols, or names that the company uses. Besides explaining the different intangible assets the company owns via an explanatory note, the business needs to explain how it has determined the intangible asset's value showing on the balance sheet. See Chapter 13 for more information on intangibles.

Assuming that Note 14 addresses the intangibles, here's a truncated example of how one looks:

NOTE 14: INTANGIBLE ASSETS:

We classify intangible assets with other long-term assets. As of December 31, 2013, our intangible assets consisted of the following: patents, copyrights, and goodwill. They are generally amortized on a straight-line basis. We perform a yearly review to determine whether useful life is properly estimated.

Consolidating Financial Statements

Consolidation refers to the aggregation of financial statements of a group company as a consolidated whole. In this section of the footnotes, the company confirms that the consolidated financial statements contain the financial information for all its subsidiaries. Any deviations, including deviations from all subsidiaries, also must be explained.

Consolidation information is always addressed early in the footnotes, usually in note 1. Here's a truncated example of how a note addressing consolidation appears:

NOTE 1: SUMMARY OF BUSINESS AND ACCOUNTING POLICIES:

Our consolidated financial statements include our parent account and all wholly owned subsidiaries. Intercompany transactions have been eliminated, and we use the equity method to account for investments in which we own common stock.

Spelling out Employee Benefits

Employee benefit plans provide benefits to both employees and former employees. One example is a health and welfare benefit plan that provides medical, dental, vision, vacation, and dependent care (just to name a few) benefits to employees and former employees.

The footnotes also spell out details about the company's expense and unpaid liability for employees' retirement and pension plans. These details include the obligation of the business to pay for post-retirement health and medical costs of retired employees.

Assuming that Note 18 addresses employee benefits, here's a truncated example of how one looks:

NOTE 18: RETIREMENT BENEFIT PLANS:

We provide tax-qualified profit-sharing retirement plans for the benefit of our eligible employees, former employees, and retired employees. As of December 31, 2013, approximately 80 percent of our profit-sharing fund was invested in equities, the rest in fixed-income funds. We have unrelated external investment managers.

Revealing Contingencies

A contingent liability exists when an existing circumstance may cause a loss in the future, depending on other events that have not yet happened and, indeed, may never happen. For example, the company may be involved in an income tax dispute. Disclosing this contingent liability is a requirement if the company will owe a substantial amount of additional tax penalties and interest if the unsolved examination ends up in the government's favor. See Chapter 14 for more information on reporting contingencies.

Assuming that Note 10 addresses the contingent liability, here's a truncated example of how one looks:

NOTE 10: COMMITMENTS AND CONTINGENCIES

As of December 31, 2013, we were contingently liable for guarantees of indebtedness owed by third parties for $2 million. These guarantees relate to third-party vendors and customers and have arisen through the normal course of business. The amount represents the maximum future payments that we could be responsible to make under the guarantees; however, we do not consider it probable that we will be required to satisfy these guarantees.

Reporting Debt

The notes to the financial statements also must disclose claims by creditors against the assets of the company. The note shows how the company is financing present and future costs. It also gives the user of the financial statements a look at future cash flows, which can affect the payment of dividends.

Assuming that Note 7 addresses contingent liability, here's a truncated example of how one looks:

NOTE 7: DEBT AND BORROWING ARRANGEMENTS

On June 30, 2013, the Company replaced short-term debt with longer-term debt. The Company issued long-term notes in the principal amounts of $50 million at a rate of 4.75 percent, due June 30, 2017.

Chapter 22

Ten Ratios for Financial Statement Analysis

*W*hy, you may be wondering, is GAAP so nit-picky? Because proper classification of accounting transactions is key for user analysis, which is the topic of this chapter. Here we take a look at key ratios that users of the financial statements perform to gauge the effectiveness and efficiency of a company's management.

The four major ratio measurements are liquidity, activity, profitability, and coverage. But you may be asking, isn't an investor interested only in how profitable a company is? Not necessarily. *Liquidity,* which is how well a company can cover its short-term debt; *activity,* which shows how well a company uses its assets to generate sales; and *coverage,* which measures the degree of protection for long-term debt, are all measurements that have to be considered along with profitability to form a complete picture of how well a business is doing.

In this chapter, I look into liquidity ratios (current and acid test), activity ratios (related to turnover), profitability ratios (ROA, ROE, profit margin), and coverage ratios.

Current Ratio

I've been an accountant for many years, but at times I've still had to look up the exact formula for some ratio analysis. The current ratio is an easy one, though: It's simply current assets divided by current liabilities.

This ratio tells you the company's ability to pay current debt without having to resort to outside financing. Let's say you're looking at a company's balance sheet. Current assets are $100,000 and current liabilities are $45,000. The current ratio is 2.2 ($100,000 ÷ $45,000). In this case, the company has sufficient current assets to pay current liabilities without going to outside financing.

If anything is difficult about the current ratio, it's making sure you include only *current* assets and liabilities. If you're unsure of what goes into each of these categories, check out Part III of this book for the skinny on current assets and flip to Chapter 14 for the lowdown on current liabilities.

The Electric Ratio Acid Test

The acid test ratio is similar to the current ratio, but it includes only quick assets. Wait, what the heck is a quick asset? A *quick asset* is readily convertible to cash or is already in the form of available cash — think money in the company's operating checking account.

To figure the acid test ratio, you first add together cash, *temporary cash investments* (like stock in other companies that the business plans to sell within one year of the balance sheet date), and accounts receivable. Then you divide that total by the company's current liabilities.

The current asset that's most often omitted from the acid test measurement is inventory.

Now, let's say that, of the $100,000 in current assets from the previous current ratio calculation, quick assets total $75,000. Dividing that amount by current liabilities of $45,000 gives you an acid test ratio of 1.67.

As a general rule, having a current ratio of at least 2.1 and an acid test ratio of at least 1.0 shows that the business has sufficient liquidity to pay current debt as it comes due.

Asset Turnover

Turnover analysis shows how quickly income-producing assets such as merchandise inventory comes in and goes back out the door. The quicker, the better! By this, I mean that, in normal circumstances, efficiently moving assets indicates a well-run business. Therefore, the asset turnover ratio measures how efficiently a company uses its assets to generate sales.

The basic formula for calculating asset turnover is net sales divided by average total assets. If net sales are $135,000 and average total assets are $87,500, asset turnover is 1.54 times. In other words, the company earns $1.54 for each $1 it invests in assets. That turnover ratio looks pretty good, but to truly give this ratio meaning, you have to compare it to asset turnover for similar companies.

Net sales is gross sales minus all discounts, allowances, and returns — see Chapter 5 for more on net sales.

A quick and dirty way to get average total assets is to add beginning and ending total assets and divide by 2. So if total assets on January 1 are $100,000 and total assets on December 31 are $75,000, average total assets are $87,500.

Inventory Turnover

This activity measure shows how efficiently the company is handling inventory management and replenishment and how fast the products are being sold. The less inventory a company keeps on hand, the lower its costs are to store and hold it. This strategy lowers the cost of inventory that must be financed with debt or *owners' equity,* or the ownership rights left over after deducting liabilities.

To compute this ratio, divide the cost of goods sold by average inventory. Suppose that the cost of goods sold is $35,000 and average inventory is $8,500. Inventory turnover is 4.12 times ($35,000 ÷ $8,500). Again, comparing this inventory turnover figure against industry averages, the higher the ratio, the better!

Accounts Receivable Turnover

This ratio shows the average number of times accounts receivable (A/R) is turned over — that is, booked and paid — during the financial period. The sooner a company collects receivables from its customers, the sooner the cash is available to take care of the business's needs.

Why is this such a big deal? Well, the more cash the company brings in from operations, the less it has to borrow for timely payment of its liabilities.

To figure A/R turnover, if accounts receivable on January 1, 2013, was $2,500 and then was $1,500 on December 31, 2013, average A/R is $2,000 ($2,500 + $1,500 ÷ 2). Net sales are $35,000 for 2013, making A/R turnover 17.5 times ($35,000 ÷ $2,000).

Return on Assets (ROA)

This ratio shows how well a company is using its assets to make money. Basically, the premise is that how well a company uses its assets to generate revenue goes a long way toward telling the tale of its overall profitability.

A business that is effectively and efficiently operated, which this and other activity measures show, generally is more successful than its less effective and efficient competition.

Figure ROA by dividing *net income,* which is revenue minus expenses (see Chapter 5) by average total assets (see Chapter 6). So if net income is $55,000 and average total assets total $87,500, ROA is 63 percent. By any accounting ratio, that number is pretty good: It shows that, for each dollar in assets, the company earned 63 cents.

However, keep in mind that different types of companies need varying amounts of assets. For example, manufacturing companies generally are top-heavy with assets, compared to law firms. Having an ROA of 63 percent most likely indicates an asset-light company. For effective ratio analysis, you need to use similar types of companies or measure ROA for the same company over a period of years. (This approach, known as trend analysis, looks at the same ratios over several time periods.)

Return on Equity (ROE)

Return on equity (ROE) measures the profit earned for each dollar invested in a company's stock. You compute it by dividing *net income* (which is revenue minus expenses — see Chapter 5) by average *owners' equity* (which is what's left over in the business after all liabilities are subtracted from all assets — see Chapter 16).

The higher the ratio, the more efficiently the company's management is utilizing its equity base. This measurement is important to stockholders and potential investors because it compares earnings to owners' investments. Having net income grow in relation to increases in equity presents a picture of a well-run business.

To illustrate, here's an ROE calculation. If net income is $55,000 and average owners' equity is $365,000, ROE is 15 percent. To make wise investment decisions, users of this information look at ROE as it trends over a series of years in comparison to other companies.

Profit Margin on Sales

Harkening to Chapter 5 and the income statement, profit margin on sales is net income divided by net sales. This ratio gives the users of the financial statements the 411 on how well the company is handling expenses: It measures the net income (revenue minus expenses) generated by each dollar of sales.

If net income is $55,000 and net sales is $135,000, profit margin on sales is 41 percent. The higher this figure, the greater the company's cash flow, which results in a better cash cushion to protect against unanticipated future cash needs.

Based on *trend analysis* (defined earlier) and industry standards, 41 percent may be good, bad, or average.

A single profitability ratio alone doesn't tell you much about a company or how it's performing compared to its competition. To get the total picture, it's necessary to do trend analysis. Doing so is usually more helpful to the user of the financial statements since everything is relative. Seeing how profitability ratios go up and down and comparing the company to others in the same industry is more meaningful than looking at one standalone ratio.

Debt to Equity

I talk about short-term and long-term *debt* (money a company owes vendors, employees, and other creditors) in Chapters 14 and 15. *Equity* shows the owners' investment interest in the company and is represented by stock and additional paid-in capital. I discuss this topic in Chapter 16.

The debt-to-equity ratio gives users an idea of how a company is financed: through debt or equity. This consideration is important because a company with a high debt-to-equity ratio can have wild fluctuations in net income due to interest expense.

For example, if debt to equity is high one year and not the next in a comparative analysis (or comparing one company to another), it clues the user of the financial statements into the underlying factor.

Most companies not in the business of lending money try to keep their debt-to-equity ratio under 50 percent, to minimize the risk of bankruptcy.

Figure 22-1 shows how to calculate the debt-to-equity ratio. In this case, it's looking good — it's under 50 percent.

Figure 22-1:
Calculating debt-to-equity ratio.

Liabilities	$35,000
Owners' Equity	65,000
Total liabilities and equity	$100,000

Debt ratio = Total liabilities / Total liabilities and equity
= $35,000 / $100,000
= 35%

Book Value Per Share

Compute this ratio by dividing *total common stockholders' equity* (all paid-in capital attributable to common stock plus retained earnings) by the number of shares of common stock outstanding. If total common stockholders' equity is $65,000 and the number of shares of common stock outstanding is 9,900, book value per share is $6.57.

This ratio is of limited use if the company's stock is publicly traded and the market value of the stock is greater than the book value. However, for your intermediate accounting class, you need to know how to calculate it and understand its limitation for publicly traded companies.

Index

• B •

• C •

• **G** •

Apple & Mac

iPad 2 For Dummies,
3rd Edition
978-1-118-17679-5

iPhone 4S For Dummies,
5th Edition
978-1-118-03671-6

iPod touch For Dummies,
3rd Edition
978-1-118-12960-9

Mac OS X Lion
For Dummies
978-1-118-02205-4

Blogging & Social Media

CityVille For Dummies
978-1-118-08337-6

Facebook For Dummies,
4th Edition
978-1-118-09562-1

Mom Blogging
For Dummies
978-1-118-03843-7

Twitter For Dummies,
2nd Edition
978-0-470-76879-2

WordPress For Dummies,
4th Edition
978-1-118-07342-1

Business

Cash Flow For Dummies
978-1-118-01850-7

Investing For Dummies,
6th Edition
978-0-470-90545-6

Job Searching with Social
Media For Dummies
978-0-470-93072-4

QuickBooks 2012
For Dummies
978-1-118-09120-3

Resumes For Dummies,
6th Edition
978-0-470-87361-8

Starting an Etsy Business
For Dummies
978-0-470-93067-0

Cooking & Entertaining

Cooking Basics
For Dummies, 4th Edition
978-0-470-91388-8

Wine For Dummies,
4th Edition
978-0-470-04579-4

Diet & Nutrition

Kettlebells For Dummies
978-0-470-59929-7

Nutrition For Dummies,
5th Edition
978-0-470-93231-5

Restaurant Calorie Counter
For Dummies,
2nd Edition
978-0-470-64405-8

Digital Photography

Digital SLR Cameras &
Photography For Dummies,
4th Edition
978-1-118-14489-3

Digital SLR Settings
& Shortcuts
For Dummies
978-0-470-91763-3

Photoshop Elements 10
For Dummies
978-1-118-10742-3

Gardening

Gardening Basics
For Dummies
978-0-470-03749-2

Vegetable Gardening
For Dummies,
2nd Edition
978-0-470-49870-5

Green/Sustainable

Raising Chickens
For Dummies
978-0-470-46544-8

Green Cleaning
For Dummies
978-0-470-39106-8

Health

Diabetes For Dummies,
3rd Edition
978-0-470-27086-8

Food Allergies
For Dummies
978-0-470-09584-3

Living Gluten-Free
For Dummies,
2nd Edition
978-0-470-58589-4

Hobbies

Beekeeping
For Dummies,
2nd Edition
978-0-470-43065-1

Chess For Dummies,
3rd Edition
978-1-118-01695-4

Drawing For Dummies,
2nd Edition
978-0-470-61842-4

eBay For Dummies,
7th Edition
978-1-118-09806-6

Knitting For Dummies,
2nd Edition
978-0-470-28747-7

Language & Foreign Language

English Grammar
For Dummies,
2nd Edition
978-0-470-54664-2

French For Dummies,
2nd Edition
978-1-118-00464-7

German For Dummies,
2nd Edition
978-0-470-90101-4

Spanish Essentials
For Dummies
978-0-470-63751-7

Spanish For Dummies,
2nd Edition
978-0-470-87855-2

 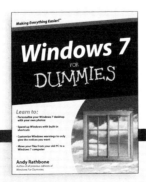  

Available wherever books are sold. For more information or to order direct: U.S. customers visit www.dummies.com or call 1-877-762-2974.
U.K. customers visit www.wileyeurope.com or call (0) 1243 843291. Canadian customers visit www.wiley.ca or call 1-800-567-4797.

Connect with us online at www.facebook.com/fordummies or @fordummies

Math & Science

Algebra I For Dummies,
2nd Edition
978-0-470-55964-2

Biology For Dummies,
2nd Edition
978-0-470-59875-7

Chemistry For Dummies,
2nd Edition
978-1-1180-0730-3

Geometry For Dummies,
2nd Edition
978-0-470-08946-0

Pre-Algebra Essentials
For Dummies
978-0-470-61838-7

Microsoft Office

Excel 2010 For Dummies
978-0-470-48953-6

Office 2010 All-in-One
For Dummies
978-0-470-49748-7

Office 2011 for Mac
For Dummies
978-0-470-87869-9

Word 2010
For Dummies
978-0-470-48772-3

Music

Guitar For Dummies,
2nd Edition
978-0-7645-9904-0

Clarinet For Dummies
978-0-470-58477-4

iPod & iTunes
For Dummies,
9th Edition
978-1-118-13060-5

Pets

Cats For Dummies,
2nd Edition
978-0-7645-5275-5

Dogs All-in One
For Dummies
978-0470-52978-2

Saltwater Aquariums
For Dummies
978-0-470-06805-2

Religion & Inspiration

The Bible For Dummies
978-0-7645-5296-0

Catholicism For Dummies,
2nd Edition
978-1-118-07778-8

Spirituality For Dummies,
2nd Edition
978-0-470-19142-2

Self-Help & Relationships

Happiness For Dummies
978-0-470-28171-0

Overcoming Anxiety
For Dummies,
2nd Edition
978-0-470-57441-6

Seniors

Crosswords For Seniors
For Dummies
978-0-470-49157-7

iPad 2 For Seniors
For Dummies, 3rd Edition
978-1-118-17678-8

Laptops & Tablets
For Seniors For Dummies,
2nd Edition
978-1-118-09596-6

Smartphones & Tablets

BlackBerry For Dummies,
5th Edition
978-1-118-10035-6

Droid X2 For Dummies
978-1-118-14864-8

HTC ThunderBolt
For Dummies
978-1-118-07601-9

MOTOROLA XOOM
For Dummies
978-1-118-08835-7

Sports

Basketball For Dummies,
3rd Edition
978-1-118-07374-2

Football For Dummies,
2nd Edition
978-1-118-01261-1

Golf For Dummies,
4th Edition
978-0-470-88279-5

Test Prep

ACT For Dummies,
5th Edition
978-1-118-01259-8

ASVAB For Dummies,
3rd Edition
978-0-470-63760-9

The GRE Test For
Dummies, 7th Edition
978-0-470-00919-2

Police Officer Exam
For Dummies
978-0-470-88724-0

Series 7 Exam
For Dummies
978-0-470-09932-2

Web Development

HTML, CSS, & XHTML
For Dummies, 7th Edition
978-0-470-91659-9

Drupal For Dummies,
2nd Edition
978-1-118-08348-2

Windows 7

Windows 7
For Dummies
978-0-470-49743-2

Windows 7
For Dummies,
Book + DVD Bundle
978-0-470-52398-8

Windows 7 All-in-One
For Dummies
978-0-470-48763-1

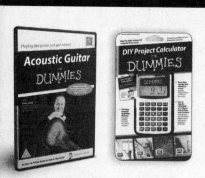